CURRENT LEGAL PROBLEMS 1988

Volume 41

AUSTRALIA AND NEW ZEALAND
The Law Book Company Ltd.
Sydney : Melbourne : Perth

CANADA AND U.S.A.
The Carswell Company Ltd.
Agincourt, Ontario

INDIA
N.M. Tripathi Private Ltd.
Bombay
and
Eastern Law House Private Ltd.
Calcutta and Delhi
M.P.P. House
Bangalore

ISRAEL
Steimatzky's Agency Ltd.
Jerusalem : Tel Aviv : Haifa

CURRENT LEGAL PROBLEMS 1988

Edited by
ROGER RIDEOUT and JEFFREY JOWELL
with
BEN PETTET as Assistant Editor

On behalf of
THE FACULTY OF LAWS
UNIVERSITY COLLEGE LONDON

Editorial Committee

Volume 41

LONDON
STEVENS and SONS
1988

Published in 1988
by Stevens & Sons Ltd.
of 11, New Fetter Lane, London
Laserset by P.B. Computer Typesetting, Pickering
Printed and bound in Great Britain by
Hazell Watson & Viney Limited
Member of BPCC plc
Aylesbury, Bucks, England

British Library Cataloguing in Publication Data

Current Legal Problems.—Vol. 41 (1988)
1. Law—Periodicals—Great Britain
340′.05   K3

ISBN 0 420—48160—5

All editorial communications should be addressed to:
The Editors,
"CURRENT LEGAL PROBLEMS,"
Faculty of Laws,
University College London,
4–8 Endsleigh Gardens, London, WC1

PREFACE

A reviewer of Volume 40 in this series regretted that he had found no discernible theme. We hope that search did not occupy too much of his time since it has never been the policy of Current Legal Problems to behave in a way different from more frequently published general periodicals. Once in 1963 the Editors carried away, no doubt, by the heady enthusiasm engendered by a prospect of lakes and mountains decided to celebrate, somewhat prematurely, the accession of the United Kingdom to the Common Market. They found that "currency" may resemble a sunbeam anticipated from a weather forecast. To suppose that that sunbeam, if trapped, will provide the desired light to a readership of widely various interests has seemed to us unrealistic.

We were surprised and apprehensive, therefore, when some of our colleagues purported to find a theme in the subject matter of four of the contributions in this volume and we look forward with interest to ascertain whether our reviewers detect it also.

Despite long experience the unexpected still surprises. Perhaps it was not hilarity, to which Alan Rodger with a rare attachment to hearsay refers, but surprise with which our colleagues learned that so distinguished and learned a practitioner proposed to deliver a paper on *Donoghue* v. *Stevenson*. The reader may share our pleasure at the result and, like us, await the day when the author's painstaking research reveals a single source of inspiration in 1930's Glasgow for *Donoghue, Bourhill* and *Muir* (see p. 9). How delighted Tony Thomas would have been to contemplate the potential enlightenment of such pure research.

Coincidentally, Sir Johan Steyn might have been thinking along the same lines when he wrote that "one of the principal causes of judicial error is a lack of knowledge of the environment of the critical decision." He has set out to enquire as to the extent to which a judge may allow such an environment to influence interpretation of a contract. Little in the law of evidence can have excited more attention than the hearsay rule and some would think it only a brave writer who, having once examined it, returns again. We hope there will be general agreement, however, that Stephen

Guest's thorough and carefully worked re-examination of the rule provides much material for continued agitation.

Barry Rider's examination of available sanctions against malpractice in the handling of corporate securities could scarcely have been more current. Many of our readers are unlikely to share the view of his lecture chairman that he is inclined to be alarmist. An exciting lecture has produced an absorbing paper.

Nine point three per cent of the Chief Constables currently in office in England and Wales are old students of this Faculty and for that reason, if no other, it seems appropriate that we should publish an interim report, as it were, on Robert Reiner's research into the office of Chief Constable which was presented to his audience as objectively and dispassionately as it now appears. Much has changed from 1859 when the Chief Constable of Bedford was the former licencee of the Red Lion, but who now are these people who exercise such powerful discretion? Readers of these preliminary results will, no doubt, await impatiently publication of the full results of this enquiry.

Sharply contrasted with this empirical research is the legal argument, surely a model of its kind, presented by Denis Galligan on the rights of an accused person to remain silent. Declarations of intention by the Home Secretary to alter the content of this right have made sharply current what has long been recognised as a problem of principle.

The Penal Crisis is a current social problem which legislature, judiciary, criminal practitioner and academic are not at liberty to ignore. Andrew Rutherford documents the history of the present crisis from a time when this country was noted for pulling down unwanted prisons to the present when the prison population exceeds even the most recent upper limits on what would be regarded as tolerable. The reader of his paper will scarcely be surprised if policy makers cannot decide whether to open or shut the front or back door. David Thomas reveals the process of sentencing which regulates the queue at the front door as a morass of complexities through which one can only be surprised at the ability of the judiciary to wade. It was unnecessary for him to reveal himself as a master of the art of the public lecture. His paper likewise discloses the fact, which we knew already, that he is the master of this subject.

Bob Hepple's well known command of comparative labour law has produced a paper on specialist labour courts in time to remind us that problems exist even if governments see no need to face them. United Kingdom Industrial Tribunals are deprived of work at a time when few would consider what they have to offer as adequate. If, one day, we are to move ahead we must make sure that we understand better than we did in 1971 what we have and what we want.

It is our policy to publish a paper from each of our visiting professors. We do not always succeed, but this year Professor Joshua Weisman and Professor Hiroshi Oda (to whom we owe a lot more than this) readily agreed. Professor Weisman reveals to us how an invention of English Law — the floating charge — has fared in an environment not dominated by the Common Law. Professor Oda, who might have been expected to write of Japan, instead produces for the reader a valuable survey of the procurator — a reviewer who became a prosecutor — in the Soviet Union. This Faculty has long recognised the need to come out of common law isolation, not only into Western Europe but to the study of the most significant of the world's other systems and this paper is a very welcome example of that work.

Finally, we are happy to accede to a request from the Race Relations Committee of the General Council of the Bar to publish the Vice-Chancellor's Inaugural Kapila lecture on the role of the civil law in controlling racial discrimination.

As usual, our thanks are due to the members of the Editorial Committee for their advice. Ben Pettet is the latest in a line of assistant editors without whose hard work these annual volumes would not be published. We are deeply grateful to him for the considerable amount of work he does, largely behind the scenes, to this end.

UNIVERSITY COLLEGE LONDON   *THE EDITORS*

CONTENTS

TABLE OF CASES

TABLE OF STATUTES

Mrs. Donoghue and Alfenus Varus

ALAN RODGER Q.C.

It is a great honour for me to be asked to give the Third Thomas Memorial Lecture here in University College. Two names above all are associated in my mind with University College, London. The first is not—as it ought to be and would be if I had a proper taste for jurisprudence—Jeremy Bentham. Rather, it is the poet and classicist A. E. Housman who was Professor of Latin at the end of last century and the beginning of this. I think in particular of the Introductory Lecture[1] which he gave in 1892, and which was really concerned with the problem confronting universities today: what is the good which we set before us as our end when we exercise our faculties in acquiring knowledge, in learning? His answer, which from a Patent Office official turned Professor of Latin was hardly surprising, came to be that knowledge in itself is good for man. Once we have recognised this, he says,

> "we shall need to invent no pretexts for studying this subject or that; we shall import no extraneous considerations of use or ornament to justify us in learning one thing rather than another. If a certain department of knowledge specially attracts a man, let him study that, and study it because it attracts him; and let him not fabricate excuses for that which requires no excuse, but rest assured that the reason why it most attracts him is that it is best for him."[2]

That passage has always stuck in my mind and remains fixed there when I hear Government ministers urging all young people to study engineering or similar subjects. While Buckland was an engineer before he took to Roman law, I shudder to think what a structure engineered by me or any of my legal acquaintances would have been like. The passage was also in my mind when choosing my themes for this lecture. I have chosen them not because they are relevant or useful, but simply because they have attracted me. I do not pretend that, when you have heard this

1

lecture, your knowledge of law will be enhanced. I hope at most that you too may find the topics not entirely unattractive. If you do, then the lecture may be appropriate for a series dedicated to the memory of Tony Thomas, the other University College name in my mind. With a complete disdain for passing fashions in the teaching of law, he would enliven the driest topic in Roman law with his insight and humour. He was besides an intensely human man interested, as every real lawyer is, in the gossip and personalities of the law. It is, I am afraid, to gossip and personalities that we first bend our attention.

When I mentioned to Andrew Lewis that I might say something about *Donoghue* v. *Stevenson*,[3] and he informed the relevant Faculty committee, there was, he told me, great merriment. Doubtless, though he was too polite to mention this, there were more than a few groans too. A Scotsman could speak of nothing else. Yet, why not? It is, after all, probably the most famous case in the whole Commonwealth world of the Common Law. It is the case which everyone knows. But one may perhaps ask: what does everybody know about it? The answer in most cases is that they know what is to be found in 1932 Appeal Cases plus a few legends as to whether or not there actually was a snail in the bottle. Still, the position is strange. I am prepared to wager that no one in this audience has ever read the decision of the Scottish appeal court on the case, far less the first instance judgment of Lord Moncrieff. Which, when you come to think of the acres of print on the case, is quite extraordinary and wholly different from, say, *Bell* v. *Lever Bros.*[4] where writers refer to the judgments in the lower courts as well as those in the House of Lords. The reason is, of course, that *Donoghue* v. *Stevenson* was not reported in either the Inner or the Outer House except in brief uninformative notes in an obscure Scottish series of reports.[5] Yet the courts below did issue opinions[6] and, while the Inner House opinions are brief, that of Lord Moncrieff in the Outer House is certainly of interest, if only because he managed to reach the same result as the House of Lords without their powers to overrule inconvenient precedents. So, although I do not propose to investigate these matters here, you can see that the knowledge of even the most blasé teacher of torts about *Donoghue* is something less than complete.

Indeed, the curiosity of lawyers about leading cases is remarkably slight. Only rarely are we treated to a feast of information such as Professor Simpson provides in his *Cannibalism and the Common Law*[7] which explores the background to *R.* v. *Dudley and Stephens*.[8] Even when the feast is laid before them, other academic lawyers partake of it only with considerable caution, as if nervous of being caught indulging.[9] Where a case has social or political interest at the time, lawyers like everyone else nowadays may see the participants on television or read their statements in the newspapers. But such cases—however important they may seem at the time—rarely have the status of a classic leading case. I think I remember seeing a picture of Mr. Anns, the plaintiff in the horrendous *Anns* v. *London Borough of Merton*,[10] in a newspaper, but no legal journal contains a behind-the-scenes interview with him. By now it is too late, for it has been plain since Lord Keith's speech in *Peabody*[11] and it is plainer than ever since Lord Bridge's remarks in *Curran* v. *N.I. Co-Ownership Housing Association*[12] that *Anns* is not going to enjoy classic status and indeed will be lucky to survive, having now been consigned by Lord Bridge to the dread category of matters which might be appropriate for consideration by the Law Commission. So we should not waste our time with the hero of that discredited authority. Despite a shaky start *The Wagon Mounds*[13] are doing rather better. Yet, while Professor Wilson of Edinburgh University on a visit to Sydney in 1986 went to look for the area where Morts Dockyard once lay, and while Mr. Weir used to tell us in his splendid *Casebook* where and when the *Wagon Mound* was built and that it sailed the seas under a different name,[14] it is only in an American casebook[15] that a student will find photographs showing firemen actually fighting the fire and a view of the dock after the fire, with a corner of the Harbour Bridge visible in the background. This seems rather a pity since such information surely brings the whole subject-matter much more to life.

Above all perhaps one feels what the hymn-writer calls "an aching void" so far as Mrs. Donoghue is concerned. Who was this woman whose alleged misfortune was to transform the Common Law? You will find no pictures of her and precious little information either.[16] The only account of which I know is in a few lines in a Sunday Times Colour Supplement published in 1976.[17] Unfortunately they contain elements of sheer fantasy so that Mrs. Donoghue's life becomes a Gothic romance. While a considerable amount of work remains to be done, I propose to begin by telling you about this most famous of litigants.

First, perhaps, it would be polite to find out what her name was. I do not mean that she was simply Mrs. Donoghue, not Mrs. M'Alister or Donoghue, or even Mrs. Donoghue (or M'Alister) as the All England Reports now call her.[18] That particular chestnut was disposed of years ago,[19] and I assume that everyone, who wishes to, knows that she was Mrs. Donoghue, her maiden name having been McAllister. But how does one spell McAllister? The invariable practice is to spell it with an apostrophe after the initial M and with one "l." Both of these variants derive from the papers in the case, but in fact Mrs. Donoghue spelled her name "McAllister."[20] Then we turn to her Christian name. In the official Scottish report, in Session Cases, she appears as Mrs. Mary Donoghue,[21] and under that name she achieved another kind of immortality when she appeared in Notes in connexion with a House of Lords Practice Direction issued by the Clerk of Parliaments in 1972.[22] On the other hand, in, say, the Scots Law Times she is Mrs. May Donoghue.[23] The English reports eschew such frivolities and omit her Christian name.[24] In fact the answer is that she was Mrs. May Donoghue.[25] So in summary the lady was born May McAllister and was at the time of the case Mrs. May Donoghue. As we shall see below, even the matter of her name is not quite so simple as that.

Having discovered her name, we may perhaps turn to her age. Mrs. Donoghue was born on July 4, 1898.[26] The famous incident of the snail in the bottle occurred on August 26, 1928, so that she was 30 at the time and 33 when the speeches were delivered by the House of Lords in May 1932.

Next, her background. In the early 1870s the Steel Company of Scotland was formed and it proceeded to build a large steelworks at Hallside, Newton near Cambuslang to the east of Glasgow.[27] The works were closed in 1980 and have now been demolished, leaving a vast cleared site. Newton has returned to semi-rural obscurity. A century ago, however, the works were attracting labourers and their families to the area. Among them were Mrs. Donoghue's parents. Her father, James McAllister, was a steelworker.[28] Her mother Mary Jane Hannah had the splendidly Victorian occupation of dyefield worker,[28] but Mrs. Donoghue's maternal grandfather was a steelworker also.[29] At the time of their marriage in 1886[30] Mrs. Donoghue's parents were living in the area and they continued to do so after they were married. The family was Protestant.[31] Mrs. Donoghue had at least an older brother John, born in the year of her parents' marriage,[32] and an older sister Mary,[33] and there may well have been others. Her brother John in due course became a steelworker like his father.[34] Mrs. Donoghue was actually born in what had been a large mansion house, Morriston House, in Cambuslang.[35] The house itself was demolished more than 60 years ago.[36] By the end of the nineteenth century it had seen better days and had been bought by a local builder.[37] The house was converted into workmen's houses and the McAllisters moved into one of these shortly before their daughter May was born in 1898.[38] We know nothing of her education, but it probably was the very basic kind of education which would have been usual at the time. Still, Mrs. Donoghue was certainly literate and indeed specimens of her signature, one of which may be inspected in London,[39] show that she wrote with a well-formed hand. Her writing is much better than that frequently encountered nowadays among people who have little occasion to write.

In 1915, when she was 17, May McAllister had an affair with Henry Donoghue, a steelworker who lived with his parents just a few doors away in a Steel Company of Scotland house in Newton.[40] The houses would have been similar to the old miners' row houses. Henry Donoghue was eight years older than May McAllister and was of Irish stock.[41] In some records indeed his father's name is given as "O'Donoghue."[42] The family probably came to Scotland when Henry was about 16.[43] As a result of the affair, May McAllister became pregnant and the couple decided to marry, which they did in Glasgow on February 19, 1916.[44] In passing, I may add that they married by one of the old forms of irregular marriage, declaration *de praesenti*, which existed in Scotland until 1940. All that they did was to declare their consent to be married before two witnesses and then apply through a solicitor for a warrant from the sheriff to register the marriage.[45] The couple moved from Newton into a flat at 29 Webster Street in part of the east end of Glasgow dominated by vast industrial buildings. The Scottish steel industry was booming due to war production and it seems possible that Henry Donoghue had got a job at the Parkhead steelworks. At all events, on July 25, 1916, Mrs. Donoghue had a son, Henry Donoghue.[47]

There followed what must have been a difficult period. In June 1917 a second son James was born. But the birth was premature and he died when less than a day old.[48] In May 1918, Mrs. Donoghue had another son, John, but again the birth was premature and he died when only two days old.[49] Mr. Donoghue had meantime joined the army as a private in the 84th Training Reserve based at Bath.[50] After the War, he returned home to Glasgow. In June 1920 a daughter, Mabel, was born, but unfortunately yet again the child was premature and did not survive, dying when only 11 days old.[51] The incidence of three premature births is consistent with the poverty of the family, especially of the mother, since premature births were relatively common among women of the lower social classes in Britain at the period.[52] There is indeed a suggestion that malnutrition may have been a factor in the death of Mabel in 1920.[53] The Donoghues had no more children, and actually from time to time their son Henry was looked after by Mr. Donoghue's relations.[54] The marriage was not at any rate a happy one.[55] Mr. and Mrs. Donoghue continued living at the same address in Webster Street until 1928 when they gave up the house[56] and separated.[57] Mrs. Donoghue went to live about a mile away with her brother John at his flat at 49 Kent Street, Glasgow,[58] in another building which no longer exists but which was close to the Barrows, the Glasgow equivalent of Petticoat Lane. It is likely that she was living there, having separated from her husband, in August 1928 when the famous incident with the snail occurred. I say this because just over two weeks after the incident, it appears, she was treated at the Glasgow Royal Infirmary,[59] which would be the appropriate local hospital for someone living just over a mile away in Kent Street. At this time also, according to the pleadings in the case,[60] Mrs. Donoghue was working as a shop assistant. At all events, we know or believe that at about ten to nine on a warm Sunday evening,[61] August 26, 1928, Mrs. Donoghue and her friend walked into Mr. Minchella's café in Paisley, a town a little to the west of Glasgow, but just a tram-ride away. As we also know or believe, Mrs. Donoghue became unwell. Her quick-witted friend noted the name and address of the manufacturer of the ginger-beer, a local Paisley manufacturer, from the label on the bottle.[62] So on April 4, 1929 Mrs. Donoghue's famous case against Mr. Stevenson was begun.[63] After various procedural hiccoughs,[64] Mrs. Donoghue won the first round before Lord Moncrieff on June 27, 1930,[65] only to be defeated in a reclaiming motion in the Second Division on November 13 of the same year.[66]

In the meantime Mrs. Donoghue had left her brother's house and had obtained the tenancy of a tenement flat at 101 Maitland Street, Glasgow.[67] Again this was in a very poor area, but situated this time close to the commercial centre of Glasgow, Sauchiehall Street. In February 1931, steps were taken to have her case dealt with as an *in forma pauperis* appeal to the House of Lords and the necessary certificate of poverty was given by the local minister, the Rev. James Deans, and two elders from Milton Parish Church.[68] As all the world knows, on May 26, 1932[69] Mrs. Donoghue's appeal succeeded. Thereafter, following further procedural adventures,[70] the case was settled, though this process was delayed by the death of Mr. Stevenson so that it was not until December 1934 that the case was finally disposed of.[71]

Going back to Mrs. Donoghue, we find her still living in Maitland Street.[72] Her mother died a couple of years later.[73] Her son Henry, who worked in the shipyards—not a good occupation on Clydeside in the Depression—seems to have lived with her there until July 20, 1937 when he married a girl from the next street. Like his parents, Henry used the method of declaration *de praesenti* and one of the witnesses to his declaration was his mother, Mrs. Donoghue.[74] Soon after Henry's marriage, Mrs. Donoghue had to leave her home in Maitland Street, for the building was demolished, perhaps because of its condition.[75] She moved south of the Clyde to a Corporation flat at 156 Jamieson Street[76]—not paradise, to be sure, but it must have been a great deal better than her old house. The house in Jamieson Street remains to this day.

We must now turn our attention briefly to Mr. Donoghue, her husband from whom she had separated in 1928. In due course he formed a relationship with another lady and in February 1936 he had a son by her.[77] Mrs. Donoghue does not seem to have discovered this until her son Henry told her late in 1941 that Mr. Donoghue was living with this lady.[78] Mrs. Donoghue did nothing about the matter at that time and it was only after the birth of a second son to Mr. Donoghue and the lady in March 1944[79] that Mrs. Donoghue instructed her solicitors—not the ones she had used in her great case—in connexion with a divorce. Enquiry agents having been despatched to obtain the necessary evidence, the divorce action was raised in January 1945.[80] It was not defended. So it was that on the morning of Wednesday, February 28, 1945 Mrs. Donoghue at last entered the doors of the Court of Session in Edinburgh, where her name would surely have been known to any of the counsel in the building.[81] But there is nothing to indicate that anyone was aware that they had a celebrity in their midst, for all went off in a routine fashion. The case was one of 10 on Lord Mackintosh's roll that day. At 11.30 a.m. Mrs. Donoghue took and signed the oath *de calumnia*, against collusion, and at 11.45 Lord Mackintosh pronounced decree of divorce,[82] though again, as with her first, better-known action, a series of delays followed and the case was not finally disposed of until the following year.[83] Mr. Donoghue had meantime taken advantage of the divorce to marry the other lady in October 1945.[84] He died in 1961.[85]

If Mrs. Donoghue had hoped that her son's marriage would bring her grandchildren and the happiness associated with them, that hope was not to be fulfilled. Her son's marriage did not prosper and Henry and his wife separated without having children in March 1941. They were reconciled in September of the following year but separated finally in July 1943 after which Henry seems to have gone back to stay with his mother in Jamieson

Street. He may have been still living there with her towards the end of 1945 and at the time of his divorce which was granted in January 1946.[86] Henry quickly remarried in April of the same year[87] and had five children of the second marriage, three girls and two boys, the oldest born in 1947 and the youngest in 1957. So it may not be too fanciful to imagine that during this period Mrs. Donoghue may have enjoyed the company of her grandchildren from time to time.

Indeed Mrs. Donoghue's life seems to have been relatively settled. She continued to live in the same house in Jamieson Street and she continued to work as a shop assistant.[89] Following her divorce she reverted to her maiden name of May McAllister and it is that name which appears on her death certificate.[90] So, as luck would have it, all the struggles of Scots lawyers to persuade their English brethren to call the pursuer Mrs. Donoghue would not really have met with her enthusiastic approval. The problem of her name does not stop there. While reverting to her maiden name, May McAllister, she was actually commonly known as "Mabel Hannah."[91] Quite why I do not know, but Hannah was the maiden name of her mother and Mabel was the name which Mrs. Donoghue gave to the daughter who died. So maybe Mrs. Donoghue would have wished her case to be remembered as *Hannah* v. *Stevenson*.

Eventually, Mrs. Donoghue died, intestate, of a heart attack on the afternoon of Wednesday, March 19, 1958.[92] She was aged 59. The place of her death is, however, significant for she died in Gartloch Mental Hospital, a rambling late-Victorian establishment on the eastern outskirts of Glasgow. So we must assume that her last days were clouded by mental illness, though I suspect that, happily, she was not in hospital for a long period.[93]

And there the story really ends. Certainly further work will permit more detail to be added and doubtless some corrections to be made. The general picture, however, will not, I think, be greatly altered. The story cannot be said to be a particularly happy one, nor is there anything to mark it out as the story of a woman who is easily the best-known litigant of the twentieth century. One is struck by how circumscribed her life would have been. Born in Cambuslang she lived her whole life in that area and in the poorer parts of Glasgow. Although she must have been to Edinburgh at least once,[94] one may well suppose that she would never have visited London, never have left Scotland at all, for people of her generation, especially those of limited means, travelled only very little. But travel she did in August 1928 from the slums of Glasgow to Paisley and there found her way into Mr. Minchella's shop. By so doing she built herself, as far as any mortal can, a monument *aere perennius*, although she herself was probably never aware of her fame. It is a sad commentary on the lofty attitude of lawyers that, although her name as such will live for evermore, not much will be known of the woman behind the name.

In many ways probably the dominant factor in Mrs. Donoghue's earlier day-to-day life would have been poverty. This can be seen at its bleakest in the affidavit which she swore on February 16, 1931 for the purposes of her appeal to the House of Lords: "I am very poor, and am not worth in all the world the sum of Five Pounds, my wearing apparel and the subject matter of the said Appeal only excepted, and am, by reason of such my poverty, unable to prosecute the said Appeal."[95] Doubtless the somewhat Biblical language was that of the Judicial Office[96] or of her solicitors, but the reality is all too stark. At the time of her case, Mrs. Donoghue was exceedingly poor. If, accordingly, she really did recover the £200 which we are told[97] was the settlement—and family rumour seems typically to have exaggerated the sum to £500[98], which is unlikely since that was the sum sued for[99]— then such a settlement must have seemed like riches indeed.

At her death in 1958 Mrs. Donoghue's total estate amounted to £364 18*s*. 8*d*., which even then was a small estate. It was made up chiefly of £292 in a savings bank account and a life assurance policy for £40,[1] doubtless taken out to cover her funeral expenses. None the less one must not exaggerate how small the estate was. It may actually have been larger than the estates of most people dying in Scotland at that time.[2] Whether the damages which she recovered from Mr. Stevenson's executors formed the nucleus of her savings we do not know.

What Mrs. Donoghue was therefore is a very poor lady who became the pursuer in a classic case. I ask you to note that two other leading cases involving individual pursuers in everyday situations also came from Scotland to the House of Lords. In fact nearly everything you need to know about negligence is to be found in these three cases. Besides *Donoghue* v. *Stevenson*, they are, of course, *Bourhill* v. *Young*[3] and *Glasgow Corporation* v. *Muir*.[4] It is indeed partly because they involve everyday situations rather than, say, events in a factory that the three cases have been so attractive and so generally useful: Mrs. Donoghue having an ice-cream soda in a café on a warm Sunday evening; Mrs. Bourhill wrestling with her basket of fish after leaving a tramcar; Eleanor Muir queuing for sweets or an ice-cream on a wet Saturday afternoon in June 1940, the very day after Paris had fallen to the German armies. Why all these particular cases should have come from the smaller Scottish jurisdiction is a question which I pose for your attention, but having posed it, I pass on to remind you of where the cases took the law of tort or delict.

In *Donoghue*, Lords Atkin and Macmillan laid down in general, perhaps too general, terms that you owe a duty of reasonable care to avoid acts or omissions which you can reasonably foresee would be likely to injure your neighbour.[5] In *Bourhill*, referring back to *Donoghue*, the House stressed that the duty is owed to those to whom injury may reasonably and probably be anticipated if the duty is not observed. So it was not owed to Mrs. Bourhill who was out of sight behind the tram. John Young could not reasonably and probably have anticipated injuring her.

Finally in *Muir* the House was presented with a hard case in which they chose to make good law. Eleanor Muir was among a crowd of children queuing for sweets or ice-cream in a Corporation tea-room in King's Park, Glasgow. The manageress of the tea-room had allowed a church outing to take their tea in a back room. Two people from the outing, with her permission, carried an urn of boiling water through the crowd of children. Somehow or other, whether by negligence or mere accident was never determined, the urn slipped and Eleanor Muir and others were scalded. Presumably because the people who carried the urn were not worth suing—they came indeed from a church near where Mrs. Donoghue lived in the 1930s—Eleanor Muir's father sued the Corporation which he sought to make liable for negligence on the part of their manageress. In effect he alleged that she should have foreseen the possibility of the urn tipping over and should therefore have cleared away the children before it was carried in. But, developing the approach in *Bourhill*, the House of Lords said No. People carry tea-urns day and daily without mishap. The manageress could, of course, foresee the *possibility* of carelessness or of a mere accident in carrying the urn, but she was under no duty to guard against either of these possibilities. "To hold the appellants liable on either basis," said Lord Wright, "would be to make them insurers, which under the authorities they are not."[6] The approach of the House of Lords remains the same, and Lord Mackay of Clashfern recently applied the tests laid down in *Muir* in an elaborate speech in *Smith* v. *Littlewoods*,[7] another Scottish appeal which is heading for all the best torts reading lists.

So *Muir* is the clearest authority that the reasonable woman need not guard against merely possible accidents which may injure the plaintiff. Although *Muir* was concerned with carelessness or an accident caused by third parties carrying the urn, we can be sure that, perhaps even *a fortiori*, there would be no liability if the

injured person was the source of the accident. Suppose that
Eleanor Muir had accidentally jogged the arm of the person
carrying the urn, while she was queuing for sweets, and so had
caused the urn to spill. The House would undoubtedly have
rejected the pursuer's claim because, even if the possibility of such
an accident could have been foreseen, the Corporation's manageress would have been under no duty to prevent it.

To well-brought-up black-letter lawyers all this is trite indeed,
and it is comfortable knowledge. Anything which seems to
contradict even part of this trite law must therefore come as
something of a shock. Nevertheless, awakening early here in
London one summer morning in 1986, I began to doubt whether
Alfenus Varus,[8] a jurist of the first century B.C., was altogether
sound on the point. This was particularly disturbing since he is a
jurist for whom I have a certain affection and who had always
struck me as a very sensible kind of a fellow. By Christmas my
worst fears were confirmed: at least on one particular set of facts
Alfenus would not have been 100 per cent behind the approach of
the House of Lords.

Perhaps in a Thomas Memorial Lecture I need do no more than
remind you that the Roman law of damage to property was
contained for the most part in the Lex Aquilia.[9] The terms of that
statute[10] seemed to require that the defendant should actually
damage the property before he could be made liable. If the
property was not actually damaged, but was just lost, say, then the
praetor would give an indirect action, an action *in factum*. So one
finds many rather tedious discussions on borderline cases, as to
whether a particular set of facts would fall under the statute itself
or under a praetorian action.

Among the texts often cited in this connexion is D.19.5.23:

> Alfenus 3 *digestorum a Paulo epitomatorum.* duo secun-
> dum Tiberim cum ambularent, alter eorum ei qui secum
> ambulabat rogatus anulum ostendit ut respiceret: illi excidit
> anulus et in Tiberim devolutus est. respondit posse agi cum eo
> in factum actione.[11]

Thomas translates the text in this way:

> "ALFENUS, Digest, Epitomized by Paul, book 3: Two
> men were walking along the Tiber. One of them, at the
> request of his walking companion, showed him a ring for his
> inspection; the ring escaped his [the companion's] grasp and
> rolled into the Tiber. He [Servius] responded that he can be
> sued through an *actio in factum*."[12]

As usually interpreted,[13] the text is thought to deal with the following case. A and B are walking beside the Tiber. A asks to see B's ring. B hands the ring to A for A to look at. A drops the ring. The ring rolls into the river and is lost. Alfenus gives B an action *in factum* against A. The point of the decision is supposed to be that, since the ring is not damaged but merely lost, an indirect action rather than an action on the Lex Aquilia is available. So interpreted the text is not very interesting.

In fact the text has been completely misunderstood. This is not the place or the occasion for a detailed analysis of the translation, but two points can be seen very quickly. First, the text does not say that anyone drops the ring. Rather, Alfenus simply tells us that the ring fell from his grasp (*excidit*). His formulation is entirely neutral. It is modern writers who introduce the idea that someone "dropped"[14] the ring and they do so subconsciously in order to bring in an element of fault. This they require to do because they think that the case is about an extension of the Lex Aquilia, which would, of course, by the time of Alfenus at least, require an element of fault.[15]

The second point to notice is that modern commentators assume that when A asks to see the ring, B actually hands it over to A. But even though this belief goes back beyond the Gloss[16] to the Basilica,[17] the text actually says no such thing. It merely says that B showed (*ostendit*) the ring to A. Now, if I show you a ring, that can be done without handing it over to you and indeed we find elsewhere in the Digest that when a jurist wishes to say that something was handed over for inspection, he says just that, using the appropriate verb, *dare*.[18]

A literal translation of the text might be:

> "When two men were walking beside the Tiber, one of them when asked showed a ring to him (*ei*) who was walking with him (*secum*) so that he might look at it: the ring fell from him (*illi*) and rolled into the Tiber. He replied that it was possible for an action *in factum* to be brought against him (*eo*)."

The case is this. A and B are walking along the Tiber. A asks B to show him B's ring. In response to this request, B holds out the ring for A to look at, but as he is doing so, the ring falls from B's grasp and rolls into the Tiber. Alfenus holds that B, from whose grasp the ring fell, can bring an action *in factum* against A.

Such a decision may strike those brought up on our law as outrageous and unsophisticated. All that A did was to ask to see the ring. Acting on that request, B showed the ring and suffered loss due to no one's fault while doing so. Surely B should bear his own loss. In *Muir* the Corporation had a tea-room in which, among other things, they invited children like Eleanor Muir to buy sweets and ice-cream. If due to no one's fault she is injured while queuing, surely she must bear that loss herself. In the Roman case, if asked beforehand, A would certainly have admitted that it was, of course, possible that the ring would fall into the river while B was showing it. But people show rings day and daily without mishap. Likewise, the manageress of the tea-room could foresee the mere possibility that while queuing one of the children might accidentally be injured by the passing urn. If that was no reason to make the manageress liable for failing to drive out the children while the urn passed by, why should Alfenus apparently make A liable just because he asked B to show him the ring and it fell into the Tiber?

The first part of the answer is that Alfenus was not thinking in terms of delict, of tort. In particular, he was not thinking of any extension of the Lex Aquilia. As some scholars have realised since the sixteenth century, and as was mentioned by Mr. Barton a few years ago, this text comes from part of Alfenus' work concerned with matters to do with consensual contracts.[19] The text therefore concerns the kind of action *in factum* which was designed to fill a gap in the Roman system of nominate contracts. We have not time to look at the various wrong theories about what extension Alfenus was considering, but must turn instead to the solution based on a proper understanding of the facts of the case.

The key to the solution is found in the Latin word "*rogatus*," "asked." The point is that B shows the ring only because he is asked to do so by A. If you turn to the opening text of the Digest title on mandate, D.17.1, you will find that Paul tells us that if a person writes "I ask" "*rogo*," there is an action for mandate.[20] So *rogare* is a word which immediately gives rise to the possibility of mandate. In our text *rogatus* signals that we are on the fringes of mandate. Here what Alfenus is doing is giving an action *in factum*, not because the situation is like the Lex Aquilia, but because it is like a contract of mandate.

This can be seen if we look at the definition of mandate. Buckland defines mandate as "the undertaking, by request, of a gratuitous service for another."[21] Now, if you think about it, all the elements are present in this case: B undertakes, at A's request, the gratuitous service of showing A the ring. So Alfenus is saying that when A asks B to show him his ring, the relationship between A and B is similar to that between the parties to a contract of mandate. You can see the same could be said where I ask you to pour me out a cup of tea. If you do so, then you are undertaking a gratuitous service for me at my request. Now Alfenus does not say that where A asks to see the ring and B shows it, a contract of mandate actually arises, but just that the relationship is similar. That is why he gives an action *in factum* rather than the proper contractual action. English law, especially perhaps because of its doctrine of consideration, does not have much difficulty in distinguishing between mere social requests and actual contracts, but you will find, say, in Germany that the courts have had to distinguish mere social arrangements from actual contracts such as mandate.[22] The crucial point here is, of course, that while Alfenus perceives that there is actually no mandate between A and B, he is prepared to grant B an action *in factum* modelled on the appropriate contractual action (the *iudicium contrarium*) to cover B's loss.

Why then does Alfenus give an action here? You must remember the origins and nature of the contract of mandate: it covers services provided free among friends.[23] For example, you agree to my request to bring some of my books the next time you are driving from Edinburgh to London. You bring the books and make no charge. That is mandate. The fact that you are really assisting me and doing the service for nothing means that I shall feel obliged to consider your interests very scrupulously. So, if, say, your car breaks down while you are carrying my books, I shall, as a friend, feel moved to share the expenses of the repair. More particularly, if, as your car enters my street with the books, it skids and crashes, again I may feel at least morally obliged to make good the damage. After all I shall say to myself "If I hadn't asked him to bring the books, he would never have driven down my street and the accident would not have occurred." Under the influence of *bona fides*, good faith, such moral scruples may give rise to legal obligations in Roman law.[24] So in the Digest texts on mandate we find discussions, which Professor Stein has studied, about precisely which losses of the mandatary the mandator must indemnify.[25] Broadly speaking, he must pay for any losses, not caused by act of God, which occur by reason of the mandatary carrying out his mandate. There is no suggestion that the mandator's liability is restricted to losses which he should have foreseen. Nor is there any reason why it should be. The mandatary is not seeking damages for breach of contract from the mandator. The mandatary is enforcing his right to be indemnified by the mandator. The nearest analogous institution in English law is Agency and an agent has a contractual right to indemnity.

Bowstead says: "... every agent has a right against his principal to be reimbursed all expenses and to be indemnified against all losses and liabilities incurred by him in the execution of his authority."[26] So, if one were dealing with an English contract of agency, far less with a Roman contract of mandate, there would be nothing startling in the proposition that the mandatary or agent could recover the loss which he suffered purely by accident in the execution of the commission.

What Alfenus is doing is drawing the analogy between this situation and a contract of mandate, and having drawn that analogy, he is going on to give B the same right of indemnity for loss as a mandatary or agent would have had under the contract. A mandatary would be indemnified for loss incurred by virtue of carrying out the mandate. So here, B will be indemnified for his loss of the ring because he incurred that loss by virtue of the fact that he was obliging A by showing him the ring. Alfenus is really doing what Lord Wright says[27] that our law does not do: he is treating A as virtually an insurer.

As I said before, to anyone brought up on *Donoghue, Bourhill* and *Muir*, Alfenus' decision is at first sight extraordinary. That is because we have been so well taught by the House of Lords. If you actually try the idea out on your non-legal friends and relations, you will, I think, find that they are much less shocked. They tend to take the view that it was really all A's "fault" in the sense that, had A not asked to see the ring and had B not been good enough to show him it, B would not have lost it. And that was really Alfenus' approach. We do not know if other jurists accepted it, but there is nothing to show that they did not. At any rate we have to accept that Alfenus was prepared by this somewhat ingenious approach to impose liability in a situation where, on our established authorities and on the usual approach, our courts would exonerate the defendant.

You may also care to notice that the liability imposed by Alfenus is hard to categorise. Since he grants only an action *in factum* he must recognise that there is actually no contract between A and B. So the liability cannot be strictly speaking contractual. On the other hand, it is plainly not delictal. At best, we may perhaps place it among the group of actions *in factum* which cluster round the edges of the true contractual actions.[28] If we were forced to place the relationship in that category in English law as a kind of non-contractual agency, then—I speak with extreme diffidence—that system would not readily allow the plaintiff to by-pass *Glasgow Corporation* v. *Muir* by invoking the law of restitution, since the appropriate measure of recovery, if any, in the absence of contract would not extend as far as indemnity.[29]

As I said at the outset, I have no desire in this lecture to do more than put these matters before you. I do not suggest that English or Scots law should be changed to reflect the approach of Alfenus. Heaven forfend that either of the Law Commissions should ever feel moved to meddle in these matters. But we have it on the high authority of an Honorary Fellow of New College and member of the Court of London University, Lord Goff of Chieveley, that jurists and judges are fellow pilgrims "on the endless road to unattainable perfection" in the law.[30] When he said this in *Spiliada Maritime*, his Lordship was really concerned to be nice to academic lawyers. This is part of a recent tendency among higher judges in England which is not shared by their brethren in Scotland and which is probably to be deplored just as much as the former tendency to be rude. Since that was his purpose, and if his words are read *secundum subjectam materiam* as we are always told that they should be, then it seems unlikely that his Lordship had Roman jurists like Alfenus in mind as fellow pilgrims. Scots law, however, is supposed to have some kind of Roman roots and it claims to have a gratuitous contract of mandate.[31] So, with luck, some day two men will go strolling on the banks of the pollution-free, post-industrial Clyde. One will ask the other to show him his ring and, as he shows the ring, it will fall into the river and be lost. If, when the claim for the ring reaches the House of Lords, Lord Goff uses the chance to adopt the view of his fellow pilgrim Alfenus, he will make for us a leading case of the classic simplicity of *Donoghue v. Stevenson*. When that time comes, I only hope that academics will not be so busy examining the merits of no-fault compensation that they will forget to wonder *who* it was who went walking on the banks of the Clyde and ended up being discussed in a House of Lords committee room on the banks of the Thames.[32]

NOTES

[1] October 3, 1892. A. E. Housman, *Selected Prose* (ed. by J. Carter, Cambridge, 1961), p. 1.

[2] *Selected Prose*, pp. 20–21.

[3] [1932] A.C. 562; 1932 S.C. (H.L.) 31.

[4] [1932] A.C. 161. For discussion of the judgments below, see, for instance, C. J. Hamson, *"Bell* v. *Lever Bros."* (1937) 53 L.Q.R. 118 and the articles which he discusses.

[5] 1930 S.N. 117 (Outer House); 1930 S.N. 138 (Inner House).

[6] To be found most conveniently in the cases printed for use in the House of Lords ("House of Lords Case"). The copy which I have consulted is in the Advocates Library, Edinburgh, but others are to be found elsewhere. Unfortunately the original Court of Session process in the Scottish Record Office (S.R.O.) has been gutted so that nothing of interest remains except the original of Lord Moncrieff's opinion in the Outer House. See S.R.O. C.S. 252/2299/2.

[7] A. W. Brian Simpson, *Cannibalism and the Common Law* (Chicago and London, 1984).

[8] (1884) 14 Q.B.D. 273.

[9] W. Twining, *"Cannibalism and Legal Literature"* (1986) 6 *Oxford Journal of Legal Studies* 423.

[10] [1978] A.C. 728.

[11] *Governors of the Peabody Donation Fund* v. *Sir Lindsay Parkinson & Co. Ltd.* [1985] A.C. 210, esp. 239 F–241 C.

[12] *Curran* v. *Northern Ireland Co-Ownership Housing Association Ltd.* [1987] A.C. 718, esp. 726 C. Happily the long retreat from the precipice continues through *Yuen Kun Yeu* v. *Att.-Gen. of Hong Kong* [1988] A.C. 175 to *Rowling* v. *Takaro Properties Ltd.* [1988] 2 W.L.R. 418.

[13] *Overseas Tankship (U.K.) Ltd.* v. *Morts Dock and Engineering Co. (The Wagon Mound)* [1961] A.C. 388; *Overseas Tankship (U.K.) Ltd.* v. *Miller Steamship Co. (The Wagon Mound No. 2)* [1967] 1 A.C. 617.

[14] *E.g.* T. Weir, *A Casebook on Tort* (3rd ed., London 1974), p. 169. Sadly, the passage does not appear in later editions.

[15] W. L. Prosser, J. W. Wade, V. E. Schwartz, *Torts Cases and Materials* (7th ed., New York, 1982), pp. 308 and 309.

[16] For literature on the case see R. F. V. Heuston and R. A. Buckley, *Salmond & Heuston on the Law of Torts* (19th ed., London, 1987), p. 345, n. 6.

[17] The Sunday Times Colour Magazine, Feb. 8, 1976, p. 30.

[18] *E.g.* at [1987] 2 All E.R. 14.

[19] Lord Macmillan, (1933) 49 L.Q.R. 1; (1945) 61 L.Q.R. 109. It is perhaps unfortunate that in *Learning the Law* (11th ed., London, 1982), p. 19, Professor Glanville Williams stresses that the form *Donoghue* v. *Stevenson* is the correct citation "when brevity is desired." In fact, this form is correct whenever the case is cited in the usual way. It is also, by the way, a pity that at p. 43 he perpetuates two errors in referring to Scottish matters, one of which was specifically mentioned by Lord Macmillan at 49 L.Q.R. 2.

[20] Birth certificate of May McAllister, born July 4, 1898, Register of Births, Cambuslang 1898, No. 385, General Register Office for Scotland. All birth, marriage and death certificates referred to below are to be found in the General Register Office for Scotland which is situated in Edinburgh.

[21] 1932 S.C. (H.L.) 31.

[22] 1972 S.L.T. (News) 143; (1972) 17 *Journal of the Law Society of Scotland* 267.

[23] 1932 S.L.T. 317.

[24] *E.g.* [1932] A.C. 562; (1932) 48 T.L.R. 494.

[25] See birth certificate referred to in n. 20.

[26] See n. 20.

[27] See P. L. Payne, *Colvilles and the Scottish Steel Industry* (Oxford, 1979), pp. 27–32.

[28] See birth certificate of May McAllister referred to in n. 20 above and the marriage certificate of her parents, James McAllister and Mary Jane Hannah, married February 15, 1886, Register of Marriages, Cambuslang 1886, No. 21.

[29] See her parents' marriage certificate referred to in n. 28.

[30] See her parents' marriage certificate referred to in n. 28.

[31] They were married by the local Church of Scotland minister. See the marriage certificate referred to in n. 28.

[32] John McAllister, born November 18, 1886, Register of Births, Cambuslang 1886, No. 436.

[33] Mary Jane McAllister, born September 28, 1890, Register of Births, Cambuslang 1890, No. 466.

[34] See n. 58.

[35] Birth certificate referred to in n. 20. For a picture of the house in about 1890, see J. A. Wilson, *A History of Cambuslang* (Glasgow, 1929), facing p. 148. For description, see p. 152.

[36] Wilson, *op. cit.*, p. 152.

[37] S.R.O. V.R. 107/169 Valuation Roll for the County of Lanark 1898–1899, Middle Ward 2, Parish of Cambuslang, p. 161 where the owner is specified as James Low senior, builder, Morriston Street.

[38] James McAllister was not a tenant in the Valuation Roll for 1897–1898: S.R.O. V.R. 107/163 Valuation Roll for the County of Lanark 1897–1898, Middle Ward 2, Parish of Cambuslang, pp. 142–143. He is entered as the tenant of the first house in the Roll for the following year. See n. 37.

[39] In the House of Lords Record Office. See nn. 67 and 95.

[40] See the marriage certificate of Henry Donoghue and May McAllister, Register of Marriages, Blythswood, Glasgow 1916, No. 1169; birth certificate of Henry Donoghue, Register of Births, Bridgeton, Glasgow 1916, No. 1144; S.R.O. V.R. 107/306 Valuation Roll for the County of Lanark 1915–1916, Middle Ward, Parish of Cambuslang, p. 5. Henry's father is Michael Donoghue, who is entered in the Roll as tenant of 99 Hallside.

[41] See marriage certificate of Henry Donoghue and May McAllister referred to in n. 40; Article 1 of Condescendence in Summons in divorce process, *May McAllister or Donoghue* v. *Henry Donoghue*, C/30/1945, S.R.O. C.S. 46/40/1946. The proof in the case may also be consulted.

[42] See Valuation Roll referred to in n. 40 above.

[43] See n. 41.

[44] See marriage certificate referred to in n. 40. They married in a solicitor's office.

[45] For details of the form of marriage, see, *e.g.* F. P. Walton, *A Handbook of Husband and Wife according to the Law of Scotland* (2nd ed., by J. L. Wark, Edinburgh, 1922), Chap. 4. For the method of registration see the Marriage Scotland Act 1856 (19 & 20 Vict., c. 96) (Lord Brougham's Act), s.2. The procedure was amended shortly after Mrs. Donoghue's marriage by the Marriage (Scotland) Act 1916 (6 Geo. 5, c. 7), s.1. This form of marriage was abolished by the Marriage (Scotland) Act 1939 brought into force on July 1, 1940.

[46] See the marriage certificate referred to in n. 40 and the birth certificate of Henry Donoghue referred to in n. 40.

[47] See birth certificate referred to in n. 40.

[48] Birth certificate of James Donoghue, born June 25, 1917, Register of Births, Bridgeton, Glasgow 1917, No. 829; died June 26, 1917, Register of Deaths, Bridgeton, Glasgow 1917, No. 564.

[49] John McAllister Donoghue, born May 16, 1918, Register of Births, Bridgeton, Glasgow 1918, No. 574; died May 18, 1918, Register of Deaths, Bridgeton, Glasgow 1918, No. 329.

[50] See birth and death certificates referred to in n. 49 which say that Mr. Donoghue was a Private in the 84th Training Reserve, Bath. Both registrations were made by Mrs. Donoghue, whose signature may be inspected on them.

[51] Birth certificate of Mabel Donoghue, born June 3, 1920, Register of Births,

Bridgeton, Glasgow 1920, No. 1035; died June 14, 1920, Register of Deaths, Bridgeton, Glasgow 1920, No. 587.

[52] See generally I. Donald, *Practical Obstetric Problems* (5th ed., London, 1979), p. 940 with refs.

[53] Her death certificate records that the birth was "premature (inanition)."

[54] Letter to the author from Mr. Thomas Donoghue (brother-in-law of Mrs. Donoghue), July 24, 1973.

[55] Condescendence in divorce process referred to in n. 41. The proof may also be referred to.

[56] *Cf.* S.R.O. V.R. 102/1401 Valuation Roll for the City and Royal Burgh of Glasgow 1927–1928, Ward 3, Survey Book 129, p. 81 with V.R. 102/1420 Valuation Roll for the City and Royal Burgh of Glasgow 1928–1929, Ward 3, Survey Book 129, p. 81.

[57] Condescendence in divorce process referred to in n. 41. The proof may be consulted.

[58] S.R.O. V.R. 102/1401 Valuation Roll for the City and Royal Burgh of Glasgow 1927–1928, Ward 4, Survey Book 168, p. 73 and for 1928–1929 V.R. 102/1420 Valuation Roll, Ward 4, Survey Book 168, p. 73. The entries show the tenant as John M'Allister, Steelworker.

[59] Art. 4 of Condescendence in *Donoghue* v. *Stevenson*, House of Lords Case.

[60] Art. 1 of Condescendence in *Donoghue* v. *Stevenson*, House of Lords Case.

[61] Art. 2 of Condescendence in *Donoghue* v. *Stevenson*, House of Lords Case. For the weather, see *Glasgow Herald* August 27, 1928, p. 10 which gives the maximum temperature at the Coats Observatory, Paisley on the Sunday as 69.3° Fahrenheit. There were 7.4 hours of sunshine.

[62] Art. 2 of Condescendence in *Donoghue* v. *Stevenson*, House of Lords Case. As Professor Heuston notes (*Salmond & Heuston on the Law of Torts*, p. 346, n. 64), Lord Macmillan indicates in his speech that the friend was a woman: [1932] A.C. 605; 1932 S.C. (H.L.) 61. The pleadings give no indication and one must assume that Lord Macmillan proceeded on the basis of what was said at the hearing of the appeal.

[63] Date of signeting of the Summons, House of Lords Case.

[64] As was noted by G. Lewis, *Lord Atkin* (London, 1983), p. 52, n. 2, the action, though originally raised against Mr. Stevenson only, was subsequently amended to add Mr. Minchella, the café proprietor, as second defender. In the light of discussion in Procedure Roll on October 18, 1929, the pursuer abandoned her action in so far as directed against Mr. Minchella on November 6, 1929. See *Donoghue* v. *Stevenson* 1932 S.L.T. 520, also the interlocutors reproduced in the House of Lords Case.

[65] 1930 S.N. 117.

[66] 1930 S.N. 138.

[67] In the Court of Session pleadings her address is given as Kent Street and this is repeated in the petition of appeal lodged on February 26, 1931: (1930–1931) 163 *Journal of the House of Lords* 128. In fact, however, she had already moved to Maitland Street, since in her petition for leave to prosecute her appeal *in forma pauperis* dated February 16, 1931 (House of Lords Record Office), Mrs. Donoghue's address is given as "residing at 101 Maitland Street, Glasgow and lately care of M'Alister, 49 Kent Street, off London Rd., Glasgow." See also S.R.O. V.R. 102/1461 Valuation Roll for the City and Royal Burgh of Glasgow 1930–1931, Ward 17, Parish of Glasgow, Survey Book 626, p. 70.

[68] Petition for leave to prosecute appeal *in forma pauperis* dated February 16, 1931, referred to in n. 67. It was presented on February 26, 1931 and she was admitted to sue *in forma pauperis* on March 17, 1931: 163 *Journal of the House of*

Lords 128 and 152–153. Thereafter the case was lodged on June 5, 1931 and on June 9, 1931 it was set down for hearing: 163 *Journal of the House of Lords* 251.
[69] On March 18, 1932 the House ordered that the case should be considered, *i.e.* speeches delivered, on April 14, 1932, but on March 22 the order was discharged: 164 *Journal of the House of Lords* 123. It was not till May 12, 1932 that the date for speeches was finally fixed: 164 *Journal of the House of Lords* 180.

[70] See 1932 S.L.T. 520.

[71] Interlocutor of the Lord Ordinary (Moncrieff) dated December 6, 1934, granting decree of absolvitor in respect of the extrajudicial settlement of the case: (1934–1935) 154 *General Minute Book of the Court of Session* 63.

[72] S.R.O. V.R. 102/1602 Valuation Roll for the City and Royal Burgh of Glasgow 1937–1938, Ward 17, Parish of Glasgow, Survey Book 606, p. 68.

[73] Death certificate of Mary Jane McAllister, died December 28, 1936, Register of Deaths, Bridgeton, Glasgow 1936, No. 410.

[74] Marriage certificate of Henry McAllister Donoghue and Lorna Calderwood Nelson, married July 20, 1937, Register of Marriages, Blythswood, Glasgow 1937, No. 1647.

[75] *Cf.* the entry in the Roll referred to in n. 72 with S.R.O. V.R. 102/1623 Valuation Roll for the City and Royal Burgh of Glasgow 1938–1939, Ward 17, Parish of Glasgow, Survey Book 606, p. 68. The entries for numbers 97, 99 and 101 Maitland Street vanish from the later Roll and so the subjects themselves must have been demolished.

[76] S.R.O. V.R. 102/1631 Valuation Roll for the City and Royal Burgh of Glasgow 1938–1939, Ward 35, Govanhill, Survey Book 1356, p. 16. The owners are the Corporation.

[77] Thomas Donoghue, born February 21, 1936, Register of Births, Milton, Glasgow 1936, No. 325.

[78] Condescendence in divorce process referred to in n. 41. The proof may also be consulted.

[79] Birth certificate of James Donoghue, born March 26, 1944, Register of Births, Govan, Glasgow 1944, No. 536; Condescendence in divorce process referred to in n. 41. The proof may also be consulted.

[80] The summons in the divorce process referred to in n. 41 passed the signet on January 15, 1945.

[81] (1944–1945) 164 *General Minute Book of the Court of Session* 160.

[82] Minute of proceedings in divorce process referred to in n. 41.

[83] July 4, 1946. See (1945–1946) 165 *General Minute Book of the Court of Session* 381.

[84] Marriage of Henry Donoghue, October 19, 1945, Register of Marriages, Pollok, Glasgow 1945, No. 1003.

[85] Death certificate of Henry Donoghue, died January 21, 1961, Register of Deaths, Tradeston, Glasgow 1961, No. 40. He was 69 years old.

[86] See averments in Condescendence in summons in divorce process, *Henry Donoghue v. Mrs. Lorna Calderwood Nelson or Donoghue*, C/396/1945, S.R.O. C.S. 258/15803/1945. Decree of divorce was pronounced on January 23, 1946: (1945–1946) 165 *General Minute Book of the Court of Session* 155.

[87] Marriage certificate of Henry McAllister Donoghue and Margaret Wright Houston, April 27, 1946, Register of Marriages, Pollok, Glasgow 1946, No. 340.

[88] The entries, all from the Register of Births, Provan, Glasgow are: Desmond McAllister, 1947, No. 1741; Evelyn, 1949, No. 1320 (a girl); Elizabeth Houston, 1952, No. 557; Margaret Houston, 1955, No. 1636 and Stephen, 1957, No. 376.

[89] See the entries in the Valuation Roll for 1938–1939 referred to in n. 76 and S.R.O. V.R. 102/2304 Valuation Roll for the City and Royal Burgh of Glasgow 1957–1958, Ward 35, Govanhill, Survey Book 803, p. 180.

[90] Register of Deaths, Provan, Glasgow 1958, No. 269; S.R.O. S.C. 36/48/875 Inventory of Estates in Court Books of Commissariot of Lanarkshire April 10 to April 24, 1958, Inventory of estate of May McAllister (formerly Mrs. May Donoghue) April 12, 1958.

[91] S.R.O. S.C. 36/52/229 Confirmation on estate of May McAllister, commonly known as Miss Mabel Hannah, Commissariot of Glasgow, April 16, 1958.

[92] See death certificate referred to in n. 89.

[93] She remained the tenant of the house in Jamieson Street and a small amount of cash was still in the house. See Valuation Roll entry referred to in n. 88 and the inventory referred to in n. 90.

[94] For her divorce. The late Lord Milligan, her junior counsel in *Donoghue* v. *Stevenson*, told the writer that he never met Mrs. Donoghue, and so she cannot have attended a consultation in Edinburgh, nor the legal debate in the Court of Session.

[95] Sworn on February 16, 1931 and attached to petition for leave to prosecute her appeal *in forma pauperis* of the same date. The affidavit is signed by her. See nn. 67 and 68.

[96] *Cf.* House of Lords Directions to Agents, 1926 edition, No. 18.

[97] *Cf. Salmond & Heuston on the Law of Torts*, p. 346, n. 65.

[98] Letter to author from Mr. Thomas Donoghue dated July 24, 1973.

[99] See 1932 S.C. (H.L.) 31.

[1] See Inventory referred to in n. 89.

[2] *Cf.* M. C. Meston, *The Succession (Scotland) Act 1964* (3rd ed., Edinburgh, 1982), pp. 11–12.

[3] [1943] A.C. 92; 1942 S.C. (H.L.) 78.

[4] [1943] A.C. 448; 1943 S.C. (H.L.) 3.

[5] [1932] A.C. 580, *per* Lord Atkin; 620–621, *per* Lord Macmillan; 1932 S.C. (H.L.) 44, *per* Lord Atkin; 1932 S.C. (H.L.) 71–72, *per* Lord Macmillan. *Cf.* Heuston, Preface to the nineteenth edition of *Salmond & Heuston on the Law of Torts*, pp. vii–viii.

[6] [1943] A.C. 465; 1943 S.C. (H.L.) 16.

[7] *Smith* v. *Littlewoods Organisation Ltd.* [1987] A.C. 241, esp. 259 D–262 D; *sub nom. Maloco* v. *Littlewoods Organisation* 1987 S.L.T. 425, esp. 432 D–433 H.

[8] For information about his career (some of it rather speculative) see R. A. Bauman, *Lawyers in Roman Transitional Politics* (Munich, 1985), pp. 89 *et seq.*

[9] See, for example, J. A. C. Thomas, *Textbook of Roman Law* (Amsterdam, New York, Oxford, 1976), Chap. 29.

[10] For Chapter Three see D.9.2.27.5, Ulpian 18 *ad edictum*; Gaius, Institutes 3.217. For recent discussion of the wording of the provision see J. A. Crook, "Lex Aquilia" (1984) 62 *Athenaeum* 67, 73 *et seq.* For the distinction between direct and indirect actions see F. H. Lawson and B. S. Markesinis, *Tortious Liability for unintentional harm in the Common law and the Civil law*, (Cambridge, 1982), pp. 14 *et seq.*

[11] In his *digesta* Alfenus records not only his own opinions but those of Servius Sulpicius Rufus, also of the first century B.C. It is not possible to disentangle the two strands. See F. Schulz, *History of Roman Legal Science* (corrected edition, Oxford, 1953), pp. 205 *et seq.* For the sake of simplicity I have chosen to refer to the author as Alfenus.

[12] *The Digest of Justinian* 2 (ed., A. Watson, Philadelphia, 1985).

[13] See for example W. W. Buckland, *A Textbook of Roman Law* (3rd ed., P. Stein, Cambridge, 1963), p. 589 with n. 3; Lawson and Markesinis, *Tortious*

Liability, p. 15, n. 109; H. Hausmaninger, *Das Schadenersatzrecht der lex Aquilia* (2nd ed., Vienna, 1980), p. 17.

[14] *E.g.* Buckland, *Textbook, loc. cit.*; A. Watson, *The Law of Obligations in the Later Roman Republic* (Oxford, 1965), p. 244.

[15] See, *e.g.* Watson, *Obligations*, pp. 236 *et seq.*; D. Daube, *Roman Law Linguistic, Social and Philosophical Aspects* (Edinburgh, 1969), pp. 143 and 153 *et seq.*

[16] In the late twelfth century A.D. John Bassian glossed *illi excidit* with "cui ostensus erat."

[17] Basilica 20.4.23.

[18] *Cf.* D.19.5.17.2, Ulpian 28 *ad edictum*; D.47.2.79, Papinian 8 *quaestionum.*

[19] *E.g.* J. Cuiacius, *Commentaria accuratissima in libros quaestionum summi inter veteres I.C. Aemilii Papiniani, Opera Omnia* (Lyon, 1606), col. 142 at col. 143 (on D.19.5.17.2); O. Lenel, *Palingenesia Iuris Civilis* 1 (Leipzig, 1889), 49; J. L. Barton, "The 'Lex Aquilia' and Decretal Actions," *Daube Noster* (ed., A. Watson, Edinburgh and London, 1974), p. 15 at p. 18.

[20] D.17.1.1.2, Paul 32 *ad edictum*. See A. Watson, *Contract of Mandate in Roman Law* (Oxford, 1961), pp. 61 *et seq.*

[21] *Textbook*, p. 514.

[22] *Cf.* Palandt, *Bürgerliches Gesetzbuch* (46th ed., by P. Bassenge and others, Munich, 1987), p. 734, commentary on Article 662 and p. 211, Introduction 2) to Article 241. For English Law, see *Chitty on Contracts* (25th ed., edited by A. G. Guest and others, London, 1983), paras. 123 *et seq.*, esp. 126.

[23] D.17.1.1.4, Paul 32 *ad edictum*; F. Schulz, *Classical Roman Law* (Oxford, 1951), pp. 555 *et seq.*; H. Honsell, T. Mayer-Maly, W. Selb, *Römisches Recht* (4th ed., Berlin, etc. 1987), pp. 335 *et seq.* (Honsell).

[24] See above all W. Kunkel, "Fides als schöpferisches Element im römischen Schuldrecht," *Festschrift Paul Koschaker* 2 (Weimar, 1939, reprinted, Leipzig, 1977), 1; also D. Daube, *Forms in Roman Legislation* (Oxford, 1956), p. 19; Honsell, *Römisches Recht*, pp. 220 *et seq.*

[25] P. Stein, "Julian and Liability for Loss Suffered in the Execution of a Contract in Roman Law," (1956) *Butterworths South African Law Review* 64, 66 *et seq.*; P. Stein, *Fault in the Formation of Contract in Roman Law and Scots Law* (Edinburgh and London, 1958), Chap. 9; Watson, *Mandate*, pp. 154 *et seq.*

[26] *Bowstead on Agency* (15th ed., by F. M. B. Reynolds, London, 1985), p. 246, Art. 64.

[27] [1943] A.C. 465; 1943 S.C. (H.L.) 16.

[28] It is similar in kind to the actions *in factum* which Professor Daube has illuminated in articles such as "Certainty of Price," *Studies in the Roman Law of Sale* (ed. by D. Daube, Oxford, 1959), p. 9 esp. at pp. 31 *et seq.*

[29] See for example Lord Goff of Chieveley and G. Jones, *The Law of Restitution* (3rd ed., London, 1986), pp. 324–325 and *Bowstead on Agency*, p. 247.

[30] *Spiliada Maritime Corporation* v. *Cansulex Ltd.* [1987] A.C. 460, 488 C.

[31] See, for example, Bell's *Principles* (10th ed., by W. Guthrie, Edinburgh, 1899), paras. 216–218.

[32] A fuller discussion of D.19.5.23 will appear elsewhere. Professor Peter Birks put up with a deluge of letters on that text and patiently discussed the point. Anne and Lindsay Muir gave post-prandial and non-legal comment on the idea of making someone liable in these circumstances. My sister, Dr. Christine Rodger, patiently drove with me around the various parts of Glasgow and its environs which feature in the tale of Mrs. Donoghue. I am grateful to all of them.

Written Contracts: To What Extent May Evidence Control Language?

SIR JOHAN STEYN

All judges are prone to error. And one of the principal causes of judicial error is a lack of knowledge of the environment of the critical decision. Such an environment may be, in a general common law case, the impact of the decision on other areas of the law; in a judicial review case, the historical and social context of a statute; in a commercial case, the way in which a particular trade or market works; and many other examples spring to mind. But the law sometimes sets limits to the extent to which a judge may be informed of, and take into account, the broad environment against which his decision will be made. My concern is with the extent to which a judge, who is confronted with a problem of the interpretation of an integrated written contract as opposed to an issue of contract formation, may allow evidence of the broader environment to control the language of the contract, and therefore to influence the answer to the question to be decided. The interesting question is not what evidence may be admitted but the substantive question of the extent to which evidence may ultimately be allowed to influence the answer to the question of interpretation. Since all language is imprecise, and the vicissitudes of contractual relations are unpredictable, even Sir James Murray's great dictionary will seldom provide the answer. Some evidence, or agreement as to the relevant facts, will always be necessary.

The critical question is: Where is the line to be drawn? The answer to that question varies greatly between different legal systems. It is interesting to contrast the approaches of the common law and the civil law. The common law classifies all issues of interpretation as questions of law. The common law rules are based on an objective approach to the interpretation of contracts. The question is not what the parties subjectively intended but what meaning would be given to the language of the contract by an ordinary speaker of the English language, who is placed in the position of the parties at the time when they made their contract. English law therefore adopts an external standard and subordinates the equity of the particular case to the policy of striving for legal certainty in the generality of cases. Proceeding from this starting point English law readily arrives at the conclusion that evidence may only be used in aid of the interpretation of contracts in limited circumstances.

The civilian approach is diametrically opposite: the purpose is to determine what the parties actually intended when they made the contract. The meaning of contracts is generally regarded as a question of fact. It is a subjective theory of interpretation. The starting point is the language of the contract. But, if there is uncertainty about the meaning of the language, or a dispute about the intention of the parties, a civilian court will take into account all material which arguably throws light on the intention of the parties.

The superiority of the English system, and the desirability of maintaining it, should not be presumed. A number of factors combine to suggest that a re-examination may not be out of place. First, the jurisprudence of the European Court of Justice in relation to the interpretation of contracts is squarely based on the civilian approach. Secondly, the practice of the common law countries is not uniform: in the case law of the United States there has been a radical departure from the common law rules as developed by the English courts, with the result that in this area of the law the United States straddles the middle ground between the traditional common law and civilian approaches. Thirdly, in relation to wills and statutes, exclusionary rules as to the use of extrinsic material in aid of interpretation have been relaxed to some extent: in the case of wills by a 1982 statute[1] to broaden the categories in which an otherwise meaningless will may be construed in the light of evidence of a testator's intention, and in the case of statutes by House of Lords' decisions[2] which have made clear that statutes passed to give effect to unenacted treaties must nevertheless, when ambiguous, be construed in the light of the treaty and its *travaux preparatoires*. Finally, even in the framework of our own system, there have been attacks on the traditional approach, and attempts to circumvent it. The time is therefore ripe to take a critical look at our rules.

There are three classes of evidence which no sensible system of law can ignore. The first is identificatory evidence. It is self-evident that evidence ought always to be admitted to relate the terms of a contract to the external world, *i.e.* to identify persons, things and concepts. Such evidence is used not in order to construe the contract but only to ascertain whether a given factual situation comes within the words of the contract. So far there is nothing to excite controversy. But one has to add that identificatory evidence may itself give rise to difficulties of interpretation in the form of a latent ambiguity, and that qualification brings me to the second uncontroversial class of evidence.

In everyday life words receive their colour from their context. Samuel Johnson illustrated that in his dictionary by defining "oats" as—

> "A grain, which in England is generally given to horses, but in Scotland supports the people."

Time, place and circumstances are relevant to the process of selecting the appropriate meaning. And our law does recognise this reality. The purpose for which such evidence is admitted is to place the court in the same contextual scene as the parties were when they signed the contract or, in the conventional idiom, "The court must . . . place itself in thought in the same factual matrix as that in which the parties were."[3] The advocate who urges the admission of seemingly inadmissible material, as a factor capable of arousing sympathy for his client's favoured interpretation, almost invariably says, "it is part of the factual matrix." But catchphrases tend to obscure the true nature of legal principles. Two questions arise. The first is *when* evidence of surrounding circumstances may be called in aid of interpretation. The second is *what* evidence may be used for this purpose. It used to be said that evidence of surrounding circumstances may only be used when there is an ambiguity in the language of the contract, or an ambiguity revealed by admitting identificatory evidence. In *Reardon Smith Line Ltd.* v. *Yngvar Hansen-Tangen*[4] the House of Lords held that in all commercial cases it is right that the court should know the commercial purpose of the contract which, it was said, presupposes knowledge of the genesis of the transaction, the background, the context and the market in which the parties are operating. But, if sufficient certainty as to the meaning of the contract can be gathered from the language alone, it would clearly not be right to reach a different result by drawing inferences from evidence as to the surrounding circumstances. In such a case the verdict must be that the resort to surrounding circumstances has proved unnecessary. It is helpful to concentrate not on what evidence a judge ought to admit as a matter of the rules of evidence, because under this heading he will admit what is arguably relevant, but on what use he may make of such material in selecting, as between contending interpretations, the appropriate one. No adequate generalised proposition is possible. All one can say is that the use which a judge may make of such materials will depend on how far the language is capable of stretching.[5] In other words, it depends on the different meanings which the language itself will let in. And it has rightly been said:

> "Language is a labyrinth of paths. You approach from one side and know your way about; you approach from another side and no longer know your way about."[6]

Where the uncertainty of the language of the contract is such that it is necessary and right to draw inferences from surrounding circumstances, it still remains to be considered what evidence of the objective setting of the contract may be allowed to influence the decision. It used to be said that the purpose of the rule is to allow recourse to objective matters and circumstances which were probably present to the minds of the parties when they contracted. If the rationale of the rule were allowed so to circumscribe the classes of evidence, which may be used in aid of the construction of contracts, a great deal of useful contextual material would be excluded. In *Reardon Smith Line Ltd.* v. *Yngvar Hansen-Tangen*,[7] a more flexible approach was adopted. It was held that when one is speaking of extrinsic evidence of aim, or object, or commercial purpose, one is speaking objectively of what reasonable persons would have in mind in the situation of the parties. In other words, the judge, who is faced with a question of interpretation, should consider all classes of evidence which arguably forms part of the objective setting in which a contract is to be construed. And it is no answer to say that the parties, or one of them, ignored the objective setting.

Given the fact that the sometimes amorphous objective setting of a contract may be allowed to influence its interpretation, the case for allowing a crystallised custom or usage to do so is overwhelming. A distinction must be drawn between custom and usage. The role of custom is deeply rooted in our legal history. It was one of the formative influences in the development of our commercial law. Today, that role has greatly diminished. Custom has played other roles: in localities where a custom was observed it enabled and still enables a court to annex incidents to a contract or to give a secondary meaning to contractual language. In order to establish a custom stringent requirements have to be met: a custom must be lawful, not inconsistent with the contract, reasonable, notorious, certain and universally acquiesced in. The stringency of these requirements is such that the role of custom in the interpretation of written contracts is nowadays of marginal importance only. But in the course of time a more flexible doctrine, permitting the use of evidence of trade usage falling short of custom, became established. The good sense of the development is clear: it is the assumption that usages are mostly taken for granted and therefore not spelled out in writing. To ignore such usages would be to defeat the reasonable expectations of parties. When will it be right for a judge to allow such a usage to control the issue of interpretation? Negatively, it is easy to agree on the proposition that trade usage ought not to be encumbered with the stringent requirements of custom. For example, in the last few years the financial pages of our national newspapers have recorded the emergence of a number of new and orderly financial and commodities' markets, with a regularity of observance of usages, which ought to be recognised in the process of interpretation. In what seems to me a maze of irreconcilable precedent, I have been unable to find any coherent analysis of the circumstances in which a trade usage as opposed to a custom may be allowed to control an issue of interpretation. Here is a task still to be performed; it will require separate and special study. All I can tentatively suggest is that in the meantime the despairing judge may not go too far wrong if he adopts the simple and liberal solution of the United States Uniform Commercial Code.[8] It defines a trade usage as "any practice or method of dealing having such a regularity of observance in a place, vocation or trade as to justify an expectation that it will be observed with respect to that transaction." But it also provides that a trade usage will only bind a person if, when he contracted, he knew of it or should have known of it. Given the doubt that exists about the precise boundaries of trade usage, it is obvious in principle that any sensible legal system must allow recourse to it in aid of interpretation of written contracts.

Two classes of evidence mark the great divide between the common law and civilian systems, *viz.* evidence of prior negotiations and subsequent conduct of the parties. In civilian systems the search is for the subjective *consensus ad idem* of the parties. The concept of rectification of a written contract is not known. Pre-contractual exchanges are freely admitted as evidence of the parties' actual intentions. But it is probably right to say that the clearer the language of an integrated written contract the less likely it is that the court will ultimately allow evidence of the negotiations to control the interpretation. And, if the parties have contracted on standard-form terms, it is in practice difficult to persuade a civilian court to depart from the ordinary meaning of the language on the basis of inferences from the evidence of the negotiations. In England the rule is different. Pre-contractual negotiations are let in by a plea of rectification. But if that plea fails the judge may not allow his interpretation of the contract to be influenced by evidence of negotiations.[9] The rule is that evidence of the parties' intentions, or negotiations, may not be received as an aid to interpretation. This rule was clearly established by the decision of the House of Lords in *Prenn* v. *Simmonds*.[10] Lord Wilberforce, who gave the leading judgment, explained the rationale of the rule. He said that the reason for the rule is not a technical one or even one mainly of convenience. Such evidence is unhelpful because the positions of the parties change until final agreement. If earlier documents use different expressions, that does not help. If the same expressions are used, nothing is gained by looking back. And, the words used may and often do represent a formula which means different things to each side, yet are accepted because that is the only way to get agreement. Lord Wilberforce also referred to the judgment of Cardozo J. in *Utica City National Bank* v. *Gunn*[11] to dispel, as he said, "the idea that English law is some island of literal interpretation." He said that the New York Court of Appeals "followed precisely the English line." But in that case the great American judge was considering the admissibility of evidence of "the genesis and aim of the transaction," and not of evidence of pre-contractual negotiations. And it is tolerably clearly established in the United States, despite its multiplicity of jurisdictions, that pre-contractual negotiations are admissible in aid of the interpretation of contracts.[12] The terrain of the debate in the United States was apparently whether an ambiguity must be shown before such evidence may control the decision. In the Restatement Second of Contracts[13] Corbin's liberal view prevailed over Williston's more restrictive view. The law of the United States has therefore developed along very different lines.

But it is necessary to examine Lord Wilberforce's pragmatic justification of the rule. It would clearly not be right to say that evidence of negotiations is always unhelpful in the search for the subjective consensus of the parties. If it were, the practice of civilian courts, and of courts in the United States would be different. All one can safely say is that in the real world such evidence seldom reveals material which satisfactorily establishes the subjective consensus of the parties at the time of the making of their contract. The real reason for the exclusion of such evidence is the philosophical starting point of English law: the purpose of the process of interpretation is not to find what the parties intended but to determine what the language of the contract would signify to an ordinary speaker of English, who is properly informed as to the objective setting of the contract. In relation to that enquiry evidence of the actual intentions of the parties, or of their pre-contractual communications, is unhelpful.

Leaving aside the case of rectification, the question arises whether the exclusionary rule is subject to any exceptions. One hesitates to add to the burgeoning field of application of the doctrine of estoppel, but it seems conceivable that in pre-contractual exchanges an unequivocal representation as to the meaning of a word or expression may be made by one party, and that the other party may sign the contract in reliance on it, thus giving rise to an estoppel. But that must be a fairly rare case. A judgment given in the Commercial Court, appeared to form the basis of another potentially more virile exception to the general rule. In *Karen Oltmann*[14] the court used pre-contractual telex exchanges as an aid to the interpretation of an ambiguous word on the basis that the exchanges revealed that the parties had negotiated on an agreed basis. It was said that the parties had given to the word the same dictionary meaning. And this conclusion was reached despite the fact that the judge held that there was no basis for rectifying the contract, or for finding that an estoppel operated. It is an exception which could easily swallow up the rule. That has, however, not happened so far and this decision can perhaps be regarded either as justified on the orthodox basis of an estoppel or as depending on its own rather special facts. So, the rule appears to be intact.

That brings me to the next category of evidence which is in the controversial area where the solutions of civilian and common law legal systems differ, *i.e.* evidence of the conduct of the parties during the performance of the contract which reveals how they understood words and expressions in the contract. An example will illustrate the point. An exporter negotiates a revolving credit line for two years with his bank to finance his export transactions at an historic rate of interest. The limit is £1,000,000. He uses the facility repeatedly; on two occasions he repays the entire sum due to the bank, thereafter he uses the facility again. Then during the two-year period a rise in interest rates makes the transaction unprofitable for the bank. The exporter wishes to use the facility again. The bank then says "once you have repaid the entire sum the facility is at an end." The merchant says "But you did not say that when the market was in your favour." To the lay mind, and in particular a businessman, such evidence is not only relevant but of great persuasive value. In civilian systems such evidence is regarded as an important source of reliable information as to the true intention of the parties. In the United States such evidence is called "practical construction," and is given great weight as an aid to construction.[15] In England, on the other hand, such evidence is inadmissible as an aid to construction. If such evidence is admitted on the basis of pleas of variation or estoppel, and the pleas fail, the evidence as to subsequent conduct must be ignored. In the seventies the House of Lords was on two occasions asked to reconsider the rule.[16] But on each occasion the traditional rule was reaffirmed. It may be useful, however, to explore the reason for the exclusionary rule. For Lord Simon of Glaisdale in *Schuler A.G.* v. *Wickman Machine Tool Sales Ltd.* the principal reason was that subsequent conduct is equally referable to what the parties meant to say as to the meaning of what they said.[17] Lord Wilberforce stated the objection as follows:—

> "The general rule is that extrinsic evidence is not admissible for the construction of a written contract; the parties' intentions must be ascertained, on legal principles of construction, from the words they have used. It is one and the same principle which excludes evidence of statements, or actions, during negotiations, at the time of the contract, or subsequent to the contract, any of which to the lay mind might at first seem proper to receive."[18]

It cannot be doubted that such evidence may be helpful if the object of the enquiry is to determine the subjective consensus of the parties. Given that English contract law eschews that as an object of interpretation but instead seeks to determine the ordinary meaning of the language, in its objective setting, the result inevitably follows that such evidence cannot be allowed to influence interpretation. Evidence of the subsequent conduct of the parties, like evidence of prior negotiations, could only become admissible as an aid to construction if the objective theory to the interpretation of contracts was abandoned.

In taking stock of the merits and demerits of the different approaches, one has to accept that in a hard case the decision of a Continental and an English judge may be different.[19] Which is the better system? The disinterested idealist would probably say that the civilian approach represents a search for complete and perfect justice between the parties, and is therefore to be preferred. He would say that contractual disputes ought to be resolved in the light of all the facts of the case, and that the self-denying ordinance prescribed by the objective theory of interpretation results, from time to time, in a denial of justice. And he would probably say the English approach must occasionally result in an interpretation which neither party put forward. The answer of the English lawyer is pragmatic: he seeks to justify the objective approach on practical grounds. He points out that as between the parties to the contract the English approach tends to make the resolution of issues of interpretation more predictable, and, he would add, predictability is a matter of the greatest importance in commerce. He says that in an increasingly complex commercial world, a written contract between two parties is frequently linked with other contracts, and often forms the basis of other dealings. Third parties must necessarily take written contracts at face value. The interests of trade are therefore advanced by the objective theory. He says the resolution of contractual disputes is rendered less time-consuming and costly under the English system of allowing only limited resort to extrinsic evidence. Justice is more important than time and money. But the administration of civil justice cannot sensibly be organised on the basis that time and money do not matter. Moreover, the English lawyer says that it is an entirely defensible philosophical stance to say that under our system, the parties to a contract assume the risk of the interpretation which an impartial court or arbitral tribunal may place on their words. And, finally, he points to the popularity of English standard forms of contract in international commerce and to the remarkably high incidence in international transactions of an express choice of English law as the proper law of the contract and, in other cases, of the inclusion of a London arbitration clause. The English commercial lawyer says, and I agree, that the English approach has been vindicated in the international market-place, as well as in the hard school of international commercial litigation and arbitration.

NOTES

[1] Administration of Justice Act 1982, s.21(2)(a).

[2] *Fothergill* v. *Monarch Airlines Ltd.* [1981] A.C. 251; *Gatoil International Inc.* v. *Arkwright—Boston Manufacturers Insurance Co. Ltd.* [1985] A.C. 255.

[3] *Reardon Smith Line Ltd.* v. *Yngvar Hansen-Tangen* [1976] 1 W.L.R. 989 at 997C, *per* Lord Wilberforce.

[4] *Supra* at 995H, *per* Lord Wilberforce.

[5] *Fustis Mining Co.* v. *Bear* 239F. 976.

[6] Wittgenstein, *Philosophical Investigations* (1953), para. 203.

[7] *Supra* at 996E–F, *per* Lord Wilberforce.

[8] Section 1–205. See also Joseph H. Levie, "Trade Usage and Custom under the common law and the Uniform Commercial Code" 40 N.Y.U.L.R. 1101.

[9] On the other hand, it may be permissible to have recourse to pre-contractual exchanges for the limited purpose of identifying the objective setting of the contract. See *Prenn* v. *Simmonds*, [1971] 1 W.L.R. 1381 at 1385A, *per* Lord Wilberforce.

[10] *Supra.*

[11] (1918) 118 N.E. 607.

[12] Farnsworth, *Contracts*, 1982.

[13] s.212.

[14] [1976] 2 Ll.L.R. 708. See also *Polaris Aktieselskap* v. *Unilever Ltd.* 39 Com.Cas. 1 at 9, *per* Lord Atkin.

[15] Farnsworth, *op. cit.*, s.7.13.

[16] See *Whitworth Street Estates (Manchester) Ltd.* v. *James Miller & Partners* 1970 A.C. 583; *Schuler A.G.* v. *Wickman Machine Tool Sales Ltds.* 1974 A.C. 235.

[17] *Supra*, at 263F.

[18] *Supra*, at 261B.

[19] One is alive to the dangers of generalising about foreign legal systems. Fortunately, I had the advantage of the comments of Dr. Albert Jan van den Berg, a distinguished Dutch lawyer, on a draft of this lecture.

Hearsay Revisited

STEPHEN GUEST

In a recent article, I argued that the hearsay rule should be confined strictly to the most obvious interpretation of the words in which it is most frequently expressed: "a statement other than one made by a person while giving oral evidence in the proceedings is inadmissible as evidence of any fact stated."[1] I argued that although the only clear rationale I could discern for the rule—a perceived necessity for cross-examination to enhance reliability—could extend to cases escaping the words of this definition, any extension of the definition would lead to a uselessly wide characterisation of the rule. The alteration suggested by certain infamous problem cases[2] would allow in effect that *any* reports of conduct from which states of mind, particularly belief, could be inferred would be hearsay. I therefore argued that to make best sense of the rule a line should be drawn so that the hearsay rule excluded only *statements* (which was to include greetings, etc., in which there is a "propositional content") made out of court and intended by counsel to be used to prove their truth.[3]

It seemed to me that this conclusion would serve two purposes. It would exclude the clearest expressions both of deception in the form of lying and mistaken judgments both of which are characteristically made in the form of statements. Further, it would leave the rule as the following handy rule of thumb:

(i) first, find whether an out-of-court statement has been made;

(ii) second, find whether that statement is being offered as proof of its truth.

This rule of thumb has the advantage both of avoiding the problem cases, such as the sea-captain who inspects the ship (*per* Parke B. in *Wright* v. *Tatham*)[4] and the "silent" cases (*e.g. Bessela* v. *Stern*)[5] where no statements are made. A further advantage is

33

that the application of the rule thus characterised involves the relatively unproblematic examination of the public meaning of the statement (which may include what is entailed by the statement) and counsel's purpose in putting the evidence forward. This proposed rule of thumb method gives a clean cutting edge to an otherwise perversely difficult rule and it achieves this at the same time as cohering with the way the rule has been repeatedly formulated in terms of "statements" and "facts stated."[6]

I shall here defend my conclusion against two different approaches to characterising the problem of implied hearsay. The first is Tapper's idea that conduct falling within the hearsay rule is that intended to be assertive of some fact[7] and the second is Professor Tribe's view that the hearsay rule should be confined to the exclusion only of unreliable evidence.[8] But it is first necessary for me to clarify and develop what I called the *"reductio ad absurdum"* of allowing some non-stating behaviour to be caught by the hearsay rule and it is to this argument that I shall now turn.

Actions as *"reports"* of judgments or other mental states

The idea is this: if we are to declare *some* uncertain reported acts as hearsay, where do we draw the line? If a line cannot be drawn then any report of such acts, put forward in court to prove the truth of some proposition about the actor, becomes hearsay. The position is reduced to absurdity because the following case, uncontroversially regarded as a case of direct testimony, would then have to be classified as hearsay: D is observed by W to stalk P with a dagger and then plunge it into P, killing him. This set of circumstances clearly falls within my extended version of Cross's classic rule which was: "Conduct (including stating) other than that of a person while giving oral evidence in the proceedings is inadmissible as evidence of any state of mind to be inferred from that conduct."[9] W's evidence in court on oath, about which he may be cross-examined, is good evidence that D intended to kill P, however, and there is no question of it being hearsay (at least at the ordinary, practical, courtroom level). On the other hand, W's report that he had overheard D, at the time of the stabbing, shout "Death to you, P" or "I'll cut out your gizzard, P," would be regarded as a clear case of hearsay, although because it comes under the *res gestae* category of statements of intentions accom-

panying acts, it would be admissible.[10] (But, of course, admissible
only by way of exception to the hearsay rule.)

The above is a compelling argument. It must follow that a line
has to be drawn somewhere between the hearsay statement, for
example, "The man who threw the stone went over there,"[11] and
my example of stalking and stabbing. As I have suggested, that line
should be drawn at the point where no *statement* has been made by
the party out of court. But consider the following, perhaps more
academic, difficulty. What if a report of a witness who has
observed a "stalking and stabbing," is really a report of a report,
evidenced in the action, of an inner mental state of the person
stabbing? Why not, if the sea-captain who inspects his ship is, in so
doing, reporting his belief that the ship is sea-worthy? Using this
parallel, the man who stabs "reports," by his actions, his intention
to kill (or do grievous bodily harm). It is necessary, then, to
consider this argument because if it is correct our ordinary
assumptions about direct reports of intentions, etc., from the
observance of non-verbal actions are wrong.[12]

The classic formulation requires that the purpose for introducing the out-of-court report be to prove the facts stated. The truth
of the hearsay statement is important because, since these sorts of
statement are not self-verifying, its probative value depends on the
likelihood of a correct judgment having been made by the speaker.
For example, "The man who threw the stone went over there" is
without probative value if stated by a foreigner who just happens
to be reading out a line in a phrase-book. Similarly, in the sea-
captain's case, the probative value—the truth of the proposition
"the ship is sea-worthy" is dependent on the sea-captain's having
inspected the ship as well as his competence. The overall picture
then is of the statement, or conduct from which the proposition is
to be inferred, detached from the mental state of the speaker, or
actor. In the first case it is the person's *seeing* the man who threw
the stone and, in the second, the sea-captain's *judging* the ship to
be sea-worthy.

But how realistic is this sort of argument? In the case of D, who
stalks and stabs P, it seems that there is no question of a judgment
of a similar sort. It sounds pedantic, if not ridiculous, to say that D
made a judgment that he had an intention to kill P and then
carried that intention out. Rather, it seems that in observing his
actions we can go *straight* to his intention merely by applying,
correctly, the intention-laden words "stalking" and "stabbing."
The idea that D has an intention "in his mind" that somehow is
"reported" by D's behaviour, is the result of a view that nowadays
seems too simple to help us understand the direct ways we ascribe

responsibility and the various ways we can explain the workings of the mind.[13]

It is useful to compare the way the law of hearsay treats reports of people's mental and physical states. It classifies statements of intention, emotion and sensation as hearsay, along with "the man who threw the stone"-type judgments. It is significant that where such statements are made in the *res gestae* the evidence is admitted because of the greater likelihood of reliability.[14] In the case of intention, if the statement of intention is made during the disputed action it is admissible to explain the action, provided that the statement is made by the person carrying out the action.[15] But it is clear that is only necessary where the action is equivocal, that is, requires explanation. So, for example, in our case of D stalking and stabbing P, because the action is relatively unequivocal, the probative force of his yelling "Die, P!" is unimportant because superfluous although from a purely academic point of view, "Die, P!" may confirm the earlier observation that D "stalked" before he "stabbed." It should be noted, too, that there is less likelihood of deception in the case of non-verbal actions, for these require more obvious dramatic acting, although the witness is available for cross-examination on this point. "Was this really 'stalking' or was it an elaborate game of hide and seek?" "Did the dagger drop accidentally when D, seized of an imbecilic momentary interest in entomology, reached for a butterfly over P's head?" and so on, and so on.

The non-verbal stalking and stabbing case, in my view, raises no hearsay question. The matter is therefore one merely of relevance. Direct observation can be made of a person's intention at the time of doing the act and also shortly before and after the act, for example, in D's case, of "stalking" and, say, concealment of the offence. The cases show that this parallels neatly with a person's statement of his intention being relevant to show that he had a later existing intention or performed a later act carrying out that intention.[16] D's statement that "he intended to cut P's life short," made on December 1, would tend to suggest that he had that same intention on December 2, when P in fact dies. And so presumably, for the non-verbal case, would evidence of D's having spent December 1 firing a rifle at a photograph of P, when P dies on December 2 of a bullet wound inflicted by D (and D's defence is that the rifle went off by accident). Here there is clearly no need to analyse the situation in terms of "stated" reports of internal events.

Emotions and sensations are more difficult. It is sufficient for present purposes to note the following about the relationship between a person's statement of his emotion and the ability of other people to correct those statements. It is possible for someone to say of another "that is not anger you feel but simply jealousy," referring here to the fact that we can be confused in our judgment about, in this case, our relationship with another person. This sort of situation may have little practical impact for hearsay, for jealousy or anger can both be motives for committing offences. But consider the following. D is reported to have said "I feel guilty about P's death." Is the *feeling* of guilt probative, if faithfully reported by D, to suggest that D caused P's death? It is always possible that a psychological explanation of D's feeling can make better sense than he can make of it himself. For example, D may neurotically think that P was a "better" man than D, and that it is unfair that he, D, continues to live while P is dead, even though D was elsewhere when P died, or D killed P as the result of an accident. The fact that we can describe D here as "neurotic" shows that we have independent criteria for judging *how we should take* his faithfully reported statement that he "felt guilty."[17]

We could also consider the following. D is reported to have said "I am fine and fully in control." The witness knows that D has two separate drugs, which, unknown to D, can in their combined state, produce a sense of euphoria and a false sense of control. Here the overall judgment of the witness is better than the truthfully given report of D. Put simply, statements made truthfully by a person of the emotions he feels are corrigible, that is, are not decisive of the question whether he in fact has that emotion.

Much of the same kind of arguments can be applied to statements of physical sensation, although the force of these may not be so strong. First, it is clear that we can make judgments about other people's sensations. The semi-conscious, or unconscious, victim "writhes in pain," we say, without thinking of first asking him. This is because we have learned how to use pain-ascribing language by observing what happens to people, and what they do, when they *say* they are "feeling" pain, and seeing how that mimics a feeling we have when those same things happen to us and we do those same things.[18] We can say, too, that a person is making too much fuss about the pain they feel as if we knew what pain they are likely to be suffering given the circumstances. And if we become convinced that a person *is* genuinely suffering more pain than we would expect, we say that he is, perhaps, "unusually sensitive."

It follows from this analysis that the idea of statements of intention, or emotion, or physical sensation being reports of some kind of internal event to which only the speaker has access, is misleading. Further, and more strongly, the idea that the actions *themselves* be a *report* of the "internal event" (of having such an intention, and so on) is confused because the actions themselves constitute direct evidence that there is an intention (or an emotion or a physical sensation). The conclusion is that all our actions are potentially evidence of the intentions, etc., we have, and only some of these constitute reports.

Since reporting entails the use of language, employing public conventions and rules, the stalking and stabbing case shows that the *reductio ad absurdum* argument succeeds. If the hearsay rule is extended to exclude as hearsay all actions from which mental states can be inferred, the reported observation of stalking and stabbing is hearsay. Since *that* conclusion is absurd, the extension to the hearsay rule is not justified and, because a statement was not made in the sea-captain case, that case did not involve a question of hearsay.

Tapper and intentionally assertive conduct

An alternative approach to the idea of implied hearsay is supplied by Colin Tapper in the latest edition of *Cross on Evidence*.[19] It goes some way towards clarifying the problem but nevertheless contains a significant confusion. First, he usefully substitutes the idea of "assertion" for that of "statement" in the classic formulation.[20] "Assertion" is less ambiguous than "statement" is between "statement" as an utterance (A's statement being identical to the act of A's stating) and as an assertion (A's statement being identical to *what* A asserted). "Assertion" refers directly to the proposition, that is, the thing that is being asserted. So, for example, when John states "I am Catholic" and Mary states "John is a Catholic," both are asserting the one proposition—let us call it the assertion—that John is a Catholic. It would therefore be useful for lawyers to employ "statement" in the *Subramaniam*-type cases where the thrust of the assertion is not being proved, only the fact of statements—utterances—being made, and to employ "assertion" in the *Gibson*-type cases, where the truth of the assertion is being relied upon (namely, *that* the defendant threw a stone).

This amendment to the classical definition is useful. Tapper also argues that the hearsay rule operates only to exclude those cases, as hearsay, where there is present "a primary intention to assert," and his analysis assumes that this test will successfully deal with the problematic cases such as the sea-captain case and the case of *Rice*.[21] He concludes in the latter case, for example, that the airline ticket agent, unidentified, did not primarily intend to assert anything about a flight, or about a passenger, when he issued an airline ticket. Rather, Tapper says, the ticket was "primarily intended to be used as a valid warrant for travelling on an aeroplane." It was, therefore, a piece of real evidence and the Court of Appeal was right not to exclude it as probative of the fact that the defendant, whose name appeared on the ticket, travelled on that flight. Thus, Tapper concludes, "the presence of an intention to assert provides the most defensible watershed between hearsay and non-hearsay both as a matter of logical coherence and of practical commonsense."[22]

The difficulty with this approach lies in the ascertaining of the primary intention to assert. How are we to ascertain what the ticket agent's intention was, first of all? And secondly, what does "primary" mean? We can consider these two problems together by asking the following question. How would we adduce evidence *against* the fact that an unidentified ticket agent intended to assert that a person who gave the name Rice made a booking on a particular flight? Perhaps we could show that typically ticket agents see their role as that only of issuing travel warrants and that this fact increases the probability that the ticket agent in this case "saw himself" as only issuing a travel warrant. But that is hardly satisfactory, especially given my earlier argument that statements about a person'a intentions, and so on, are corrigible, that is to say, are open to alternative explanation. In this particular case, it would be relatively easy to establish that "issuing a travel warrant" can be broken down to "confirming that a person, who gave a particular name, booked a particular flight," and thence with another short step to "*asserting* that a person, who, etc...." Perhaps another way to ascertain whether the ticket agent had the relevant intention would be to read the ticket itself. But does that show with any clarity at all that she did not have that intention? Surely not. It is a statement that a person with a particular name was booked to travel on a particular flight. It is, at the very least, unclear whether this can be characterised as an intentional assertion of these facts. And, in any case, if we take the ticket itself as evidence of the intention to assert we have to take it, according to the hearsay rules, as a hearsay report by the agent of her inner mental state. Such a report may be admissible by virtue of the *res gestae* exception referred to in the first section. But, there is a blatant illogicality with this approach. In order to work out whether the evidence is hearsay because it is "primarily intended to be assertive," we have to *breach* the hearsay rule in order to examine the statement of intention. To put it another way: there is an illogicality in making the definition of hearsay dependent on the question of intention when that question may depend on evidence inadmissible as hearsay.

More obvious difficulties arise over the idea of a "primary" intention, mirroring the sorts of difficulties encountered in other areas of law over the distinction between "direct" and "indirect" (particularly in the criminal law).[23] The difficulty is always to avoid a tautologous distinction based on theoretical convenience such as defining "primary" so as to mean "that intention which serves to distinguish the problematic cases." If "primary" does not have this meaning, what meaning does it have? An unidentified person, in fact an accomplice, yells "The man who threw the stone went over there." His intention is to mislead potential witnesses by pointing in the opposite direction to which the defendant makes his escape. Panicking, he becomes confused, however, and in fact points in the direction the defendant has gone. What is the unidentified witness's *"primary* intention to assert?" Was it to assert a misleading statement as to the direction (which failed)? Or was it to assert a statement which (in fact) was not misleading? Here it just seems that Tapper's analysis is unhelpful. It allows the prosecution to introduce the statement, because it was not evidence of a primary intention to assert, *and* the defence to say that it was hearsay, for the opposite reason. The point is that the problem cannot be solved by any intuitive appeal to the meaning of "primary" and "secondary."

Tapper's approach confuses the intention a person has in saying something with the intention he may be taken to have, given what he has said. It was with this distinction in mind that I originally amended Grice's well-known definition of meaning so as to cover the sort of case where a person conveys to others by use of language the impression that he believes something that he in fact does not.[24] The amended definition then allows for the ascertainment, by public rules or conventions, of the meaning of a statement independent of the intentions of the speaker. The fact is that we cannot work out what a speaker's real intentions are (*a fortiori* whether they are "primary" or not) solely by looking at the words he uses. It has, instead, to be discovered in a different and public way. Put in another way, what a speaker "means" publicly might not coincide with what he "means" privately. Of course, this is not to say that the sense of what he meant to say and what his statement meant are unrelated because, clearly, characteristic cases of meaning will be understood from intentional and correct employment of the rules and conventions of language.

The following, then, is the way in which my analysis applies to the case of the witness who in confusion unintentionally points in the right direction instead of the wrong direction. His action amounts to a statement of identity, as I have previously argued, namely that "D went in the direction W pointed." If this statement is to be used in order to prove that D went in that direction, then it is hearsay. This coheres with the rationale for the rule: we cannot cross-examine the witness to discover whether the evidence is reliable.

Tapper's view is that the "implied conduct" examples given by Baron Parke in *Wright* v. *Tatham* should not be regarded as cases of conduct intended to be assertive and therefore not as hearsay. His view is that, if they were, "hearsay so extensively defined would go unrecognised, and injustice would occur on account of the anomalies." This statement echoes my *reductio ad absurdum* argument earlier, but goes no further. My analysis has the advantage of being more direct and eliminates the confusions inherent in determining a primary intention. There is no assertion or statement being made, for example, when the sea-captain inspects the ship and then embarks on it with his family. Tapper cannot say without argument, too, that this situation cannot be regarded as intentionally assertive of some fact, at least in the sense that the sea-captain intends that his actions provoke a belief in an observer. He may have been performing an elaborate deception, having the (primary?) intention to convey to others that he thinks the ship sea-worthy, although he thinks it is not (say, for allowing a fraudulent insurance claim). It is just that because he does not do this by means of an intentional employment of the public device of language that we should not, in my view, regard his conduct as coming within the hearsay rule.

Tapper comes some way towards my view of the matter although he leaves the matter unanalysed. He talks throughout of "implying into" or "from" conduct what it is that is asserted, for example, "implied assertions ... will be considered according to whether they are implied from writing, speech or conduct."[25] This phraseology is in the lawyerlike—and not ungrammatical— manner employed in, for example, contract cases whereby terms are "objectively" implied into bargains independently of the "subjective" views of the parties.[26] This way of thinking about the problem is consistent with my analysis because it allows for objectivity—the public convention or rule-applying domain—in the ascertainment of the meaning of certain types of conduct.

Triangulating hearsay

An approach more difficult to deal with takes as its starting point the rationale of the hearsay rule. At the borderline of my definition, cases within the rule seem indistinguishable, in terms of rationale, from those just without. Thus the nagging objection arises that it would be irrational to exclude one sort of situation but to include the other. I shall deal with this approach by trying further to strengthen the argument for my analysis being correct. I cannot, however, defend my conclusion against the criticism that my rule of thumb will produce penumbral cases in practice. No lawyer could, of course, provide in advance an uncontroversial answer for every case that came under a rule. My claim is rather that I can narrow the penumbral range by concentrating enquiry on the question of whether there has been a *statement*. This is a much narrower (and consequently more achievable) aim than the test of *reliability*, for example, suggested by Tribe.

Professor Tribe has provided the clearest and most useful discussion on the rationale of the hearsay rule.[27] He represents the problems of unreliability inherent in the reception of hearsay evidence with a triangle.

B (belief of actor responsible for A)

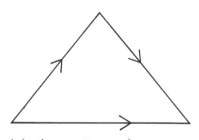

A (action or utterance)   C (conclusion to which B points)

The three points of the triangle represent, A, the "action or utterance" in question; B, the "belief" of the person who produced the "action or utterance"; and C, the proposition the truth of which counsel wishes to persuade the court. A problem of hearsay arises only when the court cannot, to use Tribe's term, "go directly" from A to C and has to rely on B.

The great advantage of Tribe's approach is that it considers the importance of the question of what is unreliable about second-hand evidence. First, there is the problem of relating the action or utterance to the belief or other appropriate state of mind of the actor. This raises the separate problems of ambiguity and insincerity. Secondly, once these problems are answered, the problems arise of the actor's erroneous memory and his faulty perception.

The triangle is therefore undoubtedly "an analytic aid of considerable clarifying and simplifying power."[28] But it does not, I think, make the best sense of the hearsay rule as it presently exists within the United Kingdom statute and common law. It fails to draw attention to the nature of the action or utterance constituting point A on his triangle and the consequent inferences that may be drawn from it. We can, for example, think of a clear and famous example where the hearsay rule, as standardly understood, fails to fit Tribe's analysis. Consider *Myers* v. *D.P.P.*[29] An unidentified foreman entered engine block numbers into a record book. Because we have absolutely no evidence to suppose that such action is ambiguous or was insincere (the obstacles between A and B), or that the foreman had an erroneous memory or faulty perception (the obstacles between B and C), it seems that we can "go directly" from the foreman's statements in the record book to the conclusion that the engine block numbers represented the engine numbers of certain stolen vehicles. But this is a classic example of hearsay and the House of Lords, deciding upon precisely these circumstances, was not prepared to say that it failed to be hearsay because of the inherent reliability of the evidence. We can criticise the reasoning in *Myers* by saying that this evidence ought not to have been deemed hearsay. But would anything in our common law have been lost as a result? Consider the handiness—the practical thrust—of the hearsay rule. If *Myers* had created a new definition of hearsay which allowed "inherently reliable" evidence in court, a great inroad would have been made into the rule because given the great elasticity of the concept of reliability (and the difficulties, evidenced by the cases, in establishing clear categories) each disputed instance of putative hearsay would be open to potentially time-consuming debate. I am inclined to the view that the best course was that followed when Parliament, shortly after the decision, reversed its effect by a very specific legislatively created exception covering records made in the course of trade.[30] Tribe's analysis does not place sufficient weight upon the "rule of thumb" use of the hearsay rule which allows lawyers to focus on excluding, quickly and without further discussion, statements made by those not before the court. I originally referred to this as a possible advantage of the ossification of the rule, namely, that courts simply do not have the time to allow lengthy and protracted arguments on whether evidence is sufficiently reliable in all cases.

Penumbral cases

I claimed my account gives a "cutting edge" to the rule and that this should not be taken to mean that my account can therefore dispose uncontroversially of every case. It should, however, draw attention to the sorts of questions that are relevant, which are those concerning whether a statement has been made. Here, given the analysis that it is statements which most clearly express deception or mistaken judgments, arguments within the umbrella of questions relevant to whether a statement has been made are perfectly proper. So, for example, although my view is that *Teper* v. *R*.[31] was correctly decided, because I thought that there a statement was made expressing a proposition about identity, I could concede, without giving up my analysis, that the statement made ("your house burning and you going away from the fire") did not entail such a proposition. One could argue, as indeed, counsel appeared to argue in that case, that exclamations, greetings, and so on, cannot constitute assertions of identity. But the argument should involve the following consideration. Given the rule's central reliance on the identification of a statement hiding a deceptive or mistaken judgment, was what was said sufficiently like a statement, given the problem of lack of possibility of cross-examination, to declare it to be hearsay? It is wrong to think that courts and lawyers do not or should not argue like this. The rules are not to be identified with the words themselves although the words in which the rules are expressed provide highly relevant arguments about what these rules are.

On the other hand, where the case envisaged wholly escapes the language of the rule so that no one would be prepared to say that the conduct amounted to a statement, it seems to me that the question of whether the evidence is too unreliable to be included is altogether a different matter. The problem simply escapes the language of the rule. Let us postulate the existence of a provision in a statute that prohibits "vehicles" from certain municipal parks and let us assume also that the clear rationale is physical protection of the pedestrians. Cars would clearly be excluded. But not so clear are the cases of skateboards and prams, although they are arguably vehicles that can be dangerous. But assemblies of rioters are clearly dangerous to pedestrians but just as clearly not vehicles and so, of course, the rationale of the provision in the statute cannot jump to deeming the rioters to be "vehicles." An important way of putting this point is to say that there is, in our legal system at any rate, a strong presumption (some would say conclusive) that rules be confined to the words that purport to express them.

The question is then: do the problem cases such as the Parke B. cases escape the language of the rule? I have already expressed the difficulty I have with finding statements or assertions in these cases. What does a person say by saying nothing? Does a person state (or assert) that a ship is sea-worthy by inspecting the ship and then sailing away on it? No, he merely inspects the ship and then sails away!

Surely, any proposal to exclude as hearsay, conduct which does not constitute a statement has to be legislative and reforming in purpose. But a trend of the last two or three decades has been the removal and not the extension of the hearsay rule's application! I can therefore claim, both in the light of this trend and the unexamined and dubious proposition that ordinary people cannot assess the weight of hearsay evidence, that a merit of my analysis is that it is restrictive rather than extensive of the hearsay rule's scope.

NOTES

[1] See Guest, "The Scope of the Hearsay Rule" (1985) 101 L.Q.R. 385.

[2] For example, *Wright* v. *Tatham* (1837) 7 Ad. & El. 313; *Lloyd* v. *Powell Duffryn Steam Co. Ltd.* [1914] A.C. 733; *Ratten* v. *R.* [1972] A.C. 378 and *Bessela* v. *Stern* (1877) 2 C.P.D. 265.

[3] I defined "statement" as the "the product of a speaker's intentional and correct use of public conventions or rules used for communicating meaning." *Supra*, n. 1, p. 389.

[4] *Supra*, n. 2.

[5] *Ibid.*

[6] See *Cross on Evidence* 5th ed. (1979) p. 6; Civil Evidence Act 1968, c. 64, s.1(1); *Subramaniam* v. *Public Prosecutor* [1956] 1 W.L.R. 965 (Malaysia) and *Ratten* v. *R. supra*, n. 2 (Australia).

[7] *Cross on Evidence* 6th ed. (1985) (ed. C. Tapper) pp. 459–475.

[8] Tribe, L. H. "Triangulating Hearsay" 87 (1974) Harvard L.R. 957.

[9] *Supra*, n. 2, p. 400.

[10] See *Thomas* v. *Connell* (1838) 4 M. & W. 267.

[11] See *R.* v. *Gibson* (1887) 18 Q.B.D. 537.

[12] Which is the more obvious answer to the riddle "Why did the chicken cross the road?" "It wanted to cross to the other side"? Or: "It intended to convey to us the impression that it wanted to cross to the other side"? The latter introduces a complication which we rule out as absurd because unnecessary.

[13] See Ryle, G. *The Concept of Mind* (1949) Hutchinson, particularly Chap. 1.

[14] See *O'Hara* v. *Central S.M.T. Co.* 1941 S.C. 363; *Ratten* v. *R.* (*supra*, n. 2) and *R.* v. *Nye & Loan* (1977) 66 C.A.R. 252.

[15] See *Cross on Evidence* 6th ed. 583–584.

[16] See *Sugden* v. *Lord St. Leonards* (1876) P.D. 154; *R.* v. *Buckley* (1873) 13 Cox C.C. Compare *R.* v. *Thomson* [1912] 3 K.B. 19 and *R.* v. *Wainwright* (1875) 13 Cox C.C. 171.

[17] I should not be taken to mean that all such declarations are "neurotic." A well-documented and understandable (*i.e.* not neurotic) phenomenon of feelings of guilt without accompanying responsibility occurred and occurs amongst Jewish survivors of German war atrocities, for example.

[18] See, *passim*, Wittgenstein: *To Follow a Rule* (1981) ed. Holtzman & Leich. Routledge.

[19] *Supra*, n. 7.

[20] So the 6th ed. of *Cross on Evidence* cites the rule as: "an assertion other than one made by a person while giving oral evidence in the proceedings is inadmissible as evidence of any fact asserted." (p. 38).

[21] [1963] 1 Q.B. 857.

[22] *Supra*, n. 7, p. 461.

[23] See, for example, *R.* v. *Steane* [1947] K.B. 997.

[24] See Grice, H. P. "Meaning" (1957) Phil.Rev. 377, and *supra*, n. 1, pp. 389–392.

[25] *Supra*, n. 7, p. 459.

[26] See *Photo Production Ltd.* v. *Securicor* [1980] A.C. 827.

[27] *Supra*, n. 8.

[28] *Supra*, n. 8, 961.

[29] [1965] A.C. 1001.

[30] Criminal Evidence Act 1965, s.1(1) (12 Statutes 970). (Now see: Police and Criminal Evidence Act 1984, ss.68–69). In *Myers*, Lord Reid said that the "only satisfactory solution [was] by legislation following a wide survey of the whole field." [1965] A.C. 1022.

[31] [1952] A.C. 480 (British Guiana).

Policing the City—Combating Fraud and Other Abuses in the Corporate Securities Industry

BARRY A. K. RIDER

Ensuring the integrity of the financial services industry cannot be an end in itself. The purpose of such efforts must be to protect and nurture investor confidence, without which the capital markets are little better than casinos.[1] Professor L. C. B. Gower, in his discussion document on investor protection,[2] commented "it is not much use having regulations unless they are enforced." He repeated several times during the course of his study of the British financial services industry that to have rules and regulations which were either unenforced, or in practical terms unenforceable, was not only a delusion but entirely counter-productive.[3] Whilst criminologists and philosophers may be prepared to argue that unenforceable rules, in some circumstances, may be useful as providing a normative or educational conditioning,[4] in the real world of financial dealings, often motivated by the baser human desires, it would only be the most academic who would seek to tolerate such a regime of self-deception.[5]

In this paper the present author seeks, with some trepidation, to evaluate the new scheme of regulation and enforcement ordained by the Financial Services Act (F.S.A.) 1986, in the context of the Government's desire to promote investor confidence, both domestically and internationally, "by ensuring that the financial services sector is, and is seen to be, a 'clean' place to do business."[6] This assessment is attempted, as has already been admitted, with trepidation, as the City is particularly sensitive to comment on its ability to restore confidence in the integrity and, thus, efficiency of its markets. Indeed, within a few days of delivering this paper a spokesman from the Securities and Investments Board Ltd. (S.I.B.) challenged the appropriateness of seeking to discuss this subject, before the new regime had been brought fully into force.[7]

Whilst it is true that the effectiveness or otherwise, of the new scheme of regulation will be determined in the course of experience, surely it is appropriate to review the policy and institutional issues involved, which have already been determined.

The philosophical issues

Although securities regulation has become an industry itself in the United States of America, and to a lesser extent Canada and Australia, few would seek to justify regulation and supervision as ends in themselves. On the other hand, relatively little has been written by lawyers, or for that matter anyone else, on the philosophical and other justifications for regulation. Whilst it is not difficult to find in "expert" reports and legislative statements references to the need to protect investors from fraud,[8] and occasionally themselves, there is generally little recognition of the fact "that the character of securities legislation will affect the development of financial institutions and their efficiency in performing certain economic functions."[9] It is hard to escape the notion that in some jurisdictions legislation has been enacted and fancy supervisory authorities established, more to generate an appearance of sophistication than for any more meaningful purpose.[10] A good illustration of the confusion and sophistry which often manifests itself in debates on regulation of the securities markets is the almost international obsession with outlawing insider dealing.[11] Few jurisdictions have sought to cut through the often ambiguous and contradictory arguments for regulating insider abuse and base control simply on the overwhelming need to foster confidence in the essential integrity of the market.[12] To fasten on impractical and inappropriate concepts of compensation and restitution has obscured the essential wrong and confused the development of more effective enforcement devices.[13]

In the context of the British securities industry, it has long been accepted that the preservation and maintenance of confidence is a primary factor.[14] The Government in its White Paper, *Financial Services in the United Kingdom*,[15] emphasised the responsibility on those charged with protecting and advancing the nation's financial services industry, to ensure that investors had confidence in the integrity and fairness of the system. However, the Government also espoused the objectives of promoting efficiency, competitiveness and flexibility. Whether these are wholly compatible objectives remains to be seen.[16]

Regulation in perspective

Concern over abuses in the markets, and the effect that this will inevitably have on confidence reposed in the integrity and efficiency of such is certainly not new.[17] Even Homer referred to "tricksters dealing in countless and worthless trinkets" to the scandal of the market. The ancient Chinese, and to some extent even the ancient Egyptians, imposed rules and regulations on their markets to prevent certain abuses such as cornering and misrepresentation.[18] In Britain there were laws as early as the reign of Edward I seeking to ensure the integrity of public markets and the ancient offences of forestalling, engrossing and regrating[19] probably to some extent survive in conspiracy to defraud.[20] Commissioners appointed by Parliament in 1696, reported that "the pernicious art of stockjobbing hath of late so wholly perverted the End and Design of companies," and they illustrated their comments by specific examples of promotional frauds, insider dealing and market manipulation.[21] Perhaps one of the most outspoken condemnations of the early financial services industry in Britain is that of Daniel Defoe in "The Anatomy of Change Alley—a system of stockjobbing proving that scandalous trade as it is now carried on to be knavish in its private practice and treason in its public." He commented "there is not a man but will own t'is a complete system of knavery, that t'is a trade founded in fraud, born of deceit and nourished by trick, wheedle, forgeries, falsehoods and all sorts of delusions."[22]

In fact, there are many examples of attempts to regulate some of these malpractices in the eighteenth and nineteenth centuries.[23] To some degree the regulations imposed, at least on brokers and stockjobbers in the City of London, were if anything by their terms stricter than under the F.S.A. 1986. For example, under the statute of 1697 stockjobbers had to obtain a licence, swear an oath to deal "without fraud and collusion," adhere to "good practices" and record transactions. They were also required to post bonds of £500, which could be forfeited for "misconduct." Draconian penalties were also provided, including a fine of up to £500, disqualification and public censure.[24] Interestingly it was also a specific offence, punishable by a fine of £50, for anyone to deal with an unlicensed broker. As with similar attempts to improve the standing of the embryo financial services industry the weak point was enforcement. The chairman of the London Stock Exchange was uninhibited enough to report to the Select Committee on Foreign Loans of the House of Commons in 1875 "we disregarded for years Sir John Barnard's Act and we are now disregarding in equal measure Mr. Leaman's Act."[25] Indeed, it has been observed that one of the results of outlawing option and forward transactions was the development of the Stock Exchange practice of reducing written records to the minimum—leading to the time honoured motto "my word is my bond."

The prelude

Whatever the merits of the uniquely English system of supervision over the City, which existed before the F.S.A. 1986,[26] it became increasingly clear that there were significant gaps, and certain activities which were subjected to quite strict control overseas were substantially unregulated in Britain. However, the most serious weakness in the British system was in its apparent inability to ensure effective enforcement of such rules as existed.[27] The Roskill Committee stated "the public no longer believes that the system . . . is capable of bringing the perpetrators of serious fraud expeditiously and effectively to book. The overwhelming weight of evidence laid before us suggests that the public is right."[28] The institutions, such as there were, charged with official regulatory and supervisory responsibilities were either totally under-resourced or uninspired. The once highly effective structure of unofficial and self-regulation had been substantially undermined by the breakdown of social homogenity in the City, international-isation of the securities industry, effective removal of exchange control and the advent of individuals who were prepared for one reason or another deliberately to "buck the system." During the last three decades there has been an increasing degree of awareness, both inside and outside the City, that deficiencies in enforcement are bringing the whole system of control and regulation into disrepute. Scandals which in fairness would have severely tested any reasonable system of control, served to underline the inability of the existing institutions to keep the City "clean."[29]

Whilst it is true that the City has had its fair share of "crooks," it is important to retain a degree of proportion. Scandals occur in all markets and, in one form or another, in every type of economy.[30] It should be remembered that more people are executed in, for example, the USSR for "economic crimes" than for any other type of offence.[31] The media in Britain by sensationalising the abuses that did occur, compounded the ever present threat to investor and public confidence. Perhaps, not surprisingly when enforcement and supervision was discussed it was in the context of institutional considerations. Thus, much discussion took place as to whether or not, it would be desirable to establish a regulatory authority modelled on the US Securities and Exchange Commission (S.E.C.). Few apparently recognised the fundamental differences between the securities industries in both countries, and the nature of the regulatory problems. Sadly, there are many examples throughout the world where inappropriate legislation or regulatory models have been simply "borrowed" from other countries without due regard to the special and peculiar local conditions. Although some adjustments were attempted, and some effort was made to improve co-ordination of regulation,[32] if not the effectiveness of actual control, by the time Professor Gower had been appointed to review investor protection it was obvious that enforcement would have to receive very serious consideration in the context of any new scheme of regulation.

What is perhaps surprising is that in considering this little regard appears to have been had to the perceptive observations of the Royal Commission that reported a hundred years earlier, under the chairmanship of Lord Penzance. This commission reported[33] that inquiries into fraud and abuse should be undertaken "promptly by some public functionary and enforced by law" and that the rules and regulations of the market should be under the supervision of "the President of the Board of Trade or some other public authority." It is also rather surprising that one of the greatest problems in developing a system of policing the securities markets, that of the international character of the securities business, received such limited attention.[34]

Concentration on the criminal law as a means of controlling abuses in the securities industry has led to far too little attention being given to other, and almost certainly more effective devices. Whilst it is true that in Britain, as elsewhere, the criminal law has not proved to be a particularly effective tool in this area, it is increasingly being recognised throughout the world, that given the nature of modern business traditional economic offences, prosecuted within traditional evidential and procedural constraints, are virtually non-justiciable.[35] For example, at the last four Common-

wealth Law Ministers' Meetings,[36] Ministers recognised that the
sophistication of economic crime is such as to be practically
beyond the reach of most law enforcement agencies, operating
within limited jurisdictions and mandates, with even more limited
budgets and resources. Given the constraints of jurisdiction;
problems of securing and admitting evidence, particularly from
overseas; securing fugitives, surmounting all the vagaries of the
trial process, and often the reluctance of judges to take economic
crime seriously, it is necessary to reassess the utility of the
traditional criminal process in this area. It must also be recognised
that our traditional conception of the type of person who
perpetrates fraud or abuse on the securities markets may well be
misconceived.[37] The Stock Exchange has expressed the view that
organised insider dealing syndicates are operating in the London
markets from the relative safety of offshore havens, utilising all the
practical and legal advantages of bank secrecy and confidentiality
laws. It is also known that organised crime has in recent years
increasingly moved into low risk high reward securities offences.
There have been cases where inside information has been
exchanged for drugs, and organised criminals have themselves
indulged in various forms of market manipulation and promotional fraud. The Yakuza in Japan have developed their own form
of corporate gangsters—the Sokaiya who have already become
active in North America and Britain. The securities and commodity futures trading markets have become increasingly attractive to
organised criminals not only as sources of revenue, but also as
facilities for laundering the vast amounts of money that are today
generated through other forms of crime. No government has any
real idea of the amount of such money in circulation, although in
the USA, Federal authorities have estimated that organised crime
could be producing in excess of US$150 billion a year. As the
United States Presidential Commission on Organised Crime has
observed every financial institution and market is at risk from
penetration and laundering activities.[38] This has also been recognised by the British Government, The Stock Exchange[39] and more
recently the Institute of Chartered Accountants.[40] When the
threat presented by organised crime and international economic
crime syndicates is considered in the context of the seeming
inability of traditional criminal justice and regulatory systems to
deal effectively with something like insider dealing[41] the often
half-hearted response of those charged with protecting the
integrity of our markets becomes at best questionable.

Whilst governments like to emphasise "their determination to
fight economic crime and abuse with all the means at their

disposal" and, indeed, to undertake this as a matter of "urgency and priority"[42] when one considers that the General Secretariat of ICPO-Interpol is only able to provide five officers to co-ordinate the fight against fraud for the whole world,[43] and the budget for the Commonwealth initiative[44] is about the same as that for keeping a police motorway patrol car on the road, the joke becomes a little sick![45] It is in this context that a meaningful evaluation of "policing" the City must take place.

Regulation cannot be divorced from the special characteristics of the relevant market and institutions. No two markets are the same and, thus, there are few if any universal models and certainly no panaceas. The British financial services industry has gone through a revolution in the last two decades and the so-called "big bang" is merely one of the repercussions. Internationalisation of the markets and their intermediaries, has created regulatory problems very different to the essentially domestic considerations of the past. With internationalisation and tremendous developments in informational and transactional technology, the markets have become much more interdependent. Continuous trading on the main markets of the relevant time zones has led to "follow the sun trading." Transactions can be executed with the aid of computers and sophisticated communications networks in a number of jurisdictions simultaneously. Indeed, the implications of all this were dramatically illustrated during the precipitous market crash in the autumn of 1987. No matter how remote or insignificant, every market was drawn into the spiral downwards. Whilst Professor Gower, to some extent alluded to these developments his treatment of them was *en passant*. The Government in its own White Paper and in modifying Professor Gower's proposals[46] ignored them. Consequently, there was virtually no discussion of perhaps one of the most important issues to effective regulation.[47]

The new order

Having regard to the circumstances surrounding the introduction of the Financial Services Bill, and the pressure to provide a viable legal framework for the many fundamental changes that were in the course of taking place, the Government must be congratulated on the job that it did.[48] The Act provides the legal authority for a scheme of regulation which, at least in conception, is probably as

viable as any.[49] This is all the more surprising given the lack of
profound philosophical thought in the preparation and planning
of it.

The Act seeks to keep out of the markets and the financial
services industry those of dubious repute and intentions. Professor Gower himself recognised the importance of prevention. A
system of prevention which is both effective and efficient, is likely
to be far more cost effective. The Government took the view that
"no regulatory system can, or should, relieve the investor of
responsibility for exercising judgment and care in deciding how to
invest his money."[50] If an investor decides to invest in a highly
speculative security after he has had the benefit of adequate
disclosure then "he cannot look to any regulator to make good the
losses arising from his own misjudgment." On the other hand, the
Government accepted that *"caveat emptor"* was no longer
sufficient, and it is today necessary to provide measures which seek
to reduce the likelihood of fraud, and encourage high standards of
conduct in investment business. Thus, the F.S.A. seeks to ensure
that those in the financial services business are "fit and proper"
persons and conform to rules which ensure professional standards
of stewardship, care and probity. The rules that are set down,
primarily through the intervention of the Securities and Investments Board Ltd. (S.I.B.) and the various self-regulatory authorities aim at a higher and more exacting standard of conduct than
would be practical in a general statute. The Government also
accepted Professor Gower's view that the rules should not only be
clear and precise—so that everyone knew where they stood, but
also enforceable and actually enforced. Thus, a primary requirement before the essentially self-regulatory scheme can be "sanctioned" is that not only is there the willingness, but the ability, to
police the various rules. Within the new regime there is also a shift
from supervision and regulation into "prudential" control, particularly in regard to financial soundness and solvency. The various
authorities "ordained" to administer the day-to-day operation of
the Act and its rules are also charged to develop effective
procedures for surveillance and monitoring. In other words,
enforcement is to be proactive and not merely reactive. Where loss
is caused to investors the emphasis is on indemnity and compensation. In addition to relatively strong compensation schemes, quite
wide ranging provisions imposing civil and restitutionary liability
are provided. Finally, the F.S.A. itself provides new and far
reaching enforcement and investigatory powers for the Department of Trade and Industry (D.T.I.) and the various new
authorities.

Cleansing the city?

Let us now examine certain of these aspects in a little more detail. The desire of Professor Gower and the Government, that the various rules promulgated under the Act should be simple and clear has proved forlorn. Whilst the S.I.B.'s Regulations are on the whole well drafted, they are certainly not simple, and the very nature of the subject-matter inevitably renders a good proportion so technical as to be obscure. It remains to be seen whether the plethora of rules and regulations that are being churned out will be accorded any great attention by practitioners, once the dust has settled. The present author has been surprised by the attitude of many practitioners who seem to be of the opinion that most of the voluminous new sets of rules serve little other purpose than meeting the requirements of the F.S.A. for the various self-regulatory authorities to obtain recognition from the S.I.B. and then continue much as they did before.

The importance that the Act, and now the City, attaches to prevention is laudable. Keeping persons of dubious integrity out of the markets is obviously more cost effective than seeking to unscramble their devious operations and repair the damage once their true nature comes to light. The Act places a responsibility on the S.I.B. and the various self-regulatory authorities to satisfy themselves that persons permitted to undertake investment business are in fact fit and proper persons. In other words, applicants for authorisation, or the equivalent, must be "vetted." Unfortunately, there would appear to be little realisation within the new authorities, except the established professional bodies, of what this entails. It is unclear how the S.I.B. and most of the other authorities will actually check applicants, other than in the conventional way of simply verifying references. It is obvious that there are no resources for any form of "positive vetting." The experience of banking authorities in vetting applicants for banking and deposit taking privileges, particularly at the "bottom end" of the market, has not been impressive. Many overseas jurisdictions have had to admit that reliable information is simply not available at an international level. On several occasions Commonwealth Ministers of Finance and Attorneys-General have called for vastly more co-operation in this regard. Given the rather ambiguous nature of the S.I.B. and the various other authorities charged with this onerous responsibility it remains to be seen whether foreign agencies will be willing, or for that matter able under their own domestic laws, to provide meaningful assistance. Several foreign agencies have already expressed some disquiet about the essentially private nature of the S.I.B. and the almost commercial orientation of some, at least, of the self-regulatory authorities. Indeed, under the Act the self-regulatory authorities are allowed to "contract out" some of their supervisory and monitoring responsibilities to private concerns. When one considers the profound problems that police and other official agencies have in securing assistance for specific criminal investigations through established networks, the new authorities are going to have an "uphill struggle" to discharge their "vetting" function.

Disquiet has already been expressed in some quarters as to the reliance that certain of the self-regulatory authorities will apparently place on "audits" and inspections by outside private firms. Indeed, in regard to one such organisation complaints have already been made to the DTI concerning the lax way in which investors complaints and inquiries are being dealt with and the conduct of certain officials of this authority. There have even been allegations as to the appropriateness of certain "council" members sitting in judgment on matters in which their firms would appear to be interested. In one instance a report has even been submitted through the Director of Public Prosecutions. None of this serves to give the outside observer great confidence in the competence, or perhaps even the integrity, of the new system.

The importance of intelligence is not only in regard to "vetting." It is equally significant to the discharge of the various monitoring and prudential responsibilities. There is little evidence that any more thought has been given to this. Although the S.I.B. does intend to constitute an "intelligence committee" it would appear to have little idea of the sort of investment that is required to constitute even a limited intelligence function. At the international level there is minimal co-operation, and although the International Association of Securities Commissions and Similar Organisations (IASCO) has discussed, at its last four meetings, the setting up of an ongoing programme for the exchange of information, nothing of any substance has emerged. The British Government has set up an annual meeting of representatives from a few overseas regulatory authorities, but these last only two days and were dismissed by at least one influential participant as "nice little tea parties." Whilst it is the D.T.I.'s intention to develop these informal meetings it cannot be supposed that this is likely to provide an adequate facility for the exchange of intelligence on a timely basis. It has been said that the ICPO-Interpol network might be deployed to this end. However, the constitutional and resource constraints on the General Secretariat of Interpol would rule this out. Senior representatives of the S.I.B. have had one meeting with the special unit established in the Commonwealth Secretariat, to develop preventive intelligence against serious economic crime, but this initial contact has not been followed up.

As experience has shown in other areas of commercial and fiscal vetting, given the wide use of nominees, frontmen and the sophistication of organised crime, to ensure effective vetting it is necessary to undertake inquiries and make assessments on a much more thorough basis than is clearly being anticipated. By section 179 of the Act, information received by the D.T.I., S.I.B. and certain other authorities, in the discharge of their responsibilities under the Act is restricted. It is a criminal offence for it to be divulged except with the consent of the person to whom it relates. Naturally there are certain exceptions and the most important are those provided for in section 180. These exceptions include a host of specific agencies, including the self-regulatory authorities, where it is necessary for the discharge of their proper functions. Furthermore, under section 180(6) the D.T.I. may authorise disclosure to foreign regulatory authorities. Whilst this provision is to be welcomed, sadly, it is the case that the British authorities do not enjoy a reputation for being over-willing to share information. Indeed, some foreign authorities have encountered so much difficulty in securing co-operation they have resorted to sending their own officers to London to undertake very basic inquiries at considerable expense and inconvenience. It is hoped that the D.T.I. will use this statutory authority to promote a climate of co-operation which is vital if the international markets are to be protected.

The British Government, following the lead of U.S. authorities, has entered into two Memoranda of Understanding (M.O.U.) with the S.E.C. and Commodity Futures Trading Commission in the U.S.A., and the Ministry of Finance in Japan.[51] It is understood that negotiations are also in an advanced stage with certain other jurisdictions including Australia. These M.O.U.s are not treaties, but simply undertakings to supply information and intelligence where such is permissible under the domestic law, and relevant for the exercise of supervisory and enforcement functions. Whilst the agreement with the U.S.A. may be expected to work well and to strengthen what were already good informal lines of communication, it remains to be seen how effective these bilateral arrangements will be with other jurisdictions. For example, in Australia it has now become recognised that even in the domestic context something more than merely the exchange of information is required and a facility for analysis of information and co-ordination is desirable at a Federal level. By analogy the bilateral approach of the M.O.U.s will not provide the facility of a multilateral or truly international initiative.[52] It also remains to be seen how effectively the new regulatory regime will be interfaced into these bilateral arrangements given their ambiguous constitutional position. Finally, before leaving this particular aspect of enforcement, the important new powers of the Director of the Serious Fraud Office, under the Criminal Justice Act 1987, to secure and transmit evidence, on the request of foreign prosecuting authorities, must be mentioned. Whilst the provisions of this Act and those in the Criminal Justice Bill, now before Parliament, facilitating investigation and prosecution of serious fraud offences must be welcomed, it again remains very much to be seen how effective these powers will be in practice. The institutional constraints on this office do not augur well. Furthermore, there does not appear to be the degree of political and institutional support that has proved to be so vital in establishing similar offices in, for example, Hong Kong[53] and Singapore.[54]

Having regard to the amount of discussion that has taken place on fraud it is perhaps surprising that more was not attempted in the F.S.A. in terms of substantive law.[55] The only substantive general anti-fraud offence is section 47. Section 47(1) essentially re-enacts section 13 of the Prevention of Fraud (Investments) Act 1958. This makes it an offence to induce an investment arrangement by misrepresentation. Section 47(2) extends this offence to where the misrepresentation is by conduct, rather than misstatement. Section 13 was never a really effective anti-fraud provision[56] and it would seem that one of its most serious weaknesses has been carried over into the new provision. In *Tarling No. 1* v. *Government of Singapore*,[57] the House of Lords accepted that a proven intention to stabilise or correct the market constituted a defence to an allegation that the person responsible was seeking to induce a transaction by virtue of, for example, a misstatement. Whilst the Act does seek to regulate stabilisation, by empowering the S.I.B. to draw up rules setting limits, this only applies to section 47(2) and not section 47(1).

There are, of course, a host of other specific statutory offences under the F.S.A., but most relate simply to the mechanics of regulation, such as failure to secure authorisation, misstatement in the filing of reports and other documents and misstatements in investment related documents. Given the importance of disclosure of information it is important that the provisions ensuring the integrity of this information are adequately enforced. This has not been a priority in the past. Often far too little attention is given to such offences, which tend to be dismissed as merely "technical" in character. Not only are many filing and reporting obligations critical to the credibility of the disclosure philosophy, but invariably the first sign that a major fraud or abuse is being perpetrated is a misfiling or late filing of some routine report. Proper enforcement at this level can have important implications for effective prevention and loss minimisation.

Offences under the F.S.A. can only be prosecuted with the consent of the D.T.I. or D.P.P., except that the S.I.B. itself is empowered to bring prosecutions for offences designated by the D.T.I. The S.I.B. has indicated that it will probably only seek to prosecute offences relating to authorisation and not more general provisions under the Act.[58]

Of far greater practical significance in ensuring probity and integrity is the conduct of business rules promulgated under the Act by the S.I.B. and the various self-regulatory authorities.[59] The expedient of providing conduct of business rules specifically tailored to particular aspects of the financial services industry is highly advantageous. Even the Royal Commission sitting under Lord Penzance in 1877 recognised this. Although in the vast majority of cases there is no direct criminal liability for breach of a specific conduct of business rule, disciplinary sanctions are provided, and there is the prospect of civil liability. The S.I.B. and the various self-regulatory authorities are specifically charged with the responsibility of monitoring due compliance with their rules.

Mention has already been made of the importance that the Government attached to compensation schemes so as to provide investors with assurance that proper obligations imposed on financial intermediaries will be met. In addition, the Government accepted that it was desirable to deploy the civil law not only in its traditional role of providing compensation, but as a restitutionary and in some cases as a prophylactic device. The significance of civil actions in the U.S.A. for enforcing the Federal securities laws, and other economic legislation, has long been recognised. Such actions are quick, cheap, and flexible. The standard of proof is easier to attain, and the rules of evidence and procedure are more facilitative of enforcement than in a criminal trial. In the U.S.A., the S.E.C. has long encouraged civil actions by aggrieved investors and corporate issuers, and has itself developed its own jurisdiction to bring civil enforcement actions for injunctive and restitutionary relief. Indeed, these actions have been most effective against

fraudulent and abusive conduct by corporate insiders. In the vast
majority of cases pursued under the various anti-fraud provisions
the S.E.C. has brought a civil rather than criminal action. Because
of the efficacy of these actions, and no doubt the cost implications,
many defendants are prepared to settle and "consent" to an
injunction enjoining future violations of the law and agree to
divestiture of their "profits." The F.S.A. provides both the D.T.I.
and the S.I.B. with the power to bring similar enforcement actions
in the English courts seeking injunctions and restitution orders.
These powers extend to where the defendant has engaged in
unauthorised investment business, violated the conduct of business rules, or certain other provisions of the Act. The D.T.I. has
had powers under the Companies Act and other legislation to seek
orders in the Civil courts for many years, but there has been few
instances where it has even considered using them. It remains to
be seen whether the S.I.B. will be more adventurous. Sir Kenneth
Berrill, the Chairman of the S.I.B., has indicated that the S.I.B.
will be willing to utilise these powers and he has even indicated
that although the S.I.B. does not have any enforcement role under
the Company Securities (Insider Dealing) Act 1985, in appropriate
cases this may be an area where such an action could be
entertained.[60] It is debateable whether this will always be feasible
under the terms of Section 61, but Sir Kenneth's zeal must be
commended.

A potentially even more significant provision is found in section
62 of the Act. This provides a statutory tort action for breach of
the provisions of the F.S.A. and rules promulgated under it, by
anyone damnified by the breach. In the U.S.A. the willingness of
the Federal courts to allow implied civil actions to enforce the
provisions of the securities laws has played a major role in the
development of the law. On the other hand, given the costs and
procedural problems in mounting such actions the present author
is not as convinced, as some appear to be,[61] that such actions are
likely to become common place. It is, however, interesting that the
implementation of this section in so far as it relates to the conduct
of business rules of the various self-regulatory authorities was
postponed for six months to allow those bodies a breathing space
to refine their procedures. There is clearly some fear that
litigious investors or fellow intermediaries will grasp this new
sword.

New powers of investigation and inspection abound in the
F.S.A.[62] Before a self-regulatory authority is recognised and, thus,
sanctioned by the S.I.B., the S.I.B. must be satisfied that the
relevant body has, under its own rules, the power and ability to

monitor and enforce compliance. The D.T.I. and S.I.B. are given extensive investigatory powers in the Act itself. Although there is little point in detailing these provisions here, it may be appropriate to express the present author's grave concern as to whether the S.I.B., in particular, is prepared to wield these important powers with determination and dedication. The S.I.B. has shown little interest in enforcement. Sir Kenneth himself has been reported in the press as stating "I am regulator, a watchdog and a policeman— in that order." It is rumoured that the S.I.B. is most reluctant to recruit personnel who show any sign of being "enforcement minded" and has instructed its head hunters accordingly. Whilst it is still early days, the S.I.B. has so far only provided itself with the most basic investigatory facility. Most of its lawyers are either drawn from academia or are inexperienced. It would seem there is little alarm on the part of those who have been systematically abusing the system.

The Government does deserve congratulations for including in the F.S.A. relatively strong provisions for the appointment of inspectors to inquire into cases of suspected insider dealing.[63] In the past, both Conservative and Labour Governments resisted the notion that special investigatory provisions were required for insider dealing cases, on the rather illogical basis that if such powers were not required for murder why should they be justified in an insider dealing investigation.[64] It is also welcome that the courts have already been prepared to interpret these provisions in a sensible and realistic manner.[65] One provision of particular interest is that curtailing the ability of witnesses to decline to identify a foreign principal on the basis of their ignorance, or that to divulge such would be contrary to the domestic laws of the relevant overseas jurisdiction. Under section 178, it is not a reasonable excuse for such a person to refuse to identify another on either ground, where the laws of that other jurisdiction would permit disclosure if that other person had he consented, seemingly whether he had in fact so consented or not. Whilst this is to be welcomed, it does not necessarily avoid the problem of a chain of nominees, and it may well be in practice that inspectors will in some cases have to be satisfied with the second link. It is an offence to make false statements to the inspectors, and there is the power to freeze and even "cancel" securities the ownership of which remains hidden.

Of course, there are always problems when the investigation needs to proceed out of jurisdiction. The procedures for mutual assistance in criminal matters are embryonic[66] and in the vast majority of cases under the F.S.A. a criminal offence may not even be in issue. One of the problems in this area is, that often the offence will be of a technical nature and consequently it may well be impossible to establish "double criminality" within the jurisdiction from which assistance is sought. Thus, in the Westland Helicopter's case the Swiss authorities were unable to assist the investigation of possible offences under the Companies Act 1985 relating to disclosure of substantial interests in shares because there was no similar offence in Swiss law.[67]

Mention must be made of the associated problem of jurisdiction. Given the international nature of today's securities business, strict adherence to traditional and restrictive concepts of jurisdiction are anachronistic and, indeed, dangerous. As has already been pointed out, this is not a matter upon which there was much discussion during the concept of the present regime. A senior civil servant has observed that "the fundamental purpose of the F.S.A. is to create a safe environment in which those who consume investment services within the United Kingdom can do so with confidence."[68] Thus, the philosophy of the Act, in so far as there is a cogent one, is simply to control the financial services industry within our traditional territorial jurisdiction. Where such impinges "on activity outside the United Kingdom" our controls, according to the same writer, should "go no further than is justifiable in accordance with established rules of international law and the principles of international good manners." The problem is that many of these rules are in today's world anachronistic and the crooks do not observe good manners![69] For far too long, jurisdictions that do have the resources and ability to curtail the operations of the international fraudster have been willing simply to enjoin their more egregious conduct within their own parochial jurisdiction—caring little for the havoc that is visited on their neighbours.[70] Where a country provides a "home" for such financial operations, it should according to the most basic concepts of "good neighbourness"—let alone "good manners"—attempt to ensure that its hospitality is not being abused to provide a haven for those desiring to loot and cheat others.[71] Surely this is not an extravagant expectation in the interdependent world within which we now have to co-exist?

The F.S.A. does not seek to apply to investment businesses operating outside the United Kingdom, and consequently the various criminal offences and other sanctions are subject to the traditional territorial limitations.[72] Section 47(4) preserves the decision in *Secretary of State for Trade* v. *Markus*[73] that section 13 of the Prevention of Fraud (Investments) Act 1958, now essentially section 47(1), creates a form of "result" crime.[74] Thus, it may be relevant to Acts outside the United Kingdom where the result is within territory. The provision prohibiting unsolicited calls[75] has an extended territorial reach. It can apply to calls from or to the United Kingdom. On the other hand, it is important that this prohibition can only give rise to civil liability and is not a criminal offence.

Whether the traditional and somewhat parochial approach to regulating the City, which is by all standards one of the world's leading financial centres, is adequate remains to be seen.[76] In the present author's view it is not.

Qui custos?

Whilst the new regime is reasonably ingenious, and on the whole it is difficult seriously to fault either the legislation, or the various rules made under it, it is sad that more attention was not given, at this critical stage, to thinking out some of the more fundamental and philosophical aspects of securities regulation in the very different world markets of today. There is little that is novel in the Act, or for that matter in the rules. Many of the "new" concepts had already surfaced in the Licensed Dealers (Conduct of Business) Rules 1983.[77] It is also unfortunate that the opportunity was not taken to explore more effective ways of policing the securities industry. For example, it has long been suggested that increasing and strengthening the obligation on companies to make timely disclosure of material information, and possibly providing a specific right of action by an issuer against certain insiders who trade on the basis of inside information, would be far more cost effective than the present reliance on criminal penalties under the Companies Securities (Insider Dealing) Act 1985.[78]

The most serious criticism that can be made against the new system is the lack of attention that has been given to the institutional devices for supervision and enforcement. The various new bodies have seemingly neither the desire, nor the resources, adequately to assume more than a cosmetic role in preventing and policing abuse in the City. Little if no thought has been given to improving the machinery of detection and investigation, and what thought has been given to such issues as vetting and international co-operation has been peripheral and ill-informed. Already private litigants have brought actions against individual officials, and in at least two cases against the new authorities themselves. It remains to be seen whether political support will endure, and whether adequate resources will be made available to contest these early challenges. Few have considered the implications of such direct assaults and the ever present threat of judicial review.[79] In the present author's view the new system cannot be effective until proper attention is given to these practical issues. It may well be that the cracks will not appear until the present encumbants have moved on, but with little doubt they will increasingly be noticed at home and abroad. The City, and for that matter society, deserves better from those into whose hands it has entrusted stewardship of a precious and precarious national interest.

NOTES

[1] Professor L. C. B. Gower in his response to the question "Is not the City just a casino . . . " comments "some of the activities of the City may bear a considerable resemblance to those of a casino. . . . (E)ven so, there is surely much to be said for a regulatory system which should ensure that the roulette wheel is not rigged," L. C. B. Gower "Big Bang" and City Regulation 51 M.L.R. (1988) 1.

[2] *Review of Investor Protection—A Discussion Document* (1982) H.M.S.O., at 3.41.

[3] *Review of Investor Protection*, Report Pt. 1 Cmnd. 9125 (1984) at 10.12 *et seq.*

[4] See generally H. L. Packer, *The Limits of The Criminal Sanction* (1968) Stanford University Press, Pt. 1 and G. Borrie, "Law and Morality in the Market Place" (1987) J.B.L. 433.

[5] B. Rider, *Corruption—in Perspective* (1987) I.C.A.C., Government of Hong Kong.

[6] *Financial Services in the United Kingdom—A New Framework for Investor Protection* Cmnd. 9432 (1985) at 3.1.

[7] *Securities Regulation and Law Report* B.N.A. Vol. 19, (1987) 1846.

[8] With reference to the "New Deal" legislation in the U.S.A. see L. Loss, *Fundamentals of Securities Regulation* (1988) 2nd ed., Little Brown, 25 *et seq.*, and generally, J. Howard, "Securities Regulation: Structure and Process," (1978) in *Proposals for a Securities Market Law for Canada*, Vol. 3, (1979) Government of Canada. The same is also true in regard to judicial pronouncements. See, *e.g. R. v. Littler* 65 D.L.R. 3d 443.

[9] *Report of the Attorney-General's Committee on Securities Legislation in Ontario* (1965) commonly referred to as the *Kimber Report*.

[10] See generally the accounts in B. Rider and H. L. Ffrench, *The Regulation of Insider Trading* (1979) Macmillan, in regard to some of the smaller and less developed jurisdictions.

[11] See B. Rider and H. L. Ffrench, "Should Insider Trading be Regulated? Some initial considerations" (1978) 95 S.A.L.J. 79 and *supra*, n. 9, at Ch. 1.

[12] B. Rider, *The Unacceptable Insider* (1987) Legal Research Foundation, University of Auckland.

[13] See for example the novel approach in Hong Kong, B. Rider "The Regulation of Insider Trading in Hong Kong" (1976) 17 Mal.L.Rev. 310 and (1977) 18

Mal.L.Rev. 157; and B. Rider "Insider Trading: Hong Kong Style" (1978) 128 N.L.J. 897.

[14] See for example *The Conduct of Company Directors* Cmnd. 7037 (1987), para. 22 discussed by B. Rider, "The Conduct of Company Directors" (1978) 128 N.L.J. 27.

[15] *Supra* at n. 6.

[16] See L. C. B. Gower, *Review of Investor Protection, Report* Pt. 11 (1985) H.M.S.O. at 5.17 and B. Rider "Protecting the Prudent Investor" (1985) 6 Co. Law 54 and B. Rider "Analysis and Appraisal of The City Revolution" in *The Practical Implications of The Financial Services Act* (1986) C.C.H.

[17] See generally B. L. Anderson and A. J. H. Latham (eds.) *The Market in History* (1986) Croom Helm and M. Silver, *Economic Structures of the Ancient Near East* (1985) Croom Helm.

[18] For example, the rules relating to stabilisation of the commodity markets in China which outlawed persons from rural areas purchasing more than a shih of rice in Peking, see G. Boulais, *Manuel du code chinois* (Varieties sinologiques series No. 55, Shanghai, 1924) at 754b. Indeed, even strikes by ferrymen were punished as interfering with the proper function of the markets, see the memorial of the Governor-General of Kiangsu, concerning Hou Ming-chang, who was duly decapitated for "restraining trade," see *Hsing-an hui-lan*, Shanghai, 6.10/20b–21a. For ancient Egypt see for example, D. Lorton, *The Judicial Terminology of International Relations in Egyptian Texts Through Dynasty XVIII* (1974) John Hopkins University Press.

[19] See J. W. C. Turner (ed.) *Russell on Crime* (1964) 12th ed., Stevens & Sons, Chap. 100.

[20] See Law Commission Working Papers Nos. 56 (1982) and 104 (1987), see also A. Arlidge and J. Parry, *Fraud* (1985) Waterlow at 8.01 and R. Pennington, *The Investor and The Law* (1968) MacGibbon & Kee, 290 *et seq.*

[21] *House of Commons Journals*, November 25, 1696.

[22] See generally E. V. Morgan and W. A. Thomas, *The Stock Exchange—Its History and Functions* (1962) Elek, Chap. 1 and R. C. Mitchie, *Money, Mania and Markets* (1981) John Donald.

[23] See *supra* at n. 22.

[24] See generally B. Rider, D. Chaikin and C. Abrams, *Guide to The Financial Services Act (1987)* C.C.H. Chap. 1.

[25] *Select Committee on Loans to Foreign States*, 1875, Evidence of S. H. de Zoete, 477.

[26] See generally B. Rider (ed.) *The Regulation of The British Securities Industry* (1979) Oyez and B. Rider and E. Hew, "The Regulation of Corporation and Securities Laws in Britain—The Beginning of the Real Debate" (1977) 19 Mal.L.Rev. 144.

[27] See L. C. B. Gower, *supra* at 3: T. Hadden, *The Control of Company Fraud* (1968) P.E.P.; T. Hadden, "Fraud in the City; Enforcing the rules" 1 Co. Law (1980) 9; L. H. Leigh, *The Control of Commercial Fraud* (1982) Heinemann; M. Levi, *Regulating Fraud* (1987) Tavistock and B. Rider, "Self-regulation: The British approach to policing conduct in the securities business; with particular reference to the role of the City Panel on Takeovers and Mergers in the regulation of insider trading" (1978) 1 *Journal of Comparative Corporate Law and Securities Regulations* 319. B. Rider, "Enforcement" in *Company Law for The Senior Executive* (1980) Crown Eagle.

[28] *Report of The Fraud Trial Committee* (1986) H.M.S.O., para. 1.

[29] See generally M. Clarke, *Regulating the City* (1985) Open University and T. Hadden, "Fraud in the City: The Role of the Criminal Law" (1985) Crim.L.R. 500.

[30] See generally B. Rider, *The Promotion and Development of International Co-operation to Combat Commercial and Economic Crime* (1980) Commonwealth Secretariat.

[31] See also, by way of example, The Resolution of the Standing Committee of the Chinese National People's Congress regarding the severe punishment of criminals who seriously undermine the economy, adopted by the 22nd Session of the Fifth National People's Congress March 8, 1982, see also B. Rider "Combating International Commercial Crime—A Commonwealth Perspective" (1985) 2 L.M.C.L.Q. 217, B. Rider "Commercial Crime" in *Proceedings and Papers of The 7th Commonwealth Law Conference* (1983) Hong Kong at 433.

[32] See *Report of the Committee to Review the Functioning of Financial Institutions* Cmnd. 7937 (1980) Chap. 22, and T. Hurst "Self-Regulation versus Legal Regulation" 5 Co. Law (1984) 161, B. Rider and E. J. Hew, "The Structure of Regulation and Supervision in the Field of Corporation and Securities Laws in Britain" (1977) *Revue de la Banque* 79 B. Rider "The British Council for the Securities Industry" (1978) *Revue de la Banque* 303.

[33] *Report of The Royal Commission on the Stock Exchange* (1878) Govt. Printer.

[34] See generally S. Hebenton and B. Gibson, "International Aspects of Securities Legislation" (1978) in *Proposals for a Securities Market Law for Canada*, Vol. 3 (1979) Government of Canada; *Internationalisation of the Securities Markets; Report of the Staff of the U.S. S.E.C.* to the U.S. Senate Committee on Banking, (1987) S.E.C., and B. Rider and D. Chaikin, *Mutual Assistance in Criminal Matters: A Commonwealth Perspective* (1983) Commonwealth Secretariat and B. Rider, *Final Report to the Government of Barbados on the Securities Exchange of Barbados and a Regional Capital Market* (1979) C.F.T.C.

[35] See B. Rider *supra* at 31, and B. Rider, "Prosecuting Economic Crime" (1987) International Bar Association.

[36] Commonwealth Law Ministers' meetings in Winnipeg, Canada (1977); Barbados (1980); Colombo, Sri Lanka (1983) and Harare, Zimbabwe (1986). Similar sentiments have been expressed by Commonwealth Senior Law Officers of Small Jurisdictions at their meetings in the Isle of Man (1983) and Port Villa, Vanuatu (1985) and at several meetings of Commonwealth Ministers of Finance. See also *Report of the UNCTAD Secretariat on Maritime Fraud* (1985) TD/B/C.4/AC.4/8.

[37] See A. Shipman and B. Rider, *International Organised Crime* (1987) International Chamber of Commerce and *Organised Economic Crime* (1986) Commonwealth Secretariat, B. Rider, *Economic Organised Crime* report to the U.S. Presidents Working Party on Drugs, (1988) and *Communique of the Commonwealth Law Ministers' Meeting* (1986) para. 59; " . . . Ministers an increasing trend of organised crime becoming involved in economic offences, as these offered high rewards with relatively little risk of apprehension." Similar observations have been made at the last three General Assemblies of ICPO-Interpol.

[38] *The Cash Connection: Organised Crime, Financial Institutions and Money Laundering, Interim Report to the President of the U.S.A.*, (1984) President's Commission on Organised Crime, U.S. Govt. Printer at 52 para. 1. See also B. Rider, "Organised Economic Crime and Money Laundering," *Organised Crime and the Financial Markets*, Australia (1987) Crown Agents/Commonwealth Secretariat.

[39] Letter to Member Firms from M. E. Fidler, Secretary to the Council of The Stock Exchange, October 14, 1986.

[40] *Statement* (TR 681) December 14, 1987.

[41] See generally B. Rider and H. L. Ffrench *supra* at n. 10 Chap. 16, and B. Rider, *Insider Trading* (1983) Jordans.

[42] *Communique*, Commonwealth Law Ministers' meeting, Colombo, Sri Lanka (1983).

[43] See B. Rider, *The Role of ICPO-Interpol in Combating International Economic and Commercial Crime* (1980) Commonwealth Secretariat. There are additional officers concerned with counterfeiting and theft offences.

[44] See B. Rider, *supra* at n. 31.

[45] Commonwealth Law Ministers resolved at their meeting in Harare in 1986, that the mandate of the special office set up to "spearhead" the international fight against international economic crime should have its mandate extended to organised crime and "recognising the important and unique role of the Commonwealth Unit in facilitating the fight against serious international crime . . . Ministers emphasised the need to ensure at all times that the Unit was adequately resourced to enable it to meet the growing needs and expectations of governments"; *Communique* (1986).

[46] See generally *supra* at n. 24 Chap. 2.

[47] See *supra* at n. 34.

[48] Professor Gower takes a rather different view and considers that the main "teething troubles" are likely to arise from blemishes in the F.S.A. See generally L. C. B. Gower *supra* at n. 1, at 20.

[49] See generally *supra* at n. 24 and A. Whittaker and G. Morse, *The Financial Services Act 1986* (1987) Butterworths.

[50] *Supra*, at n. 6 at 3.3.

[51] See generally G. Kerrigan, 7 Co. Law (1986) 272 and *supra*, at n. 24 Chap. 13.

[52] See the editorials in 7 Co. Law (1986) at 130 and 226.

[53] B. Rider, *Report on the Detection, Investigation and Prosecution of Commercial Crime in Hong Kong* (1981) Hong Kong Government.

[54] G. Knight, "The Detection and Prosecution of Economic Crime in Singapore" (1988) *Economic Crime in the Financial Markets*, Crown Agents.

[55] In this context reference should be made to the Law Commissions Working Paper No. 104 on *Conspiracy to Defraud* (1987).

[56] See B. Rider, "The Crime of Insider Trading" (1978) J.B.L. 19.

[57] (1980) 70 Cr.App.R. 77.

[58] *Annual Report of the S.I.B.* (July 1986) 5.

[59] See generally *supra*, n. 24, Chap. 6.

[60] Address at Park Lane Hotel, January 28, 1987 conference organised by The British Institute of Securities Laws.

[61] See for example "Save us from Section 62" by A. Large in *Financial Times* September 29, 1987.

[62] See *supra* at n. 24 at 187–195.

[63] Ss.177 and 178.

[64] B. Rider, *Insider Trading* (1983), Chap. 6 and B. Rider "Insider Trading—A Question of Confidence" 77 L.S.Gaz. (1980) 113.

[65] *Re an Inquiry under the Company Securities (Insider Dealing) Act 1985*, House of Lords, December 10, 1987 (1987) 137 N.L.J. 1181 and P. Tridimas "The Financial Services Act and the Detection of Insider Trading" 8 Co. Law (1987) 162.

[66] See B. Rider and D. Chaikin, *supra* at n. 33 and T. Huckle, *Mutual Judicial Assistance and Economic Crime—A Special Study* (1985) Commonwealth Secretariat. Reference should be made in this context to *The Commonwealth Scheme for Mutual Assistance in Criminal Matters* (1986), 12 C.L.B. (1986) 1118.

[67] This has been a major problem in the enforcement of U.S. laws especially in regard to insider dealing, see D. A. Szak, "International Co-operation in Insider Trading Cases" 40 *Washington and Lee Law Review* (1983) 1149 and L. Frei.

"International Mutual Assistance in Criminal Matters under the Swiss Federal Act" (1982) 8 C.L.B. 794.

[68] J. B. K. Rickford, a Solicitor at the D.T.I., *Developments in the U.K.— Securities Regulation, an International Perspective* paper presented to a conference organised by the Centre for Commercial Law Studies, Queen Mary College (1986).

[69] See for example M. G. Yeager, "The Gangster as White Collar Criminal: Organised Crime and Stolen Securities" in *The Crime Society* (1976) Meridian and generally *Report to the U.S. President, The Impact: Organised Crime Today*, (1986) President's Commission on Organised Crime.

[70] See for example the U.S. S.E.C.'s settlement with I.O.S. Sec. Ex. Act Rel. No. 8083 discussed in B. Rider and H. L. Ffrench, *supra* at n. 10 Chap. 16.

[71] See for example the memorandum submitted by the Government of Zambia to The Commonwealth Law Ministers Meeting in Colombo, Sri Lanka (1983) and Harare, Zimbabwe (1986) on economic crime and the third world; *Minutes and Memoranda*, Commonwealth Secretariat.

[72] See generally B. Rider (ed.) *supra* at n. 26, Chaps. 10 and 11.

[73] (1976) A.C. 35.

[74] See generally A. Arlidge and J. Parry, *Fraud* (1985) Waterlow, Chap. 11. See also s.47(5) in regard to s.47(2) which applies the same rule to manipulation by conduct.

[75] See s.56.

[76] See in this regard *Jurisdiction over Fraud Offences with a Foreign Element—A Consultation Paper Prepared by the Criminal Law Team of the Law Commission* (1987) which unfortunately does address itself directly to investor protection offences, although its recommendations in regard to its listed substantive offences must be welcome.

[77] S.I. 1983 No. 585.

[78] See for example B. Rider, "Insider Trading—A Question of Confidence" 77 Law Soc.Gaz. (1980) 113 and *supra* at 11.

[79] See generally A. C. Page, "Self-Regulation—The Constitutional Dimension" 49 M.L.R. (1986) 141; R. Baldwin and C. McCrudden, *Regulation and Public Law* (1987). Weidenfeld & Nicolson Chap. 13. J. Beatson "Financial Services—who will regulate the regulators?" (1987) 8 Co. Law 34; T. Lowe "Public Law and Self-Regulation" (1987) 8 Co. Law 115 and Sir Henry Woolf, "Judicial Review in the Commercial Arena" (1987) 8 Co. Law 167.

The Right to Silence Reconsidered

D. J. GALLIGAN

I

In the course of a judgment in the Supreme Court of Victoria, Mr. Justice Starke recently made a remarkable statement. "In my opinion," he said, "the right to silence is a fundamental principle of the criminal law and is not to be overridden by any other so-called doctrine or other principle."[1] It might be commonplace that the right of silence is a fundamental principle, but what makes the statement remarkable is that it is rare to find judges or legislators or academics prepared to affirm the right with such unreserved confidence. References to the right tend to be oblique and indirect, made in hurried passing, as if to pause might raise awkward questions. When direct confrontation becomes unavoidable, safety is secured by reference to the "so-called" right to silence, as if by that qualification an escape route is left open. On other occasions refuge is found by resort to one of the last weapons in the lawyer's armoury, the Latin maxim, which here is inappropriate since *nemo tenebatur prodere seipsum* refers to the related but different privilege against self-incrimination. More remarkable perhaps is the fact that Parliament, in an extensive review of pre-trial investigations resulting in a comprehensive statute, followed by a detailed code of practice, makes no direct reference to the right. Yet many provisions of the Police and Criminal Evidence Act 1984 make sense only on the basis that there is a right of silence, and although there is express reference to other rights, such as the right to consult a solicitor, rights which are related closely to the right of silence, there is no reference to that right itself.

Yet the right of silence has been the subject of discussion and debate for a generation. It was the subject of the Eleventh Report

69

of the Criminal Law Revision Committee (1972),[2] a report which met with such objections that its proposals for restricting the value of the right were never enacted. The issue was again the main subject of the Royal Commission on Criminal Procedure (1982) which made recommendations more or less opposite those of the Criminal Law Revision Committee.[3] That two official enquiries should produce such contrasting results is hardly surprising, since the camps have long existed. To those in opposition, the views of Jeremy Bentham remain the starting point. Bentham did not write specifically about the right of silence, but from his opposition to the privilege against self-incrimination, it is not difficult to imagine what his attitude would have been.[4] The late Rupert Cross who did much to revive discussion of the principles of evidence, called the right a "sacred cow"[5]; more recently the London Metropolitan Police Commissioner called for its abolition and wondered how the "so-called" right to silence "ever gained any sort of respectable place in the English legal tradition."[6] The Commissioner concluded by endorsing the view of one of his predecessors that the right of silence "has done more to obscure the truth and facilitate crime than anything else in this century."

The litany of criticism is extensive, but despite its persistence and the authority of its sources, despite the reluctance of the courts and Parliament to make it explicit, the right to silence is indeed a fundamental principle of English law. Its meaning and scope are uncertain, but it is difficult to deny that the core of the right is deeply embedded. There are many who share the view that the right is fundamental and that it should be secure in English law; to those it also represents deeper values which ought to be protected. But of the many issues which are raised by the right to silence, I shall consider in this essay the following few. In the first place, I shall sketch out the place that rights have in criminal justice, to show that different rights operate in different ways, and require different justifications. Secondly, I shall summarise briefly some of the empirical research which shows the role of the right to silence in police investigation. The third task is to examine, again rather sketchily, the extent to which the right of silence is recognised and protected in law. My main concern here will be to gauge the way the law regards the right to silence and to show how a fuller sense of the right might be achieved within the law. Finally, I shall identify and examine the values in terms of which the right of silence finally must be justified.

II

To those of a Benthamite persuasion, the law of evidence and procedure, indeed the investigation and the trial itself, have one principal object; to achieve an accurate assessment of guilt or innocence. As Professor William Twining has shown in his recent and acclaimed study, Bentham's approach to the law of evidence proceeds according to two basic ideas[7]: first, that rectitude, or accuracy of outcome, is the object of the judicial trial and is achieved through a flexible system of guidelines rather than rules; secondly, that while rectitude might be modified on the grounds of delay, vexation or expense, it should not be diminished, except in very special and limited circumstances, in order to preserve values external to proof, such as protecting the accused from self-incrimination or allowing him to remain silent in the face of evidence.[8] But while Bentham's approach, with rectitude at its centre, has been a major force in shaping the modern law of evidence, parts of it have remained highly contentious and much of practice has marched to a different tune. It is now well-known that most cases are disposed of in the exercise of discretion by the police or the prosecutor without reference to the courts; in many other cases, pre-trial negotiations result in a plea of guilty so that for the courts sentencing is the only task left.

However, if we put aside the many issues raised by disposition other than by trial, and if we assume that the guiding object of investigation and trial is accuracy in the determination of guilt and innocence, even then there are difficulties with Bentham's approach. The first difficulty concerns the wrongful conviction of the innocent. If the outcome of the trial is accurate, then guilt and innocence will have been decided correctly; but procedures are imperfect, so that sometimes the innocent will be wrongly convicted, the guilty acquitted. The two mistakes are different, however, because punishment of the innocent is a greater wrong than acquittal of the guilty. Bentham accepted the distinction and recognised the disutility in punishing the innocent; he urged that the judge should proceed on the presumption of innocence and "in doubtful cases, to consider the error which acquits as more justifiable, or less injurious to the good of society, than the error which condemns."[9] But beyond this he offers no precise instructions and, indeed, it is not clear that direct utilitarianism could be more precise.

An alternative approach, and one closer to English law, is to introduce the concept of right and to recognise that the accused has a right not to be wrongly convicted and punished. From this right it follows that the accused has a further right to procedures which protect against that outcome, a right often referred to as the right to a fair trial. Such procedures cannot be perfect, but they must ensure a level of accuracy which represents a relationship of proportion between, on the one hand the importance of the substantive right according to the values of society, and on the other hand the resources which society can be expected to make available in maintaining it.[10] Punishment of the innocent is then not just one set of costs to be put against another set of benefits; rather the accused has a right not to be wrongly convicted and that right must be given special protection. Many features of the criminal trial make sense viewed in this light: the presumption of innocence, the burden of proof on the prosecution, and the onus of proof beyond reasonable doubt. The same concern to avoid wrongful conviction underlies the rules and principles relating to similar facts, character, corroboration, and restrictions on cross-examination of the accused. Each rule attempts to regulate the reception or use of evidence which, if freely admitted, would create a special risk of a wrong conviction. The principle against wrong conviction explains why such classes of evidence, which are generally of probative value and therefore admissible on the test of rectitude, are either excluded altogether or admitted subject to restrictions. Moreover, the recent tendency of the courts to put the idea of a fair trial at the centre of the law of evidence, is implicit recognition of this most fundamental right.[11]

The second problem with Bentham's approach is that it does not allow the investigation or proof to be hindered by considerations the justification for which lies in values independent of and possibly contrary to rectitude of outcome. And since the right to silence may do just that, we are confronted with two different conceptions of the law of evidence. Bentham's views would be as follows.[12] To the extent that the right to silence, by discouraging false statements, serves rectitude, rather than exclude those statements in advance, it would be better for their probative value to be left to the courts. To the extent that the right to silence serves values *independent* of rectitude, the right would be an unwarranted fetter on investigation and trial. That fetter should be removed and, should the suspect choose to speak, anything said would be admissible against him; if he should remain silent, it would be permissible to draw appropriate inferences. The alternative approach to this is to accept that there are other values besides rectitude and the reduction of crime. Those other values derive from ideas about how people should be treated by the state; such ideas are associated with liberty, autonomy, privacy, and respect, and they may provide a foundation for rights. But rights have costs; since to have a right is to have a protected good, protected in the sense that the right should prevail over competing considerations which might produce marginal benefits to society as a whole. As Ronald Dworkin argues, to take rights seriously is to recognise that society cannot consistently confer a right X and yet curtail or undermine X whenever it is convenient in terms of other social benefits to do so.[13] If there is a right to silence which can be justified independently of any possible contribution to rectitude, then it may require, in areas of conflict, that marginal benefits in terms of rectitude should be sacrificed in favour of the right.

It can be seen from this brief account that the criminal trial and the rules of evidence which regulate it, can be understood in different ways. The first puts overriding emphasis on rectitude. The second modifies that emphasis by introducing the notion of a right to a fair trial and the matching idea that the trial must be tilted in favour of not convicting the innocent even at the cost of increasing the risk of acquitting the guilty. The third approach goes beyond the second by allowing that probative evidence might be lost or withheld from the trial in order to serve values independently of rectitude of outcome. The view one takes to the right of silence will depend in part on the conception of the trial with which one begins.

III

The right of silence applies to suspects under questioning before the trial and in deciding whether to give evidence at the trial. It is with the first of these that I am mainly concerned. The right of silence in relation to pre-trial matters means that the suspect is not required to answer questions from the police, whether before arrest, after arrest, or after charge. The suspect may waive his right of silence and answer questions, but he must be told by the police of his right by way of the caution, and while the police may ask questions they must not take steps to compel or require an answer.

It is common and regular practice for the police to question suspects both before and after arrest. Great importance is placed on the interrogation which is indeed an integral feature of the police investigation.[14] In a very real sense the investigation is organised around the interrogation, from which the police in general expect to obtain useful information. Indeed, despite the caution, the evidence tends to show that the police expect the right of silence to be waived and the suspect to talk. That expectation governs their whole approach to interrogation and results in subtle but pervasive pressures being applied to encourage disclosure.[15] As one researcher concluded, "the way the caution was delivered or the manner of its phrasing seemed to present the right of silence as an option that the suspect was not seriously expected to entertain."[16] The result is that police questioning of suspects occurs in an environment which militates against remaining silent and leads to the great majority of suspects breaking their silence and making incriminating disclosures. According to recent studies conducted in selected areas of England, around 90 per cent. of suspects answered police questions, with less than 10 per cent. remaining steadfastly silent.[17] Of that 90 per cent., the great majority, that is between 60 per cent. and 70 per cent., made either full confessions or damaging admissions. For a small percentage of suspects, waiving their right of silence led to clearance and release, but the great majority of those who confess are convicted, in most cases following a plea of guilty, and in a few cases by trial. There is in short a close correlation between waiver of the right, confession, and conviction.

However, this does not mean the conviction of a suspect is dependent on the right of silence being waived. It appears from research findings that, in general, successful prosecution and conviction do not depend on confession. It is crucial to the prosecution in only about 20 per cent. of cases; in the remainder, confessional evidence is important in lending support to the prosecution case and in making it easier to prove.[18] There may also be collateral benefits to the police in gaining information about other crimes and other suspects, although Baldwin and McConville argue that the claims made for collateral benefits are largely illusory.[19] Of the tiny percentage of suspects who do refuse to answer questions, the great majority are convicted.[20] The idea that the right of silence allows a significant group of hardened and guilty offenders to escape, an idea propagated by the Criminal Law Revision Committee and clung to by the police as an article of faith, appears to be without foundation. There is no evidence to support it; indeed there is plenty of evidence pointing the other way. And even if more suspects are remaining silent as a result of the provisions of the Police and Criminal Evidence Act, the numbers, as Michael Zander has recently shown, are still tiny and raise no cause for the police to be alarmed.[21]

What conclusions can be drawn from this brief survey of the evidence? One is that since the right of silence is usually waived, it has little importance and should be abolished. That conclusion is of course false. The evidence shows that most suspects, for whatever reasons, waive their rights; but the evidence also suggests, if it does not exactly prove, that a major factor in that decision is the enormous pressures resulting from the methods and organisation of investigation. The only conclusion which can safely be drawn is that under present conditions the right to silence is illusory, since it is difficult, virtually impossible, for most suspects to make an informed and voluntary decision as to whether or not to waive the right, and, even if they make that decision, to withstand the pressures in favour of waiver. The conclusion which emerges is that, if the right of silence is important in principle, then there is a duty on the community to provide the conditions which ensure that the suspect has a real choice. But since interrogation is central to the investigation, and because of the expectations of the police that a confession will be made, the provision of such conditions would require fundamental reform rather than peripheral changes. Without those conditions, the right to silence is bound to be a principle which is fine in theory but not matched by practice.

Another conclusion which might seem to be justified by the empirical evidence is that the police have no good reasons for regarding the right of silence as an obstacle to investigation. Why then their implacable hostility? Part of the explanation is that, although confessions are usually made, the right of silence nevertheless delays the investigation. Incriminating admissions might be obtained more quickly and easily if the suspect were informed that he has a duty to speak and that his silence might lead to adverse inferences being drawn by the court. Another part of the explanation for police hostility is the belief that a group of guilty offenders escapes conviction by exercising the right to silence; but despite the assertions of the Metropolitan Police Commissioner supporting that belief, there must be many officers who accept that it flies in the face of all evidence.

Neither of these explanations does justice to the fears of the police. The real explanation seems to lie in the disparity between the right of silence in principle and its application in practice. If the principle were to be taken seriously, the impact on investigation could be momentous. If the circumstances of investigation were to be changed so that every suspect, after proper advice from his solicitor, could make a free and genuine choice as to whether to answer questions, then it is probable that many would choose to remain silent. One has only to look at the law relating to the Fifth Amendment of the United States Constitution to see the potential impact of the right of silence. Indeed, it might be necessary to go further; according to research conducted for the Royal Commission, the very process of interrogation as it is now practised puts such psychological pressure on the suspect that there is little scope for free choice.[22] In order to remove that pressure, the changes to the whole process of investigation which would be needed, go far beyond the requirements of the Police and Criminal Evidence Act.

The argument should not be overstated; there has to be a sense of reasonableness in drawing a line between the conditions necessary for full enjoyment of a right and the competing demands of police investigation. But the point of the argument should be clear: if there is a commitment in principle to the right of silence, then there is a powerful case for requiring practical conditions which ensure basic enjoyment of the right. That case poses a threat to police methods, a threat which, under the Police and Criminal Evidence Act, is to some extent becoming a reality. It would be clearly better from the point of view of the police, to remove that threat by abandoning any commitment to the right of silence. The question which arises is whether the right has foundations firm enough to justify its place in criminal justice; but before considering that question, we must examine the legal status of the right.

IV

The right of silence is capable of being defined in various ways. While it may be agreed that there is a general right of silence in the sense that the suspect has no duty to speak, there is wide scope for variation as to the legal consequences that flow from remaining silent, and as to the extent to which the law ensures that the right can freely be exercised. On a narrow view, the right may mean only that the suspect has no duty to speak, but that in exercising the right he would run the risk of adverse legal consequences, such as the drawing of inferences of guilt. On a broader view, the law might not only allow silence but go on to ensure, first, that no disadvantages result from silence, and secondly, that the right is made worthwhile by legal protections which ensure that the suspect has the capacity and opportunity to exercise the right, and that, if it is waived, it is by free and genuine choice. The right, in other words, is general and abstract, concealing a bundle of more specific legal relationships. It is only by an analysis of the surrounding legal rules that those more precise elements of the right can be identified.

However, turning to English law, I wish to suggest that it is a basic principle that, subject to limited statutory exceptions, the suspect has a right of silence in that he is under no duty to answer the questions of the police or to provide information in relation to the crime in question. This is a principle of common law which is recognised implicitly rather than explicitly in legal rules, practices and decisions; it is a principle which informs and makes sense of a number of general rules of evidence. It was on this principle that the Judges' Rules were based, and it now underlies the provisions relating to the questioning of suspects pursuant to the Police and Criminal Evidence Act 1984. The right to silence is assumed and acted upon rather than specified and stipulated.

The right to silence has two parts: the first where the suspect exercises his right by remaining silent; the second where the suspect waives his right by speaking. As to the first of these, the police must inform the suspect at different stages in the investigation that he is not required to say anything. Provided that those cautions are given, the police may interrogate and they may use against the suspect any revelations of an incriminatory kind. If the suspect exercises his right by remaining silent, the basic rule is that silence alone is not evidence. Silence itself is not, in other words, the basis upon which an inference of guilt may be drawn.[23] At first sight this rule seems clear enough; the principal rationale being that since the suspect is exercising the right of silence, that silence has no evidential value in relation to the accusations against him. There is simply no logical connection between the two. The rule also has support from the principle of fairness; if adverse inferences could be drawn from silence, then the right would be so devalued as to be worthless. If it is a minimum feature of the right that the accused should not by its exercise be prejudiced, then fairness requires that no adverse inferences should be drawn. But while the evidential and fairness rationales happily coincide in relation to the general rule, tensions between the two soon appear.

In the first place, there are circumstances where it is difficult not to allow silence to slip into the evaluation of the evidence. Those circumstances are most likely to occur where the accused, after being silent under questioning, offers a later explanation, perhaps at the trial itself, which seeks to demonstrate his innocence. It is hard in such cases to resist the conclusion, which seems to be so naturally compelling, that the fact of earlier silence affects the plausibility or weight of the later explanation, just as failure to give any explanation at all must bear on the weight of the positive evidence for the prosecution. While a direction to the jury in such terms as those would seem defensible, it is difficult to hold the line between silence as a negative factor in assessing the weight or credibility of positive evidence, and silence as an item of evidence in itself, sufficient to tip the scales in favour of the prosecution.[24]

In the second place, silence might also be relevant when it is part of a course of conduct which can reasonably be taken as an acceptance by the suspect of accusations against him. Acceptance of the accusation amounts to an admission by adoption and may be received in evidence as an exception to the hearsay rule.[25] But the English courts have gone further: in *R. v. Hall*,[26] after confirming the general rule that silence is not evidence, Lord Diplock added that there might be exceptional circumstances in which adverse inferences could be drawn from the failure of the suspect, in face of an accusation, to give an explanation or to make a disclaimer. The matter was taken further when in *R. v. Chandler* the court declared that "it does not follow [from the general rule of silence] that a failure to answer an accusation or question when an answer could reasonably be expected may not provide some evidence in support of an accusation."[27] Everything turns on when "an answer could reasonably be expected." In *Chandler*, it seemed that by the presence of a solicitor, the accused was put on sufficiently even terms with the police for it to be reasonable to expect answers to their questions. The Australian courts have opened up an additional inroad into the principle that silence does not mean guilt by allowing that, in certain circumstances, silence might be allowed as evidence of a "consciousness of guilt."[28] A selective answer, for example, where a suspect might be expected to answer, could result in a "hostile inference" being drawn.[29]

The theme running through these cases is simple enough; although silence is not itself an admission or the basis for an adverse conclusion, silence may in certain circumstances be evidential. The crucial question then is when does silence have evidential value? But notice that the question is not answered by straightforward logical analysis; rather it depends substantially on the assumptions that are made about silence and in particular on what value the right carries against other considerations. On purely evidential considerations, there are circumstances, for example where the suspect is on even terms with his questioner, in which it might be expected as a matter of common sense that some explanation should be made. But to follow that approach is to undermine or at least greatly to devalue the right of silence. The unavoidable question is, how seriously is that right to be taken, how extensive is it to be. On purely evidential considerations based on common sense the suspect might be expected to behave in a certain way, while from the point of view of the right of silence, quite different behaviour would be explicable. The short point is that the conflict between the two can be resolved only by considering how much importance is to be attached to competing values, on the one hand rectitude, on the other the right of silence. The steps that English law has taken in that direction are tentative; but the resolution which is beginning to emerge is neither entirely clear nor satisfactory.

A different set of issues arises when the suspect waives the right by speaking and answering questions. According to one theory of rights, that known as the will theory, the power of waiver is part of the very concept of right.[30] This may be inadequate as a theory of rights, since some rights do not carry the power of waiver; that power, however, does seem to be a fundamental feature of some rights, including the right to silence. It follows that a legal commitment to the right in general should include protection of the power to waive. Such protections might take different forms, but the underlying aim should be to ensure that, where silence is waived, it is by the exercise of a decision which is reasonably informed and reasonably voluntary; the decision, in other words, of a moral agent knowing the facts and consequences of different courses of action and freely choosing one or the other.

The principal way in which the law protects free waiver of the right is through standards laid down in the Police and Criminal Evidence Act 1984 and the Code of Practice pursuant to it. The Code of Practice, in particular, sets out in detail the treatment of suspects under police questioning. Closely related to those standards are the rules and discretions relating to admissibility of confessional evidence. Through these the courts traditionally and Parliament more recently set standards not only of admissibility but standards which also guide the police in investigation. From an analysis of those standards and of the law relating to confessional evidence, much can be learnt about the right to silence.

The confessional rule as traditionally stated is only too familiar[31]: confessions in the sense of incriminating admissions, gained from the suspect by a person in authority, are inadmissible unless made voluntarily and without oppression. Although the tests for involuntariness at common law became rather crude and mechanical, the general approach to confessions was based on a reasonably coherent rationale: confessions would be admissible only if made in the exercise of free choice and in the absence of conditions which might undermine that free choice. The rules of exclusion based on involuntariness following a threat, promise or inducement, or oppression in the sense of stopping the suspect's will, were specific instances of that more general principle.

Most cases where exclusion was warranted, would be caught by the confessional rules; in the exceptional case which fell outside the rules, but nevertheless violated the underlying principle, a residual discretion to exclude could be invoked. However, with the enactment of the Police and Criminal Evidence Act, the law changed significantly.[32] By allowing confessions to be admitted in evidence unless something was said or done to the suspect, which in the circumstances, was likely to render the confession unreliable, the voluntariness test was replaced by a direct test of reliability. The test of oppression also changed from the common law concern with conduct which tended to weaken the will of the suspect, to the statutory definition in terms of torture, inhuman or degrading treatment, and the use or threat of violence, whether or not amounting to torture. A discretion is retained under the Act to exclude evidence the admission of which would have an adverse effect on the fairness of the proceedings; whether this is in addition to or simply restates the discretion at common law is a matter of debate.[33] In any event, the residual discretion to exclude confessional evidence would seem to be retained.

The relationship between the confessional rule and the right to silence can be seen by considering possible justifications for the rule. These are generally put in terms of reliability, the protection of rights, discipline of the police, and a residual sense of public policy.[34] The last two, in so far as they are separate from the other two, need not concern us here. As to reliability and the protection of rights, the first point to notice is that, on the view of evidence suggested earlier, that dichotomy is false. Far from being in opposition to rights, the reliability principle should be understood as expressing the accused's right to a fair trial. The right to a fair trial requires that it should be excluded when there is a risk that the evidence is unreliable and that the unreliability might not be taken properly into account by the court. This may in turn lead to an unacceptably high risk of a wrongful conviction. But since this means sometimes excluding reliable confessions and therefore good evidence, a strong case has to be made for excluding categories of evidence such as involuntary confessions. That case is made in the following way: confessions made under conditions which lead to involuntariness may be false, but there is no way of knowing the true from the false; yet confessional evidence is particularly damaging and where there is a confession, there is likely to be a conviction. But because of the high level of accuracy which is required, if the accused's right to a fair trial is not to be violated, it is justifiable that categories of risky confessional evidence should be excluded as a matter of rule. In addition, it is necessary that the court should have a residual discretion to exclude confessions which are not excluded as a matter of rule, but are unreliable for some other reason. The standard of fairness in exercising that discretion is, on this approach, based on fairness at the trial which is in turn based on ensuring a high level of accuracy.

This approach provides a cogent and principled way of understanding the confession rule. There are, however, a number of difficulties. One is that the link between involuntariness and unreliability has not been established on sound empirical evidence. That difficulty is partly met by the Police and Criminal Evidence Act, s.76, which substitutes unreliability for voluntariness. Even so, there is still the question as to what circumstances are likely to make a confession unreliable; the new test will presumably be wider than involuntariness, but it would not be surprising if the requirement of voluntariness continued to be of great significance. A second difficulty with the reliability test is that regardless of the circumstances in which the confession was made, if its reliability is established by other evidence, evidence which is often discovered as a result of the confession itself, then it should be admitted. It is somewhat irrational to exclude evidence because there is a risk of unreliability, if it is known from other evidence to be reliable. A third major difficulty with the unreliability principle is the assumption that magistrates and juries are incapable of assessing the reliability of confessional evidence. That might be the case, but we should at least keep in mind Bentham's strictures against excluding categories of risky evidence as a matter of rule, rather than leaving their probative value to be assessed, together with all other evidence, by the court. This leads to a fourth point which is especially pertinent to the right to silence. Once the admissibility of confessions is made to turn on their reliability and the subsequent accuracy of outcome at the trial, the way is open for a powerful argument against the right to silence. On such an argument, the suspect should be under a duty to answer police questions, with the court being left to decide whether the answers were reliable enough to be admitted and what warnings to give to the jury. I shall return to this point shortly, but it is at least plausible to argue that a higher level of accuracy of outcome would be achieved without violating the accused's right to a fair trial, if the right to silence did not exist. The logic of reliability once invoked, could lead to radical conclusions, conclusions which Bentham might have applauded.

Let us now consider the confessional rule in relation to the right to silence; the first point is that the very language of involuntariness and oppressiveness matches the idea that waiver of silence should be freely made. Judges of the Australian High Court have gone further by expressing voluntariness in terms of free will and emphasising that confessions will be admitted only if made in the exercise of a reasonably free decision.[35] A similar concern can be seen in the renewed emphasis of English and Australian courts on the circumstances and personality of the suspect.[36] That enquiry makes most sense if the immediate issue is whether or not the suspect has freely waived his silence, and it is concerned only indirectly with the truth of what is said. Further, this approach provides a coherent, unifying principle to the tests of voluntariness and oppression; just as the menacing threat can in the special circumstances of a police interrogation reduce the suspect's capacity to remain silent, so may oppressive tactics or conditions. And it is interesting to note that the new statutory test retains oppression as a basis for exclusion, independently of any condition of unreliability. Indeed the statutory reference to oppression as including inhuman or degrading treatment suggests that the values at stake are quite different from reliability of evidence.[37]

It is also interesting to note that the link between the rules of confessional evidence and the right to silence can be found in one of the touchstones of the modern law, *R. v. Sang*.[38] That decision has been criticised for its narrow approach to evidence obtained by illegal methods, but in the leading speech, Lord Diplock states quite clearly that the underlying rationale of the confessional rule is that "no one can be required to be his own betrayer or, in its popular English mistranslation, the right to silence."[39] However, it is not clear that Lord Diplock carried the other members of the House of Lords with him on this point, and there are numerous judgments which base the confessional rule on reliability rather than silence.[40] The many cases on this point in the Australian High Court in recent years have revealed a similar divergence of opinion, although it is not easy to find an outright statement that the right of silence is at the base of the confession rule.[41] Parliament, as we have noted, has also partly abandoned the connection between the two by substituting reliability for voluntariness; but by retaining oppression as a separate head of exclusion, it seems to be recognising that interests other than reliability must be served.

When we consider the discretionary part of the law, the case of a link between confessions and the right to silence is strengthened. Under the pre-statutory law, a confession might pass the strict test of admissibility and yet be excluded in the court's discretion. We should be clear about what is meant here by discretion: the governing standard is fairness, and the judge's only task is to decide whether that standard has been breached. Once it is concluded that its admission would be unfair, the evidence must as a matter of law be excluded. For those with an interest in the debate over the nature of discretion, this is a case of weak rather than strong discretion.[42] But the question is what is the standard of fairness? On the reliability approach it is fairness at the trial. The alternative is to interpret fairness in relation to the right of silence: that is, it is unfair to induce waiver of the right. The exclusionary rule based on voluntariness and oppression is normally adequate protection; but there may be cases where confessional evidence, without being strictly involuntary, is obtained unfairly. The suspect may be deceived or tricked or in some other way led to waive his silence. The crucial point is that, on this approach, the rules of exclusion and the discretion so-called serve the same end, namely protecting the right to silence. Indeed the rules might be seen as specific instances of the general standard of fairness, but the possible categories of unfairness are never closed. There is discretion only in the special sense that a judgment has to be made on the basis of fairness; where there is unfairness there is a duty to exclude.

Again, judicial statements do not point clearly in one direction. Lord Diplock in *R.* v. *Sang* accepts that the right to silence lies at the base of the discretion as well as the rule. The other speeches appear either to settle for an undifferentiated sense of fairness or to confine discretion to fairness at the trial.[43] Similarly it is difficult to extract one clear rationale from the varied opinions of the Australian High Court. Some of the Justices clearly limit fairness to the trial.[44] Others appear to offer tantalising hints of something more. In one of the leading cases, Justice Deane says on the one hand, that the confessional rule is based on both reliability and the privilege against self-incrimination (which he seems to use interchangeably with the right to silence); he also says on the other hand, that fairness refers not to whether the accused was treated unfairly, but whether the reception of the evidence would be unfair to him.[45] This is a nice case of ambiguity, although finally he seems to mean fairness at trial. The most interesting statement of principle comes from Justice Brennan when he says that "the unfairness of using a statement must arise from the circumstances under which it was made."[46] He goes on to say that the test is whether, in all the circumstances, the statements of the accused have been extracted from him under conditions which render it unjust to allow his own words to be given in evidence against him. There is still a certain ambiguity, but it might be suggested that statements like these are searching for and on the brink of discovering some standard of fairness other than fairness at the trial itself; respect for the right to silence would fit precisely. In other words, the ambiguity and obscurity, which pervades judicial consideration of the discretion to exclude for unfairness, would disappear if judges were to recognise that the right to a fair trial is not the only right in issue. The position in England is now governed partly by statute; s.78(1) of the Police and Criminal Evidence Act retains judicial discretion, but uses without explanation the expression "fairness of the proceeding." It remains open as to whether fairness is limited to the trial proceedings or extends to pre-trial matters.

To sum up, the argument is that the law relating to confessions can be understood in terms of two different rights: the right to a fair trial which derives from the right not to be wrongly convicted, and the right to silence. The right to a fair trial is the more fundamental right, but the right to silence can be a significant, additional constraint on the conduct of the trial. The relationship between the two rights can be expressed in this way: the right to a fair trial imposes certain restraints on the admission of evidence and the conduct of the trial; the right to silence is to that extent complementary, but adds its own, additional constraints. The main consequence of the right to a fair trial is to ensure against unreliable evidence; the consequence of the right to silence is to go further and exclude evidence which is gained by violating the right. The first test centres on reliability, the second on notions of free choice. The courts must finally decide which conception of evidence prevails, the narrower or the broader. While judicial opinions may vary, Parliament has decided that both apply. The importance of the different approaches can be seen where a confession is confirmed or supported by independent evidence; on the reliability test, the confession should be admitted since the reason for its exclusion has been removed. On the right to silence approach, the circumstances in which the confession was gained are all important, and reliability is irrelevant. Again the views of the courts in regard to this doctrine are mixed, reflecting differences as to the underlying justifications. The argument advanced here is that a commitment to the right to silence carries a commitment to this broader conception of the law.

V

English law is committed to the right of silence and, if that commitment were to be taken seriously, the costs would be substantial. The police investigation would be hampered as more suspects claimed the right and remained silent. Where the right was waived, the law would be more exacting in ensuring free and voluntary waiver. All this points to one final question: is the right of silence under police questioning justified? Is it a sacred cow, an unjustifiable relic of the past, or is it a safeguard of liberty, something without which the individual suspect would be demeaned and the society diminished?

The question can be answered in various ways. The simplest answer would be that, in common with a host of other principles and practices, the right of silence is simply part of our culture; it provides important symbols about how the individual person stands within that culture, and about how authority is constituted. The right to silence has emerged in the development of the constitution, and just as the Americans accept their written constitution, including the Fifth Amendment, so we should accept the unwritten constitution of the United Kingdom. However, on the assumption that a rather more solid foundation must be found if the right to silence is to withstand criticism, it is necessary to consider other justifications.

It seems unlikely that utilitarianism in its direct form is able to provide that foundation. We have seen that Bentham's own special version of direct utilitarianism, with its emphasis on rectitude of outcome, provides as little support for the right to silence as it does for the privilege against self-incrimination. Both are seen as impediments to obtaining and admitting probative evidence, and Bentham's prohibition on such impediments is as close to a strict rule as an arch-anti-rule theorist could allow. There is an argument that the right to silence serves rectitude by helping to prevent against false statements by innocent suspects; but even if that were true empirically, Bentham's approach would insist that the evidence should be admitted for assessment by the court. An alternative version of direct utilitarianism might put less weight on rectitude and take more account of the utilities gained in not requiring the suspect to speak; but it is hard to see that these would offset the clear gains in requiring disclosure, especially if precautions were taken to guard against false confessions.

Arguments from rights appear to offer more promise. One line of approach is to begin with the basic right not to be wrongly convicted and the derivative right to a fair trial. The right to silence could be taken as instrumental to the right to a fair trial. The right to silence and the rules of admissibility which accompany it help to ensure that it is only confessions, freely and voluntarily made, which are admitted in evidence. On the assumption that such confessions are likely to be reliable, while confessions which are in some way tainted run a higher risk of being false, the right to silence serves as a filter of evidence and in this way helps to ensure that the innocent are not convicted wrongly. That assumption might need to be verified by more empirical evidence than is now available, and there are no doubt exceptions to it; voluntary confessions will sometimes be false, coerced confessions sometimes true. Nevertheless, the right to silence and the rules of evidence which follow from it constitute a defensible approach in that, taken as a whole, they set the scales against wrongful conviction and therefore in favour of the accused's right to a fair trial.

The main difficulty with this justification for the right to silence is whether it is a very effective way of protecting against false confessions. In the first place, it might be argued that the imposition of a duty on all suspects to answer questions does not necessarily mean a high risk of false confessions. In the absence of empirical evidence it is simply hard to know. Indeed some lessons might be learnt from the present position. We have seen that although there is no duty to answer questions, the pressures on suspects to do so are considerable with the result that most make damaging admissions. There is no evidence, however, to suggest that there is a significant risk of such confessions being false and the falsehood going undetected. The second argument is more fundamental; even if there is a significant risk of false confessions, that risk would be controlled and reduced more effectively and directly, not by the right to silence, but by stringent conditions on the interrogation. A duty to answer questions in an environment which is strictly controlled and recorded, and where the suspect is guaranteed the presence of a solicitor, followed at a later stage by the careful judicial scrutiny of both the statements made and the explanations for any refusal to answer, would seem to be a sound approach to ensuring reliability. If, in other words, the question is whether the right to a fair trial, understood against the background of the right not to be convicted wrongly, is better protected by the right to silence, or by a duty to answer questions subject to stringent safeguards, it is hard to be convinced that it would not be the latter. However, the rejoinder might be made that the present conditions of interrogation are so far removed from those which would be required to ensure against unreliability, that the right to silence is, under present conditions, the best device available. Since there is small likelihood of such conditions ever being adopted, the rejoinder must carry substantial weight. And the conclusion may be drawn that, imperfect as it is, the right to silence plays an important part in protecting the right to a fair trial.

Although it might be concluded that, under present conditions, the right to silence is indispensable to the right to a fair trial, the question remains whether there is a basis for the right to silence in values independent of the trial. For many there is an intuition, somewhat unclear in its origins and scope, that even if the conditions of interrogation were improved sufficiently to ensure reliability of confessional evidence, the right to silence would still be important. One way of explaining that importance is to link the right to silence to the general principle that the state must prove its case against the suspect, not only at the trial but also in pre-trial matters. The burden of proof lies on the state and the discharge of that burden is not to be achieved by requiring the accused to provide incriminating evidence. On this approach, the right to silence is associated closely with, indeed is a particular application of, the privilege against self-incrimination.

The Royal Commission on Criminal Procedure took this general approach, concluding that the right to silence should be preserved because it helps to ensure that the burden of proof is on the prosecution.[47] To require the suspect to explain his actions would be, on this view, to reverse the presumption of innocence and the burden of proof. However, it may be thought that this argument is less than convincing. The burden of proof is hardly reversed since the prosecution would still have to prove its case, the only argument being about which bits of evidence it may use. If the suspect is allowed to remain silent, then potential evidence is denied to the prosecution. But although the burden of proof would not be reversed by requiring suspects to answer questions, the emphasis within the relationship between state and suspect would be changed, with the suspect being a source of valuable evidence. The real difficulty lies in drawing a firm line as to just where that emphasis should fall. The suspect is already required in various ways to co-operate with the police and the prosecution in providing evidence, whether by delivering up items such as books, documents, and records, or submitting to a search of person or premises, or even making available more personal information such as finger-printing or body samples.[48] In other words, the relationship between state and suspect is not absolute but one of degree and balance. Considering the many existing exceptions to the privilege against self-incrimination, the imposition of a duty to answer questions might be taken as an adjustment within the relationship between the citizen and the state which is incremental rather than fundamental. Judgments as to the precise course which that relationship should take are judgments of fine-tuning about which reasonable people are bound to draw different conclusions. Those judgments of course have to be made and justified, but finally it is quite conceivable that the balance of informed judgment would come to accept that the imposition of a duty to answer questions is tolerable and legitimate.

There is, however, another and final argument for the right to silence which seeks to provide an independent justification in terms of privacy. Privacy is a notoriously difficult concept to use with both precision and conviction, but in the remainder of this essay, I shall provide an outline of the argument and make brief reference to the main difficulties.[49] Let us be reminded of the precise question: is there a right to remain silent under police questioning, even if that means making the job of the police more difficult and the possible loss of probative evidence? In making the case for such a right, we must be clear about what is necessary: rights protect interests; to have a right is to have a justified claim that an interest should be protected by the imposition of correlative duties. To warrant that protection, an interest must invoke a value which is important enough to outweigh conflicting values and goals, and important enough to justify the imposition of duties on others.

The right to silence protects privacy, and privacy is important because it protects personal identity and autonomy. Without a zone of privacy, identity, autonomy, personality cannot exist. This is easily shown: suppose that your every action could be monitored, that every thought, urge and desire could be known and recorded, to be used for any purposes by a stranger. Identity and autonomy, let us use the general term personality, under such conditions, would be seriously distorted if not destroyed. It follows that a zone of privacy is essential to personality. For the same reasons, I have no duty to provide that kind of information about myself to another, especially a stranger; and I have an immunity from a stranger having direct access to it. The right of silence serves privacy, which in turn serves this basic sense of personality. Since we greatly value personality, that zone of privacy is important enough to justify duties on others to respect it. So, a prima facie case for a general right to silence is established.

However, privacy can be more or less extensive; with a broad spectrum of things being characterised as involving privacy. It also competes with other values and goals. If we think of privacy as an expanding circle with individual personality at its centre, then the farther a particular instance is from the centre, the less weight it carries against competing factors; the closer to the centre, the more powerful it becomes. On this basis, decisions can be made as to whether incursions are justified. Many of course are; each of us is daily called on to provide information about ourselves—within our families, to the doctor, within the university and to the state. In each case there is some sacrifice of privacy, but it is justified by a more important consideration.

In the case of the suspect, the conflict is clear: on the one side privacy, on the other crime control. So the question is, would imposition of a duty on the suspect to explain himself—his actions, thoughts, motives—strike so close to the centre of the circle of privacy to outweigh the collective interest in crime control? Judgments on this point are bound to vary, but an affirmative although tentative answer is offered on the following lines. First, the police are strangers to the suspect, which means that there are none of the duties of disclosure which result from special relationships. The only competing interest, therefore, is crime control. Secondly, suppose that the police could find out all they need to know by plugging the suspect into a machine; the process is painless but it reveals everything about the suspect—his history, actions, thoughts, and desires. That would strike at the very centre of the zone of privacy. But there is no difference in principle between using the machine and requiring the suspect to disclose the same information through speech. The means differ but the objection is the same: the police have no claim on direct access to that information and it follows that they have no claim on the suspect to lower the shield of privacy. Thirdly, the shield of privacy is of special importance when the very object of interrogation is to gain evidence which can be used to the disadvantage of the suspect. This is not, however, simply to fall back on the argument that the right to silence is justified by the privilege against self-incrimination. The argument is rather that both the right to silence and the privilege against self-incrimination finally depend on the case from privacy. This argument also helps to explain why the suspect is in a different position from the ordinary witness.

The argument from privacy provides a sound case for the right to silence. There are, however, a number of objections which I can here raise rather than discuss in full. First, the argument from privacy might appear to lead to the paradox that the more serious the alleged crime, the greater the interest in society's detecting the offender, and therefore the greater the permissible intrusion into privacy. Considering the variable strength of the claim of privacy and the obvious need to balance countervailing values and interests, it is difficult to see how a strong case could be made for an absolute right to silence. Rather the extent of the right to silence would depend on the balance drawn in each case. The rejoinder would be, however, that since it would be intolerable for that balancing act to be performed by the investigating officers in each case, the law must, as in so many other areas, draw lines which in particular cases might be over-inclusive, but which in their overall application produce the most justifiable results.

This can be related to a second difficulty: not all questions that might be asked involve a deep intrusion into privacy. But again the rejoinder might be made that usually interrogation is by way of prolonged and discursive questioning in order to provide the right context and milieu for obtaining answers to the few really vital questions. Moreover, there is the same administrative difficulty as mentioned above: it could not be left to the discretion of the police to decide whether a given question or set of questions are intrusive. The right to silence then represents an attempt to provide a generalised, but imperfect, solution. The third and final difficulty is in distinguishing between privacy as to consciousness and privacy as to bodily parts, such as finger-prints and bodily samples. It might be thought that the two stand or fall together, and that any conclusion which put both beyond the reach of the police would be unacceptable. Considering the scientific developments in "genetic finger-printing" and its importance as objective evidence, such a loss would be too great. It is not implausible, however, to distinguish the two situations and to conclude that while both involve issues of privacy, it is only privacy with respect to consciousness which is sufficiently fundamental to attract a blanket form of legal protection. This is not to accept that bodily samples however intimate, may freely be taken; it is to say only that with respect to them different lines may have to be drawn in deciding the balance of legal protection. To sum up, the problems with the privacy argument are substantial and it might well be asked whether, in accommodating those problems and in making the elaborate distinctions that are necessary, there is indeed much left of the general principle. However, the final answer of that question must be left for another occasion.

NOTES

[1] *R. v. Beljajev* [1984] V.R. 657 at p. 662.

[2] Criminal Law Revision Committee, *Eleventh Report on Criminal Evidence (General)* (Cmnd. 4991, (1972)).

[3] Royal Commission on Criminal Procedure, *Report* (Cmnd. 8092 (1981)).

[4] See the discussion in Jeremy Bentham, *Rationale of Judicial Evidence* (ed. J. S. Mill, 1827), pp. 588 *et seq.*

[5] Sir Rupert Cross, "Right of Silence and the Presumption of Liberty—Sacred Cow or Safeguards of Liberty" (1970) 11 J.S.P.T.L. 66.

[6] P. Imbert, *Policing Major Cities* September 15, 1987, p. 10.

[7] William Twining, *Bentham and Wigmore: Theories of Evidence* (London, 1985).

[8] For further discussion, see D. J. Galligan, "More scepticism about scepticism" (1988) *Oxford Journal of Legal Studies.*

[9] Jeremy Bentham, *A Treatise on Judicial Evidence* (ed. M. Damont, London, 1825), pp. 2–3.

[10] For further discussion: Ronald Dworkin, "Policy, Principle Procedure" in C. F. N. Tapper (ed.), *Crime, Proof and Punishment* (London, 1981) and D. J. Galligan, *Discretionary Powers: A Legal Study of Official Discretion* (Oxford, 1986), Chap. 7.

[11] See the discussion, for example, in *R. v. Sang* [1980] A.C. 402.

[12] For Bentham's discussion of this issue in general, see *Rationale of Judicial Evidence*, n. 4 above.

[13] Ronald Dworkin, *Taking Rights Seriously* (London, 1976), especially Chap. 4.

[14] Recent studies of police investigation are: Paul Softley, *Police Interrogation: An Observational Study in Four Police Stations* (Research Study No. 4, 1980); J. Baldwin and J. McConville, *Courts, Prosecution and Conviction*; B. Irving and L. Hilgendorf, *Police Interrogation: The Psychological Approach* (Royal Commission on Criminal Procedure, Research Study Nos. 1 & 2, 1980).

[15] See Baldwin and McConville, *Courts, Prosecution and Conviction.*

[16] *Ibid.* p. 138.

[17] Those figures and those following are based on research undertaken by Softley and Baldwin and McConville, see n. 14.

[18] Baldwin and McConville, *Courts, Prosecution and Conviction*, p. 139.

[19] *Ibid.* p. 157.

[20] See Michael Zander, "No case for destroying the right of silence" *The Law Magazine* (January 22, 1958), p. 16.

[21] *Ibid.*

[22] Baldwin and McConville, *Courts, Prosecution and Conviction*, pp. 99 and following.

[23] For discussion, see *Cross on Evidence* (6th ed.), pp. 555–6.

[24] For further analysis, see S. Odgers, "Police Interrogation and the Right to Silence" (1985) 59 A.L.J. 78.

[25] See *Cross on Evidence* (6th ed.), pp. 528–532.

[26] [1970] 1 All E.R. 322.

[27] [1976] 3 All E.R. 105.

[28] *Woon* v. *The Queen* (1964) 109 C.L.R. 529; *Merrall* v. *Samuels* (1971) 2 S.A.S.R. 378; *R.* v. *Barren* [1975] V.R. 476.

[29] *Paterson* v. *Martin* (1966) 116 C.L.R. 506, *per* Barwick C.J. at p. 511.

[30] For the account of the will theory, see H. L. A. Hart, "Bentham on Rights" in A. W. B. Simpson (ed.), *Oxford Essays in Jurisprudence* (2nd Series, Oxford, 1973).

[31] For discussion, see *Cross on Evidence* (5th ed., 1979), pp. 534–551 and (6th ed., 1985), pp. 533–556.

[32] s.76.

[33] s.78 and see P. Mirfield, "The Evidential Provision" (1985) Crim.L.R. 569.

[34] See A. Ashworth, "Excluding Evidence as Protecting Rights" 1977 Crim.L.R. 723 and S. B. McNicol, "Strategies for Reform of the Law Relating to Police Interrogations" (1984) 33 I.C.L.Q. 265.

[35] See *Cleland* v. *R.* (1982) 43 A.L.R. 619 and *Collins* v. *R.* (1980) 31 A.L.R. 257 (Brennan J.)

[36] *D.P.P.* v. *Ping Lin* [1976] A.C. 574.

[37] Police and Criminal Evidence Act, s.76.

[38] [1980] A.C. 402.

[39] *Ibid.*

[40] See the discussion in *Cross on Evidence*, pp. 536–9.

[41] *Ibid.* and *Cleland* v. *R.* (1982) 43 A.L.R. 619.

[42] The distinction is analysed in R. Dworkin, *Taking Rights Seriously* (London, 1977), Chap. 2; see further D. J. Galligan, *Discretionary Powers: A Legal Study of Official Discretion*, Chap. 1.

[43] [1980] A.C. 402.

[44] See *R.* v. *Cleland* (1982) 43 A.L.R. 619; also *Seymour* v. *Att.-Gen.* (1984) 53 A.L.R. 513.

[45] *R.* v. *Cleland* (1982) 43 A.L.R.

[46] *Collins* v. *R.* (1980) 31 A.L.R. 257 at 313. See also *R.* v. *Lawson & Lee* [1984] V.R. 559.

[47] Royal Commission on Criminal Procedure, *Report*. For Commentary, see S. B. McNicol, "Strategies for Reform ... " (n. 34) and *Cross on Evidence*, pp. 541–2.

[48] See, in particular, the provisions of the Police and Criminal Evidence Act.

[49] For discussion, see C. Fried, "Privacy" (1968) 77 Y.L.J. 475 and R. Gerstein, "Privacy and Self-Incrimination" (1970) *Ethics*, 87.

The English Penal Crisis: Paradox and Possibilities

ANDREW RUTHERFORD

"No general remarks on this subject would be complete without a tribute to the increasing care which is being shown by the Courts of Justice in investigating the circumstances of offenders and avoiding unnecessary committal to prison."[1] So commented the Prison Commissioners for England and Wales in an annual report 65 years ago. The mood of scepticism about imprisonment and antipathy to the prison system, in part initiated by Winston Churchill during his brief tenure as Home Secretary between 1910–1911, was to be sustained throughout the inter-war years. For Churchill, "abatement" of imprisonment derived more from philosophical than pragmatic considerations. His decision to reduce the time to be served of the entire sentenced prison population, in celebration of the accession of George V, was not prompted by overcrowding, which hardly existed, but by values attached to the meaning of imprisonment in a liberal society. It was after making this announcement to the House of Commons on July 20, 1910 that he made his famous declaration: "The mood and temper of the public in regard to treatment of crime and criminals is one of the most unfailing tests of the civilization of any country."[2]

Throughout the 1920s and 1930s the prison population remained at about 11,000, half what it had been when Churchill persuaded his officials that drastic reductions be sought. During this period, 25 prisons were closed and the number of prison places was cut by one-third. The English penal experience attracted much interest. In an article "The Decreasing Prison Population of England," Edwin H. Sutherland, the American criminologist wrote: "Prisons are being demolished and sold in England because the supply of prisoners is not large enough to fill them."[3] The prison population rate was 30 per 100,000 inhabitants, and with the exception of the

Republic of Ireland, was the lowest rate in Europe, considerably below Sweden at 38, not to mention 57, the rate of the latter day penal example to us all, The Netherlands.[4]

The scene today provides a remarkable contrast with that of 50 years ago. With a prison population on February 26, 1988 of 50,365 (including 1,472 people held, most inappropriately, in police cells), England and Wales had an incarceration rate of 100. The most recent comparative data, published by the Council of Europe for February 1, 1987, showed England and Wales, along with the two other jurisdictions of the United Kingdom at the top of the European table, exceeded only by Austria and Turkey.[5] During 1988, the three jurisdictions of the United Kingdom will probably head the table, followed closely by France which seems determined not to be left far behind.

Given the promise displayed over the first three decades of this century, why is it that England and Wales should now be in such dire penal straits? Consideration of the period since 1950 illustrates the rise and fall of two fallacies: that the path to prison reform lies in building new prisons, and that the supply of punishment is infinite.

During the 1950s and 1960s, the rise in the prison population, at an even faster rate than during this decade, in large part reflected the huge increase in persons being sentenced by the courts. Although the average daily prison population virtually doubled, from 21,000 to 39,000, at least some encouragement could be found in the substantial and sustained decline in the use of custody as a proportion for all persons sentenced for indictable offences. When in 1959 R. A. Butler produced his famous white paper, *Penal Practice in a Changing Society* there were 6,000 prisoners (20 per cent. of the total) held in "grossly crowded conditions," representing "a monumental denial of the principles to which we are committed." For Butler's Home Office the way ahead lay in research, "a fundamental re-examination" of the "philosophy and practice of punishment" and "a building programme of formidable dimensions and great urgency . . . planned in relation to modern requirements."[6] In the event, 20 new prisons were built but the Royal Commission on the Penal System, set up in 1964 to carry out the fundamental re-examination was as one of its members, Barbara Wootton, later put it, "doomed from the start."[7] However, at least by 1967 the Home Office's stance on prison population, then at 33,000 was that further growth should be curtailed.

The strategy which found expression in the late 1960s and early 1970s had two main components, first, the courts would make less use of custody if they had more sentencing options, and second, the executive needed additional tools with which it might reduce average time served. Hence the invention, on the one hand, of such sanctions as the suspended sentence, compensation orders and the "credible" alternative, the community service order; and on the other hand, the introduction of the parole process in 1968 and its later refinements in order, among other objectives, to have some handle on prison population size. This two-part strategy, which has essentially remained intact, was, for the most part, careful not to restrict sentencing powers but to widen the courts' choices. No attempt was made to close the front door to the prison system, instead there developed a complex and confusing mix of non-custodial penalties. Only gradually did the paradox become apparent that rapid prison population growth was coinciding with the proliferation of new alternatives to imprisonment. But if the Home Office decided to observe "keep off" notices placed by the judiciary at the prison system's front door, it regarded the prison's back door as its own special preserve.

During the early 1970s the indicators were promising. The proportionate use of custody continued to decline; and, at least for a couple of years, so did the prison population encouraging the Treasury to axe much of a prison building programme that had been agreed in 1970. However in 1974, the proportionate use of custody started to rise, for the first time since 1950. By 1976 the prison population had leapt by 12 per cent. Reducing prison population size and the proportionate use of custody were now described by the Home Office as being among its "particular preoccupations."[8] To keep the lid on, the Home Office looked mostly to encouraging earlier and more extensive granting of parole.

In July 1975 the prison population reached a record level of 40,500 and the Home Secretary, Roy Jenkins, identified for the first time a ceiling beyond which it should not be allowed to go. If the prison population were to reach 42,000 declared Mr. Jenkins, conditions "would approach to intolerable and drastic action to relieve the position would become inescapable. We must not just sit back and wait for it to happen."[9] This speech signalled a switch of Home Office attention to the prison system's front door, but this time the intent was not to widen but to restrict sentencing powers. In asking the Advisory Council on the Penal System to review maximum prison terms, Mr. Jenkins observed that while this would encompass long-term questions about criminal justice it could not entirely be divorced from the pressing need to reduce the prison population[10]—a thought that may have found an echo,

12 years later, in Mr. Hurd's mind when he asked Mark Carlisle to undertake a review of parole, remission and related issues.

Despite the continued rise in the proportionate use of custody the prison population remained just below the 42,000 ceiling until 1979. There was however to be no legislative action on maximum prison terms. In May 1977, the Advisory Council in an interim report stated that "a large number of sentences of imprisonment passed by the courts, especially in the short and medium term band of sentences, are longer than they need be."[11] Given the obvious consequences of crowding "the time has come when the courts should be invited to make their contribution to a solution of this problem."[12] The Council decided to issue an interim report so as to consolidate what it perceived to be, "a tide of opinion moving in the direction of short prison sentences."[13] With some irony, as matters turned out, the Council noted that "a further educative role is being played by the media...the time is ripe for an initiative."[14] The interim report was couched in generalities whereas the final report, which appeared nine months later, spelled out the proposed reduced maximum terms, offence by offence, bringing the new maxima closer to actual sentencing practice.[15] Given the favourable reaction to the interim report, at least by that sector of the press to notice it, the Advisory Council cannot have anticipated the roasting given to its final report, with the exception of *The Guardian*. If the tide was moving it was certainly not in the direction perceived by the Council.[16]

That the Council had matched their case for shorter sentences for most offenders with extended sentences for the really bad or dangerous few was ignored by everyone except academics, worried about this tendency of contemporary penal policy.[17] Others have objected to the Council's avoidance of principle,[18] using little more than a pocket calculator it seemed to determine the proposed new maximum terms. Louis Blom-Cooper, who chaired the sub-committee that drafted the report, in part acknowledges this criticism in his recent Tanner Lectures. "With hindsight it may be that the fundamental flaw was for the Advisory Council to suppose that imprisonment could, or should, be a yardstick by which society's response to criminal conduct would be meted out. It had proceeded upon the retention of the sentencing structure as reflected in practice."[19]

For the Advisory Council, its report on *Maximum Penalties* was to be its "last hurrah." The Home Office read the episode as a warning to keep clear of the front door to the prison system, certainly with respect to restricting sentencing powers. Furthermore, at this time, the Home Office was consumed with the deteriorating state of industrial relations within many prisons and with concerns that power had been lost to local branches of the Prison Officers' Association. It was these anxieties that led, in 1978, to the appointment of a committee under the then Mr. Justice May, with broad terms of reference, to inquire into the prison systems of the United Kingdom. The May Committee accepted Home Office evidence that the supply side had been neglected and that the prison system had been starved of resources. In a curt swipe at the evidence from the Treasury, the May Committee stated that, "it seems very likely that the over-hopeful—sometimes merely fashionable—expectations of non-custodial disposals have persistently been used to defend the allocation of inadequate resources to the prison services."[20] The Treasury had told the May Committee that, "it might be reasonable to hope that the prison population could be stabilised within say five years.... Any proposal for a major addition to capital expenditure on replacement and modernisation would need to take that prospect into account."[21] Since that pronouncement, the Treasury, on matters pertaining to penal policy, has kept its head down and Home Office ministers have been laughing all the way to and from public expenditure reviews.

Appearing just five months after Mrs. Thatcher's first election victory, the May Committee's prescription that capital expenditure on prisons be doubled found receptive ears. The supply side to the numbers problem was now in vogue, carrying with it a key ingredient of the contemporary crisis. Holding onto concerns within the Government about the rising prison population now required all the dextrous gravitas of William Whitelaw.

That Whitelaw did make such an attempt, at least for about two years, there can be no doubt. A modest prison building programme was announced in 1980, but the policy thrust was to align resources with prison population, necessitating, the Home Office stated the following year, "a substantial reduction in the prison population so as to achieve a better correspondence between the numbers of prisoners and the resources available to accommodate them."[22] The appalling features of overcrowded prisons were described by Denis Trevelyan, then director-general of the prison system, as constituting "an affront to a civilized society." This theme, much to the gratification of the Home Office, was picked up by the new Lord Chief Justice, Lord Lane, in two judgments of the Court of Appeal. In the first of these, *Upton* in April 1980, Lord Lane referred to the scarcity value of prison places, observing: "the time has come to appreciate that non-violent petty offenders should not be allowed to take up what has become valuable space in prisons. If there really is no alternative . . . to an immediate prison sentence, then it should be as short as possible."[23] In *Begum Bibi*, three months later Lord Lane said, almost paraphrasing the Advisory Council: "What the Court can and should do is to ask itself whether there is any compelling reason why a short sentence should not be passed."[24] As in *Upton* he remarked that the prisons were "dangerously overcrowded," and this seemed to be the basis of the proposition that prison space was scarce rather than deriving from the inappropriateness of prison for relatively petty offences. The judgments did have a short-term effect on sentencing practice, by inducing, as Ashworth has suggested, a general spirit of parsimony rather than by means of selective application.[25]

In isolation from other events, and with regular reinforcement from Lord Lane and his colleagues, that was not to be forthcoming, *Upton* and *Begum Bibi* might eventually have reduced the prison population by between 2,000–3,000 below what it would otherwise have been. But by the end of the year, a significant rise in numbers dealt with by the courts swamped any such effect. For Mr. Whitelaw, matters were to be brought to a head by an industrial dispute over prison officers' breakfast time allowances. By locking new prisoners out of the prison system, the ultimate front door tactic, during the winter of 1980–1981, prison officers had within a couple of months achieved a 4,000 drop in population, even allowing for prisoners held in police cells and in two army camps.[26] With the dispute settled in the mid-January of 1981, the prison population resumed its climb, prompting Mr. Whitelaw to make a remarkable speech to Leicestershire magistrates on February 13, 1981. Mr. Whitelaw declared: "Hopes for a substantial reduction in the prison population must, in my view, rest primarily on a renewed commitment to avoiding custody wherever possible and, in cases where imprisonment is thought essential, a move towards shorter sentences for all except the violent offender. I must emphasize that the case for change in these directions does not rest solely on the crisis in the prison system, grave though it is. There are also important considerations of principle which reflect a significant shift in penological thinking over the last decade or so." Referring to recent events Mr. Whitelaw noted that the dispute with the P.O.A. "demonstrated that it is possible to survive with a much lower custodial population than before." He suggested that 40,000 be regarded as the benchmark (2,000 lower than the level identified by Roy Jenkins five years earlier) "against which we have to measure the progress or otherwise which the criminal justice system is making in months to come. . . . Parliament will be most reluctant to see the prison population return to the high levels of last year when much lower numbers seem consistent with supporting the law." He made it clear that the prison system could not build its way out of its difficulties. "There is no easy way of finding a solution through more prison places. We must look, too, to the criminal justice system as a whole, of which the prison system is an integral part. And in so doing, we must look at the sentencing practice and the legislative practice which, directly and indirectly, produces the prison population. It is, I think, common ground that a continued increase in the prison population could not be sustained. So on present trends, I should be obliged to consider what legislative measures could be taken."[27]

Mr. Whitelaw described his remarks as the beginning of a new way forward, but the speech was to be the last clarion call of an era during which, on a bi-partisan basis, the Home Office had attempted to place a scarcity value on the use of imprisonment. One reading of Mr. Whitelaw's reference to legislative action was that the measures being considered were to curb sentencing powers, and this may have precipitated the break in the concord that had developed with the Lord Chief Justice. In the event, the Home Office indicated that once again it would avoid the front door and explore further adjustments to the parole process. A departmental review of parole, which had begun in 1978, was reaching its conclusion. In July 1981 the Home Office review proposed a scheme of automatic release on licence of prisoners sentenced from six months up to three years after serving one-third of their sentence. It was estimated that adoption of this measure would reduce the prison population by up to 7,000 and "in the context of the chronic and severe pressure on the prison system, and the Government's commitment to reducing it, that could be an invaluable contribution."[28]

The Home Office scheme was formally abandoned five months later with an oblique reference by the Government that, "it has become clear, from the comments which the Government has received on the scheme, that it would be unlikely to bring about the substantial reduction in the prison population . . . (for which the Government is looking)."[29] The comments that directly contributed to this *volte-face* were those of the judiciary. But, for Mr. Whitelaw, an event a month or so earlier had been just as damaging. The defeat of the platform's motion on law and order at the Conservative Party Conference was a personal humiliation. Earlier Home Secretaries, notably R. A. Butler, had had to run this macabre annual gauntlet but at least Mr. Butler did not also have to endure the public disdain of his Prime Minister. Indeed Mr. Butler once remarked that when he was Home Secretary Harold MacMillan had allowed him a free hand in a spirit of indulgent scepticism.

In the spring of 1982 it became evident that the Government's policy had undergone a significant shift, with the articulation by Mr. Whitelaw of what might be called the "open front door" policy. In March 1982 he told the House of Commons: "We are determined to ensure that there will be room in the prison system for every person whom the judges and magistrates decide should go there, and we will continue to do whatever is necessary for that purpose."[30] This phrase was to become part of the Government's penal refrain. The prison building programme would ensure that the front door remained open. While the Home Office has kept a hand on the back door, it was with a grip that had become decidedly less confident.

Leon Brittan's appointment as Home Secretary in June 1983 gave shrill endorsement to the open front door policy. Although it is possible to underestimate the extent to which penal policy had already shifted prior to William Whitelaw's departure, Mr. Brittan's contribution emphasised and reinforced the break with efforts over a 15 year period to cap prison population size. During Mr. Brittan's two years at the Home Office the prison building programme was further expanded, work on minimum prison standards was scrapped, and the short sharp shock regime extended to all detention centres in the face of damning research by his own department. But it was the tone as much as the substance of Mr. Brittan's contribution that was further to turn the screw and reinforce the more primitive instincts of his party.

Mr. Brittan's first speech as Home Secretary to a Conservative Party Conference illustrates the point. Conscious no doubt of his predecessor's humiliation two years earlier, Mr. Brittan's 1983 Conference speech must on any reckoning be among the least edifying public performances by a Home Secretary in recent times. It might be argued in Mr. Brittan's defence that his virulant series of applause seeking announcements restricting parole for particular categories of long-term prisoners was a cynical device to cushion implementation of the earlier release of short-term prisoners under section 33 of the Criminal Justice Act 1982. But it was the style and the histrionics that did the damage, certainly overwhelming whatever relief was gained by the early release of 2,000 prisoners.[31]

For Douglas Hurd, succeeding Mr. Brittan in September 1985, the enormity of the challenge could hardly be overstated. There have been some welcome steps. The preferred language has been moderate and the approach calm and circumspect. He has uncompromisingly rejected the death penalty, now it seems a regular feature of the Parliamentary timetable. But for Mr. Hurd, the penal crisis has slipped from bad to worse. The prison population has continued its relentless increase, exceeding 50,000 and then 51,000 in July 1987. Despite an increased expenditure of 70 per cent., in real terms, on the prison system since 1980, conditions endured by prisoners and staff are worse than ever. The high cost of the squalor characterising many English prisons is another paradoxical feature of the contemporary scene. Prison overcrowding has never been greater, exceeding a peak of 19,000 persons sharing single use places in 1987. But despite 3,600 additional prison places since 1980, the level of crowding and the capacity shortfall have worsened. These are different measures, and it is not always appreciated that an equivalence of prisoners and places can, and has, coincided with very high levels of crowding. Hence the ambiguity that has arisen in a stated aim made for the prison building programme. For example, in November 1983, Leon Brittan claimed that the substantial increase he had achieved in the prison building programme would eliminate overcrowding by the end of the decade. The following year Ministers were talking about "being on course" to end overcrowding. By 1985 the Home Office acknowledged to the National Audit Office that what was actually meant by eliminating overcrowding was achieving a match of available places with average population.[32] In 1986, the Public Accounts Committee concluded: "We are dismayed that even when the Home Office's objective of matching total places and prison population is achieved, there will still be overcrowding in some prisons, and that large amounts of substandard accommodation will remain in use."[33]

One measure of substandard accommodation is denial of access to a toilet—indeed the absence of such basic privacy is one of those rights surrendered on entering the prison system. The consequential ritual of "slopping out" has been defined by Christopher Train, director-general of the Prison Service, while giving evidence in 1986 to the Public Accounts Committee. "It means that a prisoner spends his nights locked up in his cell and he has a chamber pot into which he either urinates or defaecates. When he is unlocked in the morning he takes his chamber pot and walks down the landing with it and disposes of the contents of that chamber pot into a sink. That is "slopping out.' " A few moments later Sir Brian Cubbon, Permanent Under-Secretary at the Home

Office, remarked: "Could I just add one gloss to Mr. Train's description of 'slopping out.' 'Slopping out' also takes place in cells accommodating two or three people. So the reduction of over-crowding will have the advantage of reducing the amount of "multiple slopping out.' "[34]

Mr. Hurd has given no sign that penal policy will be extricated from the elephant trap of its own making. He appears to be wedded to the familiar self-defeating policy contours that have been especially evident since 1982. In July 1987, as part of a package of responses to the record prison population, he was able to announce that there would be a further "substantial" increase to the prison building programme.[35] With the public expenditure review completed in November it was revealed that there were to be 4,200 additional places, bringing the total number of places to be built between 1980–1995 to 21,000 an increase of 53 per cent., at a total cost of over £1,000 million. Times have changed since James Callaghan's days in office: "Whenever we discussed levels of public expenditure in Cabinet I never had any doubt that if the choice lay between spending on a new school or a new prison, it would be the Secretary of Education who would win and the poor Home Secretary who would lose out."[36]

Contemporary penal policy also remains attached to splitting offenders into the very bad and the not so bad. As Tony Bottoms has shown, "bifurcation," to use his term, or the "twin track approach," in the words of Home Office Ministers, has a history that extends beyond the Advisory Council on the Penal System's 1977 Report. Uncertainties and injustices associated with the idea of dangerousness have been at the crux of the criticisms of Bottoms and others. These are concerns I share but I am stressing a rather different point—that the twin-track approach is likely to fail because it is the campaign against the very serious offender that sets the mood, not simultaneous measures taken with respect to the less serious. Douglas Hurd refers to the approach being "balanced," but is this a balance that can be maintained? In January 1988 Mr. Hurd drew attention to the increased penalties in the Criminal Justice Bill, noting that the public are particularly concerned with violence and offences against children. "We have taken account of this in our policy on penalties and so have the courts in the sentences they impose. Even within the last year or 18 months there have been sharp increases in the average sentence lengths in the Crown Court for offences against the person, sexual offences and robbery. I am reinforcing the courts' decisions by restricting the grant of parole to offenders sentenced to more than five years imprisonment for violent or sexual offences." And so on. Then he gets to the balancing bit in the speech: "But custody is a last resort. . . . We must try to ensure that custody is used only when the offence is so serious that a sentence outside prison would bring the system into disrepute."[37] While on this occasion it was this part of the speech that was reported in the press, "the twin-track approach" seems to be one that inevitably and inextricably fuels expansionist pressures.

As the Home Office casts desperately around for some way out existing constraints should not be underestimated. Among these, four are prominent. Firstly there are the ideological views of the right of the Conservative Party which dominate the Government if not the Home Office. Without doubt, Mr. Hurd regards the Party, not to mention the Prime Minister, as a powerful and perennial restraint. I am not implying that the Opposition parties are bursting with alternative policies, far from it. But these parties do not carry with them the ideological baggage that so cripples the Thatcher administration on this issue. Secondly, the judiciary presents us with two problems. The first is how to shift sentencing practice so as to recognise the scarcity value of imprisonment. The second problem is to overcome the judiciary's blocking power. At about the time that the judiciary objected to Mr. Whitelaw's plans on parole in 1981, Lord Lane halted a Home Office funded study of Crown Court sentencing practice, informing the researchers that "sentencing was an art and not a science, and that the further judges were pressed to articulate their reasons the less realistic the exercise would become."[38] Lord Lane has also been a leading champion of the Crown being able to appeal lenient sentences—the proposal in his Mansion House speech of 1983 was initially, in part, and later, in full, adopted in the Criminal Justice Bill of 1987/88. His Mansion House speech to the judiciary in 1985 contributed to the setting up of the Carlisle review on parole, which was also promised in the 1987 Conservative Party manifesto. Other judges have attempted to keep the heat on the Carlisle Committee, not always, in their enthusiasm, keeping a careful grip on all the facts. Furthermore Lord Lane, acting as he sees it to protect the independence of the judiciary, has attacked proposals for sentencing councils, as well as the Home Office's idea of placing the Judicial Studies Board on a statutory basis.[39] The third constraint is the police associations. The Police Federation in particular, has sought to weaken the presumption of bail in the Bail Act 1976. The Police Federation has also been quick to comment on any appearance that the Home Secretary is suggesting limits on the freedom of the courts to impose custodial sentences. For example, after Mr. Hurd's "balanced approach" speech of January 1988, the

Police Federation stated: "We don't think that magistrates should be expected to refrain from passing sentences of imprisonment because of the organisational problems, which are not their concern, such as the failure to provide sufficient places."[40]

Finally, there is the power of the media as a restraint and especially the tabloid press in shaping public attitudes about crime and punishment, reinforcing the symbolic role of prison. As Louk Hulsman has observed, through the mass media the public are offered vicarious participation in the drama of criminal law. What is accepted as "public opinion" is then treated as a powerful restraint by some and as a mandate by others.[41]

For the Home Office the "near crisis" is that, even with another 3,000 prison places becoming operational during 1988, the gap between supply and demand is expected to grow yet wider, at least until the end of the decade. For Mr. Hurd the options are bleak—emergency release under powers contained in the Criminal Justice Act 1982 (which he rejected in July 1987), resort once again to army camps or other temporary accommodation or an extended partnership with the private sector to accelerate the prison building programme. On the demand side it seems that the Home Office will during 1988 unveil some new "tougher" sentencing options for the courts, aimed especially at young adults, possibly involving electronic surveillance and perhaps other prison-like gadgetry and paraphernalia.

In the short-term it is evident that the prison system will not be able to absorb the sort of leaps in population that occurred in 1984 and in 1987. Over the period 1984–1987, as set out in Appendix One, the 4,500 increase in prison population was equally comprised of remand prisoners and adult males with sentences of over 18 months. What is especially worrying is that these increases were not being driven by increased numbers being processed by the courts. Quite the reverse.

What the criminal justice data between 1982–1986 clearly shows is that despite substantial declines in proceedings and in numbers sentenced by the courts there has been an upward shift with respect to mode of trial, use of custody and length of sentence. Furthermore, the remand population has greatly expanded against a decline in proceedings, reflecting an increase in time spent on remand which, in part, is a consequence of the growth in the proportion of persons committed to the Crown Court, and of *these* people an increase in the proportion remanded in custody.[42] It is not known whether this trend reflects an increase in the seriousness of offences, greater severity in the decision-making or both. The shift of business to the Crown Court is striking because it is counter to Government intentions. Some light may be thrown on the reasons for this shortly by research conducted by the Home Office and on behalf of the Lord Chancellor's Department. But it is abundantly clear that if the numbers proceeded against and sentenced were to *rise*, the impact on prison population size is likely to dwarf what has so far happened during this decade.

Possibilities

The critical flaw of contemporary penal policy is the perception of the resources for punishment. In revealing contrast to some other areas of public expenditure, punishment has, over recent years, come increasingly to be viewed as a bottomless pit. However weak the logic, this flat earth penology has become influential in shaping penal policy and practice. In particular, questions about supply tend to take precedence over those of demand. The ever-expanding prison building programme is presented as the central plank of government policy. Mr. Hurd claims that the Home Office strategy is one that "bites on both supply and demand sides of the population equation.... We are working to speed up the process of justice, to produce more consistency in the grant of bail, to build up alternatives to custody for use in cases where they make sense ... (and balance against this) ... to use the existing prison estate to the fullest possible extent, and to maintain our programme of building and modernising prisons."[43]

However, demand for prison places almost certainly will not be reduced as one feature of a policy which is also intent on increasing the supply of prison places and other resources. A policy that attempts to steer a middle course, of balancing demand and supply of prison places, is unlikely to be able to withstand pressures for expansion.

Sir Brian Cubbon, speaking in New South Wales on January 24, 1988 posed the question: "Will we never find a point of intervention on sentencing decisions themselves? Can we never contemplate inserting mechanisms of "demand management" into the sentencing process, so that the volume of demand for imprisonment can be more closely tied to the available supply?"[44] Some encouragement should be taken from the fact that Sir Brian is able publicly to raise this question, for it does imply that the need for a coherent approach to demand cannot be ignored for much longer. What might these "demand mechanisms" look like?

In the first place, it is clear that such mechanisms would need to extend beyond sentencing to address all stages of the criminal justice process from the police to the courts. At both the formal and informal levels there is a huge cast of decision makers, some more visible than others, from custody officers in the police station to listing officers in the Crown Court. Particular reference should be drawn to the potential role of the Crown Prosecution Service. Indeed the C.P.S, in my view, is the Trojan Horse of the criminal justice process. The attention given to administrative and staffing problems during its start-up phase has detracted from its far reaching implications. There are four areas where the C.P.S. seems likely to be especially important, namely

(i)   discontinuance of proceedings on "public interest" grounds;

(ii) information to the magistrates' court with reference to bail;

(iii) advice to the magistrates court about mode of trial;

(iv) (depending on the outcome of the Criminal Justice Bill) involvement of prosecutors in sentencing issues.

It should certainly not be assumed that this will necessarily work for greater severity. As in The Netherlands, prosecutors may well become a powerful force for reductionist practice.

With regards to sentencing one might envisage consideration being given to mechanisms such as the call-up system, or prison waiting list, as advocated by the Home Affairs Committee in 1981[45]; the extension to adults of the custodial sentencing criteria introduced with respect to young offenders in the Criminal Justice Act 1982; some reduction in maximum prison terms; restructuring the Judicial Studies Board so that its net effect is to reduce and not to increase the use of custody, as is sometimes believed to be the case; sentencing guidelines that are tied to existing prison capacity, as in the state of Minnesota. Since 1980 when Minnesota set up a Sentencing Commission that had the task of constructing guidelines that ensured that the prison capacity of 2,100 cells was not exceeded, it has been one of the few American states to keep the lid on prison population growth.[46]

Mechanisms of this sort can only achieve so much. A more fundamental requirement is a sea-change of attitudes among criminal justice practitioners. It is for this reason that what Willem de Haan calls "the politics of bad conscience" regarding the prison system in The Netherlands is so important.[47] Some scholars have traced the development of this anti-penal thinking to the Utrecht-School whose reformist endeavours suggests de Haan were "primarily motivated by a strong empathy with the delinquent as a fellow human being."[48] While, as David Downes has stressed, "the school was (not) the sole source of anti-penal thinking—it reinforced it at a critical period."[49] By contrast, in contemporary Britain there is little sign of any such deeply embedded scepticism of imprisonment. The Oxford pilot study of Crown Court sentencers found that: "The views expressed by the majority of judges interviewed were notable for their emphasis upon individual pathology as a principal cause of law breaking and for their neglect of the possible effects of the social system and the criminal justice system in fostering criminal behaviour and confirming offenders in their criminality." In response to a general question about the causes of persistence in lawbreaking, no reference was made to any effects of imprisonment or stigmatisation.[50]

Mood shifts about punishment, however, arise and take shape around initiatives at the local level, and with practitioners to the fore, rather than from a policy lead by the centre.

Take, for example, a final paradox of the contemporary penal scene in England. Alongside the relentless increase in the prison population, between 1982–1986 there was a 50 per cent. decline in the number of juveniles held within the prison system.[51] Demographic factors account for only about one-tenth of this reduction, which is essentially the consequence of pioneering approaches to juvenile offenders. The new arrangements which have emerged as to how young people are dealt with tend to share the following features:

The reform initiatives, in most instances, have arisen within a particular locality, very often a single court or petty sessional division.

The primary thrust for change has been made by social workers, working within statutory and voluntary agencies, who themselves are directly engaged with young offenders. By providing constructive and credible alternatives to custodial sentences, projects have been able effectively to intervene at the sentencing stage. The result of the redirected decision-making arrangements is to create, on a local basis, what have become known as "custody free zones."[52]

Among social workers, in particular, a powerful anti-custody ethos has taken hold. This has taken the form of an unequivocal dissent from sentencing juveniles to custody to encompass a campaigning stance against custody.

A second example of penal practice leading policy is currently to be found in the Federal Republic of Germany, where a distinct sea-change in attitudes among practitioners has had a profound impact upon prison population size. During the 1970s and early 1980s the prison population of the Federal Republic of Germany climbed steadily. In 1983 the average daily number of prisoners was 62,000, but between 1983–1986 West Germany's prison population declined by 17 per cent. This sustained decline in the prison population, mostly remand prisoners but later apparent in the sentenced population, is evident across the country, being almost as pronounced in conservative states such as Bavaria as in the more liberal city states of Hamburg and Bremen. At the heart of this shift in practice has been widespread concern and discussion among practising lawyers.

There have been no changes in law to account for this reduction in prison population. Nor has any influence been exercised by government at either the federal or state level. A key role has been played by the German Lawyers' Association, which represents most practising attorneys. In February 1983, the Association's criminal law section organised a special conference at the Beethoven Hall in Bonn on the theme "Too Many People in Germany are Remanded." Worries about competition from more radical organisations had encouraged the Association to take a leadership position on an important contemporary issue. Excessive use of remand in custody provided the German Lawyers' Association with a rallying call, appropriate because it was safely non-partisan and steered clear or more controversial topics such as urban terrorism. The conference attracted over 200 people, including judges, prosecutors and administrators from the federal and state governments. As befitted its setting, the proceedings were carefully orchestrated. Formal presentations were made by six leading practitioners from across the country. The common theme was the need for much closer adherence to the principle of making very sparing use of remand in custody. Little dissent was expressed at the conference to these calls for a new approach. One prosecutor observed that judges did not take remand decisions lightly, but acknowledged that some remands in custody were unjustly made and that action was required to remedy the situation. Another participant has described as "euphoric" his feeling that action could be taken by lawyers about the remand numbers.

The conference attracted wide coverage in the media. The absence of comprehensive data concerning the use of remand prompted the federal government to announce the funding of a large-scale project. The position taken by federal officials was necessarily delicate. They had to be careful not to seem to be interfering with the judiciary or to be invading the province of the state governments. Although officials were informed of preparations for the conference, including having sight of draft papers, they remained in the background. At most, support for the Association's stance by ministry officials was passive.

The movement began with defence attorneys but subsequently the debate has encompassed prosecutors and the judiciary, resulting in much greater sensitivity to decisions about the use of custody. Remand in custody has become a crusading issue for practising lawyers because little confidence remained in the prison. As a means of resocialisation, the prisons have demonstrably failed to meet earlier expectations of social workers and other treatment personnel. Since 1984, as shown in Appendix Two, there has also been a marked decline in the number of sentenced prisoners. As one prosecutor has put it: "No-one believes in the prison system any more." There may well have been a complex array of factors which awoke the German Lawyers' Association from a sleepy indifference to a determination to reduce the use of remand in custody.[53] However, it appears that much of the impetus derived from practising lawyers recognising that they hold the instrument of change in their own hands, and providing a contrast with the finding that many English solicitors persuade their clients not to ask for bail.[54]

Both the example from West Germany and recent developments regarding juvenile offenders in England suggest that a crucial key to penal reform is held by practitioners, and that occasions arise when practice is able to lead to policy. In West Germany it fell not to federal or state governments but to the legal profession to seize the initiative. The early efforts to reduce the custodial sentencing of juveniles in England were taken by social workers but they have been joined by magistrates and other practitioners. In both instances, practitioners were motivated by a powerful anti-custody ethos.

What is the likelihood of the new approach to juvenile offences in England taking a broader hold? In January 1988, Douglas Hurd stated that the fact that 21 per cent. of young adults sentenced for indictable offences receive custody is "too high."[55] Sir Brian Cubbon's Australian speech must also be regarded as an encouraging straw in the wind. Much is going to depend not only in terms of action by Government but also by practitioners at the local level.

If the sights remain focused on the near crisis of getting through the increasingly acute space shortage for the remainder of the decade, the penal crisis of the 1990s will not be long postponed.

On present trends we can anticipate, between 1988–1995 two or three further major boosts to the prison building programme, perhaps adding a further 12,000 prison places to the programme commenced in 1980. This would result in a system of 70,000 prison places by the year 2000. If the prison population matched the number of places that would translate into a rate of 140 per 100,000 inhabitants. Or take the less likely scenario of no further prison building beyond what has been agreed and the prison population rising in line with Home Office projections to about 60,000, translating into a rate of 120. A prison population of this magnitude, regardless of the conditions of its confinement, casts an appalling shadow across any society that has traditionally placed a high premium on liberal democratic values.

The crisis of the prisons is often viewed in terms of the pressure on resources at the expense of value perspectives. The penal crisis goes far beyond the issue of resources and raises urgent and fundamental questions of political philosophy, including the circumstances under which the people of this country may be deprived of their freedom. As Churchill put it, in 1910, "there is a terrible and purposeless waste of public money and human character involved in all of this."[56]

APPENDIX ONE

Net gains/losses in prison population size
by selected components 1984–87

Year	Total	Sentenced		Males under 21	Females	Remand
		Adult Males 18 months or less	over 18 months			
1984	44096	11008	13512	9799	1177	8600
Gain/loss	+3196	+147	+305	+20	+20	+1350
1985	47294	11155	14928	10104	1157	9950
Gain/loss	−894	−1569	+1787	−1166	+54	No change
1986	46400	9586	16715	8938	1211	9950
Gain/loss	+2190	−1502	+2775	−833		
1987	48590	8084	19490	8105	1272	10776
1984–87	+4494	−2924	+5978	−1694	+95	+2176

June 30, 1984, 1985, 1986; September 30 1987.

APPENDIX TWO

Prison Population Trends (average daily totals) England and Wales, West Germany 1971, 1981–86, 1987 (31/7)

	England & Wales			Federal Republic of Germany		
	Remand	Sentenced	Total	Remand	Sentenced	Total
1971	4640	35068	39708	13505	33026	46528
1981	6905	36406	43311	15297	42258	57555
1982	7385	36322	43707	16365	44971	61336
1983	7651	35811	43462	15353	46941	62294
1984	8687	34608	43295	13855	47130	60985
1985	9697	36526	46223	12598	45623	58221
1986	9962	36808	46770	11626	42118	53744
1987 (31/7)	10125	40101	50226	11909	40388	52297

(+881 in police cells)

NOTES

[1] *Report of Prison Commissioners for England and Wales*, Cmd. 2307 1923–1924, pp. 6–7.

[2] *Parl. Debates*, H.C. 5th Series, Vol. 19, cols. 1353–1354, July 20, 1910.

[3] Edwin H. Sutherland, "The Decreasing Prison Population of England," (1934) *Journal of Criminal Law and Criminology* 24, p. 800.

[4] Howard League for Penal Reform, *The Prisoner Population of the World*, London, 1936.

[5] Council of Europe, *Prison Information Bulletin*, June 9, 1987, p. 23.

[6] Home Office, *Penal Practice in a Changing Society*, London, Cmnd. 645 (1959).

[7] Barbara Wootton, "Official Advisory Bodies" in N. Walker (ed.) *Penal Policy-Making in England*, Cambridge, Institute of Criminology, 1977, p. 15.

[8] Home Office, *A Review of Criminal Justice Policy 1976*, London, 1977, p. 4.

[9] Roy Jenkins, Speech to NACRO, July 21, 1975.

[10] Advisory Council on the Penal System, *The Length of Prison Sentences*, Interim Report, London, 1977, p. v.

[11] *Ibid.* p. 1.

[12] *Ibid.* p. 5.

[13] *Ibid.* p. v.

[14] *Ibid.* p. 5.

[15] Advisory Council on the Penal System, *Sentences of Imprisonment: A Review of Maximum Penalties*, London, 1978.

[16] See Marjorie Jones, *Crime, Punishment and the Press*, NACRO, 1980, esp. pp. 9–20.

[17] See A. E. Bottoms, "Reflections the Renaissance of Dangerousness," (1977) 16 *Howard Journal* 2, pp. 70–96.

[18] See Andrew Ashworth, *Sentencing and Penal Policy*, London, Weidenfeld and Nicolson, 1983, pp. 134–135.

[19] Louis Blom-Cooper, *The Tanner Lectures*, Cambridge University, typescript of second lecture, p. 33.

[20] *Report of the Committee of Inquiry into the United Kingdom Prison Services*, Cmnd. 7673 (1979), p. 59.

[21] *Evidence by H.M. Treasury, the Civil Service Departments and the Central Policy Review Staff*, Inquiry into the United Kingdom Prison Services, Volume III, Home Office, p. 16.

[22] *The Government Reply to the Fourth Report from the Home Affairs Committee, Session 1980–1981, The Prison Service*, Cmnd. 8446 (1981), p. 4.

[23] *Upton* (1980) 71 Cr.App.R. 102.

[24] *Begum Bibi* (1980) 71 Cr.App.R. 360.

[25] Ashworth, *op. cit.*, p. 357.

[26] See *Home Office Statistical Bulletin 12/81, Changes in the Prison Population During the Industrial Action by the P.O.A.*, Home Office, 1981.

[27] William Whitelaw, Speech to Leicestershire Magistrates, February 13, 1981.

[28] *Review of Parole in England and Wales*, Home Office, 1981, para. 60.

[29] *The Government Reply to the Fourth Report from the Home Affairs Committee*, Session 1980–1981, *op. cit.* p. 5.

[30] *Parl. Debates*, H.C., Sixth Series, Vol. 21, col. 1122, March 25, 1982.

[31] Leon Brittan, Speech to Conservative Party Conference, October 11, 1983. See also Mr. Brittan's reflections on this speech, "New Deal for the Prisons," *The Times*, February 17, 1987.

[32] National Audit Office, *Report of the Comptroller and Auditor General, Home Office and Property Services Agency: Programme for the Provision of Prison Places*, H.C. 135, 1985, p. 6.

[33] *Twenty-fifth Report from the Committee of Public Accounts, Session 1985–1986, Prison Building Programme*, H.C. 248, p. xii.

[34] *Ibid.* p. 9.

[35] *Parl. Debates* H.C., Vol. 119, col. 1292, July 16, 1987.

[36] James Callaghan, "Cumber and Variableness" in *The Home Office, Perspectives on Policy and Administration*, London, Royal Institute of Public Administration, 1983, p. 16.

[37] Douglas Hurd, Speech to South East London Branch of the Magistrates' Association, January 15, 1988.

[38] Andrew Ashworth *et al, Sentencing in the Crown Court, Report of an Exploratory Study*, Oxford, Centre for Criminological Research, Occasional Paper No. 10, 1984, p. 64.

[39] *Parl. Debates* H.L., Vol. 489, cols. 326–327, October 26, 1987.

[40] *The Times*, January 16, 1988.

[41] Louk Hulsman, "Penal Reform in The Netherlands: Part I—Bringing the Criminal Justice System Under Control," (1981), 20 *Howard Journal*, 157–158.

[42] *Criminal Statistics, England and Wales 1986*, Home Office, Cm. 233 (1987).

[43] Douglas Hurd, Speech to the National Association of Prison Visitors, May 13, 1987.

[44] Sir Brian Cubbon, speech to the Australian Bicentennial International Congress on Corrective Services, January 24, 1988.

[45] Fourth Report from the Home Affairs Committee, *The Prison Service* H.C. Session 412-1, 1981, para. 104.

[46] Andrew Rutherford, *Prisons and the Process of Justice*, Oxford University Press, 1986, pp. 164–167.

[47] Willem de Haan, "Abolition and the Politics of 'Bad Conscience,' " (1987) 26 *Howard Journal*, 15–32.

[48] *Ibid.* p. 19.

[49] David Downes, "The origins and consequences of Dutch penal policy since 1945," (1982) 22 *British Journal of Criminology* 348.

[50] Ashworth *et al, op. cit.* p. 27.

[51] The respective figures for June 30, 1982 and 1986 were 1,791 and 922. See *Prison Statistics, England and Wales* for 1982 and 1986.

[52] Andrew Rutherford, *Growing Out of Crime*, Penguin 1986, p. 168.

[53] These preliminary observations on recent penal practice in the Federal Republic of Germany are based on interviews carried out during 1987 with federal officials, practising lawyers and academics. I am particularly grateful to Johannes Feest and Frieder Dunkel for their comments and suggestions.

[54] Barbara Drink and Christopher Stone, "Defendants Who Do Not Ask for Bail," *Criminal Law Review*, March 1988, pp. 152–162.

[55] Douglas Hurd, Speech to the South East London Branch of the Magistrates' Association, January 15, 1988.

[56] Memorandum to H. H. Asquith, reprinted in Randolf S. Churchill, *Winston S. Churchill* Volume II, Companion Part 2 1907–1911, London, Heinemann 1969, p. 1199.

Sentencing: Some Current Questions

D. A. THOMAS

I would like you to imagine the position of a Judge of the Crown Court who is called upon to deal with a relatively simple case. The defendant is a young man of 19 charged in an indictment containing two counts. The first count charges him with possessing a controlled substance, cannabis, with intent to supply; the second count charges him with taking a conveyance, a moped, without the consent of the owner or lawful authority. He pleads guilty to both counts. The prosecution open the facts to the Judge. It seems that the defendant had gone to his local football match with the intention of selling cannabis to the spectators on the terraces. As he was queuing to go through the turnstiles he saw that the police were searching fans as they entered the ground, probably with a view to discovering weapons. Fearful that he would be detected in possession of cannabis he decided to leave the scene as quickly as possible, and in order to do so he mounted a moped which had been left lying nearby and attempted to ride off on it. Not being skilled in riding a moped he quickly came into collision with an approaching car, damaging both the moped and the car. Let us examine the legal position so far as sentencing this young man is concerned, assuming that the provisions of the Criminal Justice Bill which is at present before Parliament are in effect. As the first count in the indictment charges the defendant with a drug trafficking offence, the Judge must begin by turning to the Drug Trafficking Offences Act 1986 and consider the first six sections of that Act. The Judge must determine whether at any time during the whole of his life the defendant has benefited from drug trafficking. If he determines that the defendant has benefited the Judge is then required by the Act to assess the value of the defendant's proceeds—in other words to work out exactly how much he has received throughout his drug trafficking career—and finally assess "the amount that might be realised." This requires him to work out to the last penny how much the defendant is worth as he stands in the dock. When this process is complete, and it may take some considerable time, the Judge must make a confiscation order for whichever of the two amounts is the lesser, and fix a term of detention to be served in default if the defendant is unable or unwilling to pay. The cannabis itself which is found in the defendant's possession should be ordered to be forfeited under Misuse of Drugs Act 1971 section 27. When he has done this he must turn to the Criminal Justice Act 1982 as it will be when amended by the Criminal Justice Bill. For the offence charged in the first count in the indictment, possession of a controlled drug with intent to supply, the Judge will probably have in mind a custodial sentence, but before imposing one he must apply himself to the statutory criteria which govern the imposition of custodial sentences (soon to be known as "detention in a young offender's institution") on offenders under 21. Under the new statutory provisions he must first consider whether he would sentence the defendant to imprisonment if he were over the age of 21; if he decides that he would, he must then decide whether the defendant qualifies for custody in terms of any of the three criteria set out in what will be section 1(4A) of the Criminal Justice Act 1982. Having decided that the defendant does satisfy one of those three criteria the Judge must state in open court that he is satisfied that the defendant qualifies for a custodial sentence and indicate the paragraph of the section under which he is so satisfied and then explain in ordinary language why he is passing a custodial sentence. Before reaching these conclusions he should observe the mandatory requirements of section 2 of the Criminal Justice Act 1982 which relate to social inquiry reports. We will turn to these later.

The first offence was committed while D was trying to enter or leave a football ground and the Judge should now turn to Public Order Act 1986 sections 30 to 35. These provisions give him a power, which is discretionary, to make an exclusion order prohibiting the defendant from attending prescribed football matches for a period to be specified, if the Judge is satisfied that making such an order would "help to prevent violence at or in connection with prescribed football matches." In addition the Judge may order the defendant to attend at a police station for the purpose of having his photograph taken. Having dealt with the first offence in the indictment, the Judge must now turn his attention to the second offence in the indictment, that of taking a conveyance. Here he will find a problem, as it is clear that this offence does not satisfy the statutory criteria in section 1(4A) for the imposition of a custodial sentence. The fact that the defendant is to be sentenced to custody for another offence is not in itself a ground for imposing a custodial sentence, and no provision is made for this particular contingency, although it is an extremely common one. However, the Judge must move on and consider the question of compensation under Powers of Criminal Courts Act 1973 section 35 as it will be when amended by the Criminal Justice Bill. The Judge will be empowered to order compensation to be paid to the owner of the moped for the damage caused to the moped while it was out of the possession of the owner as a result of the offence having been committed under the Theft Act 1968. There will be power to order compensation to be paid to the owner of the other vehicle only if compensation is not payable "under any arrangements to which the Secretary of State is a party." This presumably is a reference to the arrangements made by the Motor Insurers Bureau and the Judge should at this stage satisfy himself as to the scope of the cover provided by the Motor Insurers Bureau; something which may cause him difficulty if no details of that arrangement are available to him in the Crown Court. Under the Powers of Criminal Courts Act section 35 as amended, the Judge will be required, if he does not make a compensation order, to give reasons on passing sentence why he has not made such an order. If he has already made a confiscation order under the provisions of the Drug Trafficking Offences Act 1986, this may not be particularly difficult as he will already have made an order depriving the defendant of everything of which he stands possessed. If, however, he does make a compensation order then the Judge must then turn to another statute, in this case the Administration of Justice Act 1970, section 41(8) (as this section will be when amended by the Criminal Justice Bill). The general effect of this provision is to allow the Judge to enlarge the term of imprisonment in default of payment of the compensation order which a magistrates' court would be empowered to impose if the defendant does not pay, provided that the Judge is satisfied that the normal scale of terms is inadequate. To find these terms he must turn to Magistrates' Courts Act 1980, Schedule 4 where they are set out. (The amendment to s.41(8) will probably help him here, once he has solved the puzzle which it contains: it limits the power to cases where the amount of compensation exceeds £20,000). Having dealt with the question of compensation, the Judge must turn to the question of disqualification from driving. The offence of taking a conveyance carries discretionary disqualification under Road Traffic Act 1972, section 93(2)(*a*) and Schedule 4. In addition it carries obligatory endorsement under the Road Traffic Act 1972, section 101 and Transport Act 1981, section 19. These provisions require the Judge, if the defendant is not disqualified, to endorse his licence with a number of penalty points as set out in Schedule 7 of the Act; a reference to Part 2B of that Schedule will indicate that the Judge should order his licence to be endorsed with eight penalty points. If he already has four or more penalty points on his driving licence then the Judge must turn back to the Transport Act 1981, section 19(2) under which he will be bound to impose a term of disqualification of at least six months, unless there are grounds for mitigating the normal consequences of conviction. When he has done all this, the Judge will almost certainly be faced with an application by the prosecution for an order in their favour for the payment of the costs of the prosecution. To determine whether this order should be made, the Judge should turn to the Prosecution of Offences Act 1985, section 18 to identify his powers.

In order to deal with this relatively simple case, the Judge has had to refer to 10 different statutes, comply with at least four and possibly six distinct mandatory requirements and, in addition, try to find a copy of the Motor Insurers Bureau scheme. It may be objected that this is a contrived and hypothetical case, and indeed it is, but unfortunately it is only too easy to contrive such examples of the complexity of modern sentencing legislation. Let us take another, the case of a burglar who has stolen property from a householder; the householder wants compensation for his loss but the burglar has no income, although he has a saleable asset, his car. The question for the Judge is whether he is able to make an order which will effectively give the victim of the burglary the benefit of the car. Let us again assume that the Criminal Justice Bill at present before Parliament is in effect and explore the answer to that question. If the car represents the proceeds of the theft in the hands of the thief, if for instance he has bought it with the money he has received from the sale of the property stolen from the house, then the Judge can make a restitution order under Theft Act 1968, section 28, requiring the burglar to deliver the car to the householder, who will then be able to sell it or use it according to his choice. This order can be made only if the victim applies for such an order and the facts necessary to show the existence of the power to make the order are apparent from the evidence prepared for the trial or are admitted by the defendant. If the court makes such an order it can be enforced through the ordinary power of the court to deal with contempt, as a disobedience of a court order. If on the other hand the burglar owned the car before the burglary and used it to transport stolen goods from the house then the court will have power under Powers of Criminal Courts Act 1973, section 43 (as amended by the Criminal Justice Bill) to make an order depriving the burglar of his rights in the car, and under the new provision section 43(A) (as inserted by the Criminal Justice Bill) to make an order that any proceeds from the sale of the car be paid to the victim, provided that no compensation order is made in his favour. The machinery for enforcing this order is different; the car, if it is not already in the possession of the police, must be taken into the possession of the police and sold in accordance with the Police Property Act 1897. If neither of these applies then the court will have power to make a compensation order under Powers of Criminal Courts Act 1973, section 35, on the basis that the burglar will sell the car himself and pay the proceeds over to the victim. In this case the machinery for enforcement requires proceedings in the magistrates' court under Administration of Justice Act 1970, section 41 and Magistrates' Courts Act 1980, section 76. Perhaps these two examples will be adequate to demonstrate sufficiently that the legislation under which sentencing courts operate has become over-complicated to the point of incomprehensibility, and that the problem is getting worse rather than better with each session of Parliament, as new sentencing legislation is enacted.

A number of distinct criticisms can be made of recent developments in this field. The first is the volume of legislation to which courts have to learn to adjust. Hardly a year goes by without some change in the relevant statutory provisions, sometimes on a large scale, sometimes in a matter of detail which is often easy to overlook. In 1983 the Criminal Justice Act 1982 was brought into effect and the Mental Health Act 1983 also came into force; 1984 saw changes in the parole system which had a fundamental effect on the reality of sentences and important but detailed amendments were made in the terms of imprisonment to be imposed in default of payment of fines. 1985 saw changes in a number of maximum sentences for particular offences and changes in the law relating to the disqualification of company directors. In 1985 the Prosecution of Offences Act changed the law relating to orders to pay the costs of the prosecution, and exclusion orders were introduced in the Public Order Act 1986. (These exclusion orders must be distinguished from exclusion orders made under Licensed Premises (Exclusion of Certain Persons) Act 1980). 1987 saw the commencement of the enormously difficult and complex provisions of the Drug Trafficking Offences Act 1986. In 1988, a mammoth Criminal Justice Bill is again before Parliament.

Much of this legislation can be described as unnecessary, needlessly complicated or plainly unintelligible. Consider, for example, the provision of Criminal Justice Act 1982, sections 2(2), (3) and (8):

> (2) Subject to subsection (3) below, the court shall in every case obtain a social inquiry report for the purpose of determining whether there is any appropriate method of dealing with a person other than a method whose use is restricted by section 1(4) above.

> (3) Subsection (2) above does not apply if, in the circumstances of the case, the court is of the opinion that it is unnecessary to obtain a social inquiry report.

> (8) No sentence or order shall be invalidated by the failure of a court to comply with subsection (2) above, but any other court on appeal from that court shall obtain a social inquiry report if none was obtained by the court below, unless it is of the opinion that in the circumstances of the case it is unnecessary to do so.

What conceivable purpose can there be in enacting a broad mandatory requirement in one subsection and then countermanding it in the next? This unnecessary burden on the statute book is repeated as section 20(A) of the Powers of Criminal Courts Act 1973. Is there any real need for the byzantine complexity of Criminal Justice Act 1982, section 15, dealing with the period of statutory supervision which will follow sentences of youth custody or detention centres order? A close and detailed scrutiny of the intricacies of that provision make it clear that, in any case, a detention centre order is followed by a period of three months' supervision. Why could Parliament not have enacted that in so many words, rather than leaving it concealed in the section?

The task of the Judge, or indeed of anyone else who has to work out the effect of legislation such as this, is not helped by the fondness of Parliament for obscurity of language, and particularly for legislation by reference. Is there any justification for a statutory provision to be so incomprehensible as section 30(2) of the Drug Trafficking Offences Act 1986?:

> (2) The power to make an order under subsection (1) above is exercisable if—
> (*a*) the powers conferred on the court by sections 8(1) and 9(1) of this Act are exercisable by virtue of subsection (1) of section 7 of this Act, or
> (*b*) those powers are exercisable by virtue of subsection (2) of that section and the court has made a restraint or charging order which has not been discharged;

but where the power to make an order under subsection (1) above is exercisable by virtue only of paragraph (*b*) above, subsection (3) of section 7 of this Act shall apply for the purposes of this section as it applies for the purposes of sections 8 and 9 of this Act.

One of the reasons why sentencing legislation has grown so much in recent years is a desire on the part of Parliament to make changes for their own sake. Very often new legislation is enacted for no very obvious reason. Consider, for instance, the changes in the law which have taken place in the last five years in relation to the terms which the Crown Court may impose in default of payment of a fine. Until the Criminal Justice Act 1982, the law was very simple. The Crown Court could impose a term of imprisonment of up to 12 months in default of payment of any fine, irrespective of the amount of the fine. There is no evidence that this power was in any way abused; a quick glance at the Prison Statistics will show that the overwhelming majority of persons received into prison in default of payment are received for very short periods indeed; 90 per cent. of them for terms not exceeding one month. There seemed to be every reason for leaving this provision alone, but the Criminal Justice Act 1982 amended it by applying to the Crown Court the same table of terms as applied to the Magistrates' Courts. The table set out in Magistrates' Courts Act 1980, Schedule 4 was carried over into Powers of Criminal Courts Act 1973, section 31, and became effective in 1983. One year later in 1984 by statutory instrument, the curiously named Criminal Penalties etc. (Increase) Order 1984, all of these terms were cut in half for no particular reason. The main purpose of the order was not to decrease but increase penalties; the order doubled maximum fines imposable on summary conviction and presumably for the sake of completeness doubled the financial figures in the two tables, with the result that default terms for each figure were cut in half. The current Criminal Justice Bill makes further changes. Let us take the example of a fine of £1,000 imposed by the Crown Court. In 1982 the maximum default term was 12 months; in 1983 it became 90 days; in 1984 it was reduced to 60 days and in 1988 it will be 30 days. No sensible case has been put forward for any of these changes, but they do have a serious aspect. A Judge of a Crown Court faced with the decision whether to deal with an offender by fining him £1,000, a substantial amount for most offenders, or alternatively by imposing on him an immediate sentence of imprisonment, must check the default term provided by the table before imposing the fine, because he will be required to fix the term when he imposes the fine. It is just possible that when he finds out that the default term is a mere 30 days he may be tempted to impose an immediate sentence of imprisonment instead. Changes intended to help to contain the growth of the prison population may, if they are as ill-considered as these, prove to be counter-productive and contribute to the growth rather than reduction.

The haste with which most modern sentencing legislation is enacted inevitably means that more often than not Parliament botches the job. Statutory provisions are enacted which do not fit either with each other or with existing law. Some of them are relatively unimportant. Take, for instance, Powers of Criminal Courts Act 1973, section 31(3B).

> "(3B) Where the amount due at the time imprisonment or detention is imposed is so much of a fine or forfeited recognizance as remains due after part payment, then, subject to subsection (3C) below, the maximum period applicable to the amount shall be the period applicable to the whole sum reduced by such number of days as bears to the total number of days therein the same proportion as the part paid bears to the total sum."

This section first appeared in Schedule 4, para. 2 of the Magistrates' Courts Act 1980. It was designed to ensure that when a magistrates' court was imposing a term in default of payment of a fine it would make proper allowance for any part of the fine which had already been paid. When the changes were made in the law relating to terms to be imposed by the Crown Court in default of payment of fines imposed by the Crown Court, this provision was simply lifted from the Magistrates' Courts Act 1980 and put down among the provisions relating to fines imposed by the Crown Court in Powers of Criminal Courts Act, section 31. Nobody seems to have realised that the procedure in the Crown Court is very different from that in a magistrates' court. Magistrates' courts do not normally impose a term in default of payment until default has actually occurred. In the normal way, when a magistrates' court imposes a fine, no question of imprisonment in default arises unless the fine is not paid and the normal steps for enforcement have begun. In the Crown Court the position is different; when the Crown Court imposes a fine, it must fix the term of imprisonment in default there and then. However, if we look at the provisions of Powers of Criminal Courts Act, section 31(3B) and try to work out what they mean, what becomes apparent is that they can apply only in the rarest possible case—the case in which the defendant manages to make part payment of a fine before the term in default is fixed by the Crown Court. In other words the section can only apply to the case where the defendant manages to pay the fine or part of it while the judge is in the actual act of pronouncing sentence in court.

That particular provision is a silly one but it does not cause any great difficulty, and can safely be ignored. Unfortunately, in many other cases failures of this kind to deal with details can cause practical problems to the courts. One very important question in sentencing an offender is his age, because the age limit for different kinds of sentence varies considerably. Take the question of minimum ages; for a detention centre order this is 14, for youth custody it is 15, for a community service order it is 16, for a probation order it is 17 and for imprisonment it is 21. But what happens when an offender passes a legally relevant birthday while he is waiting to be sentenced? This can happen in a number of different situations. He may be put on probation by the court and be found to be in breach of that order after some time has passed when he is a year older. The same may happen with a community service order. Alternatively, he may be convicted in the magis-trates' court and committed for sentence to the Crown Court, but not be dealt with in the Crown Court until after he has passed another relevant birthday. A further possibility is that the court may defer sentence for six months, and the defendant comes before the court to be sentenced when he is in a different age group. If we examine the relevant statutory provisions closely, we will find that they all make different provisions for this situation. In the case of a probation order, Powers of Criminal Courts Act 1973, section 6(6) provides that an offender who is to be sentenced following a breach of probation, must be sentenced as if he had just been convicted by the court of the offence for which the probation order was originally made—in other words he must be sentenced on the basis of his age as it now is. On the other hand, section 16(5) of the same Act, dealing with breach of community service order, requires an offender who is before the court for breach of a community service order, to be sentenced on the basis of his age on the date when the order was originally made. In other words, if the offender is put on probation at the age of 20 and is dealt with at the breach of the order at the age of 21, he must be sentenced on the basis that he is now 21; if however he is made the subject of a community service order at the age of 20 and is in breach of that order after he has passed his twenty-first birthday, he must still be sentenced as if he were only 20. It is not easy to see the logic of this difference and it is obvious that practical difficulties can arise, particularly where the offender is subject to both of these orders at the same time and is in breach of both of them. Similar confusion surrounds the procedure of committal for sentence. An offender who is committed for sentence under Magistrates' Courts Act 1980, section 38 must be sentenced when he appears at the Crown Court on the basis of his age on the date of his appearance (see Powers of Criminal Courts Act 1973, section 42(1)). The court must sentence him as if it had just convicted him of the offence on indictment. If, on the other hand, he is committed under Criminal Justice Act 1967, section 56, he must be sentenced in the Crown Court on the basis of his age on the day on which he was convicted before the magistrates' court. The same conflict may arise, although the whole purpose of Criminal Justice Act 1967, section 56 is to allow an offender to be committed for his less serious offences so that they can be dealt with at the same time as those for which he was committed under Magistrates' Courts Act 1980, section 38. Similar practical problems can become obvious in the case of deferment of sentence, but in this context Parliament seems to have hedged its bets. Powers of Criminal Courts Act 1973, section 1(8) simply provides that the powers of the courts to deal with an offender when he appears before the court on the expiration of the period of deferment "include" the power to deal with him in any way in which the court could have dealt with him on his original appearance. The question is whether they *exclude* a power to deal with him which the court would have had if he had just been convicted. The Judge is left to work this one out for himself.

A further example of sloppiness and failure to attend to detail in the enactment of sentencing legislation and the practical problems this can create for those concerned in dealing with offenders, concerns the revocation of parole licences. Under the parole system as it was originally established, a prisoner became eligible for release on licence only when he had served a minimum period of 12 months or one-third of his sentence, whichever was the greater. If he was released on licence and his licence was revoked by order of the Crown Court, he would not become eligible for release on licence again (although he might be released on reaching his remission date) until he had served a further 12 months. This provision (Criminal Justice Act 1967, section 62(10)) was intended obviously to harmonise the parole eligibility of the offender in relation to the sentence he received for his later offence and the sentence which he was serving, and from which he had been released on licence. When in 1982 the Criminal Justice Act empowered the Secretary of State to reduce the specified period, and when in 1984 the Secretary of State did reduce that period from 12 months to six, this provision was overlooked. The result is that under the law as it stands at present, revocation of an existing parole licence by the Crown Court following a conviction or a further offence means that in many cases the offender will find that his eligibility for release on licence from the new sentence has been put back, in many cases from six months to 12 months. The effect of revoking his licence affects his new sentence as well as his old one. The result is that courts are required in this situation to consider whether it is fair and just to impose this restriction on the offender. In other words, as a result of sloppiness and oversight in the design of legislation, yet another twist had been added to the already tortuous processes through which the Judge is required to go.

These matters of detail are all symptoms of a broader tendency to enact legislation without thorough thinking through of its consequences. Legislation is often rushed through with many details added as the Bill goes through Parliament as last-minute after thoughts. The present Criminal Justice Bill is as good an example as any of this. Several major changes in the law relating to sentencing are the result of amendments introduced at relatively late stages in the passage of the Bill through Parliament. For instance, the significant changes in the law relating to custodial sentences on young adult offenders, which will merge the existing youth custody sentence and detention sentence order (after a mere five years) into a single sentence of detention in a young offenders' institution, were introduced as a Government amendment during the Committee stage in the House of Lords, in a Bill which had previously passed through the House of Commons (before being lost as a result of the General Election) without any mention of this matter. The changed statutory criteria for the imposition of custodial sentences on young adults were introduced for the first time in the House of Lords; there was no reference to them in the original version of the Bill which passed through the Commons, and they do not appear to have been discussed at any stage in the passage of the Bill through either House. This is symptomatic of the absence of any clear policy in the Government's thinking and of the absence of any in-depth analysis of the practical consequences of what it is asking Parliament to enact. The present Criminal Justice Bill contains what is perhaps the most bizarre example of all. Clause 102 of the Bill will amend the law relating to compensation in two unrelated respects. First, it will allow the courts to make compensation orders in cases where death has resulted from the offence (the courts will not have this power where the offence is causing death by reckless driving).

Secondly, and distinctly, the same provision will require any Judge who fails to make a compensation order when he has power to do so to give reasons on passing sentence explaining why he has not exercised the power. But has anyone thought of the combined effect of these two requirements? Allowing a court to make a compensation order where death has resulted from the offence will allow courts for the first time to make compensation orders in murder cases. (This in itself will not do very much for the relatives of murder victims, as the Bill confers no greater benefit on them than they are already likely to receive from the Criminal Injuries Compensation Board; the limit on such awards to a maximum of £3,500 may well result in the relatives of some murder victims feeling that insult has been added to injury). However, all persons convicted of murder receive a mandatory sentence, either life imprisonment, custody for life or detention during Her Majesty's pleasure (incidentally, why is it necessary to have three names for what is essentially exactly the same thing?). There is no better way of damaging a man's financial prospects than by sentencing him to imprisonment for life. But the law will shortly require a Judge, who has sentenced a man to life imprisonment for murder, solemnly to say (as the statute requires him to do) that he is not making a compensation order because, having regard to the means of the offender, he is not satisfied that the offender will have the resources from which to pay compensation within a reasonable time. A moment of high seriousness will be reduced to farce.

These criticisms are essentially matters of form rather than substance, but there are a number of deeper criticisms which must be made. The first of these is the absence of any logical structure in modern English sentencing legislation. The statutory framework fails to reflect any penological principle and frequently requires Judges to make decisions for which no logical reason can be given. If we look back to the 1960s it becomes clear that at that time sentencing legislation offered reasonably clear choices between punishment (in the form of imprisonment or fines), and treatment or individual prevention (in the form of a variety of sentences such as probation orders and Borstal training). While it may be that the premises of the system were open to question, if the premises were accepted the sentencer could follow a logical process of reasoning towards a particular form of sentence in the individual case. Subsequent legislation has led increasingly to the destruction of that logical system; new forms of sentence have been introduced with no clear penological basis, or with a basis which is confused or ambiguous. One example is the suspended sentence, another the partly suspended sentence.

Consider the process which the Judge is expected to follow in reaching the decision to impose a partly suspended sentence. First he must determine that a sentence of immediate imprisonment is necessary and justified for the offence; then he must determine the length of that sentence; next determine that the sentence cannot be fully suspended; next decide that the sentence can be suspended in part; and, finally, decide what part of the sentence is to be suspended and what part to be served. Making sense of this complex progression is not made any easier by knowledge of the fact that the decisions taken by the Judge have no real relationship to the realities which the prisoner will experience. The result of remission, credit for time served on remand, and until recently parole eligibility, means that the sentence as served will be very different from the sentence as pronounced; a sentence of two year's imprisonment with half to serve and half held in suspense means in reality that the offender will serve one-quarter of the sentence, as he will receive remission of half of the half which he is ordered to serve in the first instance.

The fact that it is extremely difficult to give any reasons for making any but the first two decisions in this process means that it tends to become wholly illogical, and the chances of establishing any coherent general criteria for the use of this form of sentence, as for many others, are remote.

As this example illustrates, a further difficulty facing the sentencer is the degree to which the decision of the court has become remote from the reality of the sentence which the offender will undergo, as a result of the complex interactions between the rules relating to parole eligibility, remission of sentence and the reduction of sentences on account of time served on remand. This has been particularly exacerbated by the extension of the parole system under the amendments introduced by Criminal Justice Act 1982, section 33.

The vast expansion of the numbers of prisoners eligible for release on licence has led to a simplified procedure which results in recommendations for release for almost 80 per cent. of prisoners eligible under section 33 those serving between 12 months and two years at present. The effect is to reduce or eliminate differentials between different offenders which have been decided by judges after expensive open court procedures, and to introduce anomalies and injustices. These result primarily from the refusal to allow time on remand to count towards the minimum "specified period" of six months which every prisoner must serve before becoming eligible for release on licence. Two examples will make the point clear. Consider first the case of a prisoner sentenced to 18 months' immediate imprisonment after spending six months in custody on remand. He must serve the minimum specified period of six months before becoming eligible for release on licence; assuming he is released on licence at the earliest possible date he will have been in custody for 12 months under that sentence. His co-defendant sentenced to the same term for the same offence who has been on bail throughout the proceedings must serve the same specified period of six months before he too becomes eligible for release; he will complete the custodial part of his sentence in half the time which his less fortunate co-defendant has spent in prison. This offender however may consider himself more fortunate than my second example, a man sentenced to 15 months' imprisonment who has spent 13 weeks in custody on remand before conviction or sentence. This man also will be required to serve the specified period of six months before becoming eligible for release on licence. Although the time spent in custody on remand does not bring forward the date on which he becomes eligible for release, it does bring forward his remission date, which is the date on which his licence would terminate, and in his case the result is to bring that date to within the period of 30 days from the date on which he will become eligible for release on licence. Because it is the policy of the Home Office not to allow the release on licence of a prisoner who would have less than 30 days on licence, this offender will be required to serve out the sentence until his remission date. His co-defendant who has received the same sentence and who has been on bail throughout the proceedings will be released earlier. In his case the remission date will fall four months after the date of sentence and leave him with an available licence period of four months. There will therefore be no obstacle to his release on licence. There can surely be no defence or justification of a system in which the fact of an offender being in custody before trial or sentence not merely fails to shorten, but actually prolongs, the period during which he must remain in prison under the sentence.

A third, and to my mind, most disturbing element in current sentencing legislation is what can only be described as a slide towards mandatory provisions. For many years Parliament made no serious attempt to lay down criteria for the guidance of sentencers, beyond some very broad formulae. Criminal Justice Act 1948, section 17 contained a broadly based exhortation to avoid imprisoning certain classes of offenders, which is now carried forward as Powers of Criminal Courts Act 1973, section 20; the legislation relating to suspended sentences has included mandatory provisions (subject to an escape route) governing activation, and we have become accustomed to mandatory disqualification from driving in various circumstances. Since 1982 the mandatory element in new sentencing legislation has become more of a dominant theme, together with often ill-considered attempts to structure and guide the discretion of the sentencer. Criminal Justice Act 1982, section 1(4), added to the Bill as an afterthought, marked the beginning of a trend, which is also evident in the Public Order Act 1986. This Act contains a provision empowering a court to make an exclusion order prohibiting the offender from attending football matches, but only if it is satisfied that to do so would "contribute to the prevention of violence or disorder at or in connection with prescribed football matches." What other reason could there possibly be, one is tempted to ask, for making such an order? The Drug Trafficking Offences Act 1986 is replete with mandatory provisions. If the offender is convicted of a drug trafficking offence, the court must proceed to take the complex route described by the Act, and must complete all its stages before passing on to deal with other aspects of sentence. The equivalent legislation for Scotland, Criminal Justice (Scotland) Act 1987, is discretionary; the court is empowered, but not required, to make an order for the confiscation of an amount equal to the offender's proceeds of drug trafficking, and is not debarred from proceeding to the main business of sentencing before completing any inquiries necessary for this purpose. If the Scottish court requires further information before coming to any decision connected with the making of a confiscation order, it may postpone that decision for up to six months after the date of conviction without delaying sentence. If Parliament is content to trust Scottish Judges with discretion in these matters, why cannot English Judges be trusted in the same way? It may be that the Drug Trafficking Offences Act 1986 will prove to be a potent weapon against major drug traffickers, but there is no obvious necessity to force the courts to apply it to all cases, including very small ones where the proceeds to be recovered will certainly be less than the cost in court time of following the steps prescribed by the Act.

The current Criminal Justice Bill reflects the same tendency towards mandatory provision and ill-considered attempts to structure sentencing discretion by stipulating statutory criteria. For instance the Bill amends Powers of Criminal Courts Act 1973, section 43 (which allows a court to order an offender to be deprived of property which he has used to commit, or facilitate the commission of, an offence) by extending its application to a wider range of offences, and removing some of the procedural barriers to its use; but the amending provision also introduces a statutory requirement that the court in considering whether to make such an order shall have regard to the value of the property concerned. One wonders why Parliament considers such a provision necessary. Does it consider that any person capable of taking office as a Judge or magistrate is incapable of working out such a criterion for himself? What remains to be seen is the procedural effect of introducing such a statutory requirement. Will it be held that a court is prevented from making such an order unless it has specific evidence before it of the value of the property concerned? I for one cannot see how a court can fulfil a statutory obligation to have regard to the value of a particular piece of property unless it has some evidence to consider. The result may be that the making of such orders will become less rather than more common, as apparently Parliament intends that it should. As I have mentioned earlier, the Bill contains provisions which will require courts to give reasons for not making a compensation order in any case where a court refrains from making a compensation order where there would be statutory power to make one. I have already referred to the absurd consequences which will result from the combination of this amendment and the amendment allowing courts to award compensation in the cases where death has resulted from an offence, but apart from this it is difficult to see anything to be gained from such a statutory provision. I know of no evidence which suggests that courts are reluctant to make compensation orders, quite the reverse; it is not uncommon to see a court, in its anxiety to compensate the victim, make a compensation order which the offender has no chance of paying. The reason why compensation orders are not made more commonly than they are is the simple and obvious one that not all offenders have the means to pay for the damage that they have done to their victims. A mandatory requirement to state the reason why a compensation order is not being made will do nothing to change this, or to make any funds available to victims; it will simply require a monotonous refrain to be added to almost every sentence, to the effect that the court is not making a compensation order in this case because, having regard to the means of the offender (and statute requires the court to have regard to the means of the offender) the court is not satisfied that he has the resources from which to pay compensation within a reasonable time.

Without doubt the most important mandatory provisions in the current Criminal Justice Bill are those which apply to imposition of custodial sentences on offenders under the age of 21. These provisions were not included in the original Criminal Justice Bill when it came for the first time to the House of Commons before the general election; they were introduced separately as a private member's bill in the House of Commons, and subsequently incorporated into the Criminal Justice Bill when it was reintroduced in the House of Lords. So far as I have been able to ascertain there has been no discussion of these provisions at any stage during the progress of the Bill through either House, and no attempt has been made to explain or justify the need for them. They are introduced against the background of a significant drop in the number of offenders under 21 sentenced to youth custody or detention centre orders. The number of youth custody sentences declined from 17,188 in 1985 to 14,936 in 1986 and the number of detention centre orders similarly declined from 11,534 in 1985 to 8,909 in 1986, representing a substantial drop in the number of offenders under 21 received into custody in the year. While this change probably reflects the declining size of the relevant population, rather than a change in the sentencing practice, it does not support the case for strengthening the statutory restraints on the imposition of custodial sentences on offenders in this age group. There can be little doubt that the new criteria, if they are enacted in their present form, will give rise to a wide range of legal difficulties, and the time of the criminal courts will be consumed more with discussing the details of the statutory requirements than with the general merits of the case. The new criteria are based on the provisions of Criminal Justice Act 1982, section 1(4), which is considerably extended. The court will have to decide first whether it would impose a sentence of imprisonment on a hypothetical offender aged 21 or more for the same offence committed in the same circumstances. This should not in itself cause too much difficulty as judges are quite used to sentencing exercises. Having cleared this hurdle the judge must next consider whether the offender is qualified for custody under one of the three limbs of what will be section 1(4A). The first of these is that the offender has a history of failure to respond to non-custodial penalties and is unable or unwilling to respond to non-custodial penalties. On the face of it, this provision seems to require that the offender should have some sort of a record and an unfavourable social enquiry report; but there may be more to it than that. Consider the case of a 19-year-old who has been before the court on a number of previous occasions; he has been conditionally discharged, fined, made the subject of a care order, put on probation and ordered to perform community service. Does he qualify under this provision? His counsel will undoubtedly argue that a conditional discharge is not a non-custodial penalty, as a conditional discharge may be imposed only if the court considers it "inexpedient to inflict punishment" (Powers of Criminal Courts Act 1973, section 7). So far as the fine is concerned, let us assume that the offender paid the fine; is there any other response which the law may reasonably require? The care order may be held not to be a custodial sentence as under Children and Young Persons Act 1969, section 24(2) a local authority in whose care a child is placed may "restrict his liberty to such extent as the authority consider appropriate." It may well be therefore that a care order is not a non-custodial penalty. A probation order is made "instead of sentencing the offender"; like a conditional discharge it may well be that a probation order is not a penalty for this purpose. This leaves the community service order, which is undoubtedly a non-custodial penalty, but perhaps counsel will argue that one breach does not constitute "a history." What will the courts make of the expression "failure to respond?" Does this mean that there must be a breach of the order or non-compliance with its terms? Is it sufficient if the offender complies with the requirements of the order and refrains from offending while it is current and then returns to his old habits as soon as the order has expired? What of the offender who is in breach of the order after doing well for some period of time immediately after it was made; a common occurrence. Can he claim that he has responded to the order even though he has failed to maintain his response throughout the whole period for which the order was to remain in effect? It may well be that some of these arguments will not prevail, and the courts will take a robust common-sense approach, but there can be little doubt that this criterion potentially increases the range of legal technicalities which courts will have to consider, without necessarily improving the quality of the ultimate decisions which are made. The second limb of section 1(4A) will also cause difficulties. The court must be satisfied that a custodial sentence is necessary to protect the public from "serious harm"; but what precisely is "serious harm" for this purpose? Arson, rape, murder, undoubtedly constitute "serious harm," but what of the more common instance of the persistent burglar? In the final analysis, the application of this criterion will require a subjective judgment of the individual sentencer.

Whatever detailed objections may be made to legislation of this kind, and there are many, what is in question is the general principle. There is no constitutional objection to legislation of this kind; the judiciary cannot claim any prerogative to exercise an unfettered discretion in sentencing. The powers which Parliament gives them can properly be limited or constrained in any way.

However, if there is to be what amounts to a major change in the style of sentencing legislation it is highly desirable that this should be a considered change of which all the implications—and particularly procedural and evidential implications—have been fully thought through before the legislation is enacted. What we are seeing at the moment, sadly, is a casual slide from one half-thought-out precedent to another, which produces as an end result the kind of morass which I described at the beginning of this paper. There are many problems with the English sentencing process, some of which may properly be laid at the door of the judiciary; but Judges can operate only within the framework established by Parliament, and if that framework is unsound then unsound decisions will be made within it. The solution is not to continue with the piecemeal construction of a grotesque and shapeless statutory edifice, devoid of coherent principle or logic, replete with unnecessary legal technicalities and ambiguities. The time has come to review the structure from first principles and to reconstruct a simpler and more intelligible statutory framework within which the judiciary may reasonably be expected to achieve consistent and acceptable sentencing practices.

In the Office of Chief Constable

ROBERT REINER

Introduction

"Policing in this country is run by an extra-constitutional
and (in theory) informal body—the Association of Chief
Police Officers."

This was the dramatic claim made a couple of years ago by an
editorial in the *New Statesman*, under the graffiti-inspired headline
"ACPO Rules is not OK."[1] The editorial encapsulates the most
conspiratorially inclined pole in the spectrum of concern about the
accountability and control of police forces which has developed
apace amongst civil libertarians in the last decade.[2]

As I tried to show in my 1985 book *The Politics of the Police*,
policing in Britain has become thoroughly politicised, the subject
of acute political controversy and debate. I hesitate to say a
political football, because the ball seems to be so consistently
hogged by one side.

There is nothing novel about the politicisation of policing in the
grand sweep of British history. But the recent clashes over the
police follow an era in which the police had come to be "like the
Royal Family ... regarded as above politics," in the words of
Leslie Curtis the Police Federation Chairman.

Bipartisan accord over the principles of policy governing crime,
"law and order," and policing has been rudely shattered, and is
now just one more relic of the lost age of cosy consensus.[3] Many
specific issues about the police have aroused concern and
controversy: methods of dealing with public order, the use of
firearms, corruption, violations of the rules protecting suspects'
rights, rising levels of serious crime and the declining proportion of
crimes which are cleared up, the treatment of ethnic and other

minorities. These and many other questions have been pin-pointed by a series of *causes célèbres*. But underlying them all is the issue of the accountability, or more bluntly, the control of policing. It is a question of the greatest possible constitutional significance, and indeed is the litmus test of the quality of a political order—for policing, the application of the state's monopoly of legitimate force, is the sharp end, the bottom line of all governance.

The *Final Report of the Royal Commission on the Police* in 1962 summed up its view in a celebrated sentence. "The problem of controlling the police can, therefore, be restated as the problem of controlling chief constables."[4] Much of the sociological research which has been done on the processes of law-enforcement in action have called this unidirectional, top-down approach into question. It has come to be generally understood that the impact of organisational and legal rules on police practices on the ground is tenuous and problematic, mediated by a complex filter of immediate situational pressures, and by the cop culture of the canteen and the streets.[5] Nonetheless, the policies and organisational structures constructed by chief officers are a crucial, if not complete, determinant of policing practices. Chief constables have been at the nub of debate, most luridly in the conspiratorial versions of their role encapsulated in the quotes with which the article began. In the last two decades systematic research on the lower ranks of police organisations has accumulated rapidly, and remains one of the few growth centres in today's impoverished social science world. But our knowledge of the senior ranks, of the policy-making levels, remains sketchy and anecdotal, a pot-pourri of chance revelation, scandal and the much-publicised remarks of arguably unrepresentative media celebrities in the rent-a-quote business. If I may humbly follow Lord Denning's precedent and cite my own past statements as authority:

> "The character of police work at the senior levels of the organisation is the greatest gap in the growing body of knowledge which social scientists have accumulated about the police."[6]

If it is true that chief constables have become, in Duncan Campbell's words "a power in the land,"[7] then we ought at the very least to know who chief constables are, and what they think. But "while we have some knowledge of the social origins and previous careers of recruits, we do not have this information for senior officers."[8] In this paper I will present some preliminary results from an empirical study of contemporary chief constables, which I have conducted over the last year, with the aid of a grant from the Nuffield Foundation. In some respects, as will emerge, the conclusions I have come to so far, paradoxically, undercut the obvious importance of my subject of study. In a nutshell what I will argue is that debate has tended to under-emphasise the growing control of policing by central government. Critics and supporters of the status quo have underlined the autonomy of chief officers, understandably in view of some well-publicised clashes with local police authorities which have been much ventilated. But in the process the role of central government has been occluded by the emphasis on constabulary independence. Even in the conspiratorial views it is the influence of ACPO on government which is stressed, not the reverse. In the 1962 Royal Commission's Report there was a long memorandum of dissent by Professor A. L. Goodhart.[9] It argued for a national police force, regionally administered. At the time it was widely regarded (not least by the majority on the Commission) as powerfully argued, but politically unacceptable. This may well remain the verdict today. But with hindsight it seems as if the alternative to Professor Goodhart's *de iure* national force, with explicit structures of accountability, has turned out to be covert national influence, with no accountability for the *de facto* co-ordinating role of central government. I will return to these considerations at the end. But first I want to review what is known about the history and legal powers of the office of chief constable, and the preliminary results of my own recent research. I must emphasise that these results are tentative ones. I have not yet completely finished my fieldwork, and have only begun the analysis of the mass of material gathered.

(i) *The History of the Office of Chief Constable Until 1964*

The term "chief constable" was only applied uniformly to all (provincial) chief officers of police after the Police Act of 1919.[10] Prior to 1919, the term "chief constable" was only standard in referring to county forces. In borough forces the usual term was "head constable," although there was a variety of other nomenclature: "superintendent," "head officer of police," as well as "chief constable" in a growing number of boroughs.[11] The difference in title corresponded to differences both in formal legal position, and in social status and background, between county and borough chiefs. These differences remained after the assimilation of names by the 1919 Police Act, right down to the Police Act of 1964, albeit in more attenuated form after the Second World War.

The first modern police force, the Metropolitan Police, was established by the 1829 Police Act on a pattern which was not followed for provincial forces, and remains unique. Its administration was placed in the hands of two justices, (later called commissioners in 1839; since 1856 there has only been one). The police authority to whom the commissioner was (and remains) accountable is the Home Secretary. When in 1888 the London County Council was set up providing elected local government for London, it was specifically decided that the control of the police should remain with the Home Secretary, because of the unique national and "imperial" functions of the Met., a decision which was the subject of much partisan controversy at the time.[12]

When the first provincial borough forces were established, by the 1835 Municipal Corporations Act, no mention was made of chief or head constables. The new municipal corporations elected as a result of the Act were required to appoint a sufficient number of their members to constitute a watch committee (together with the mayor, appointed as a justice). The watch committee in turn was instructed to appoint a "sufficient number of fit men" to act as constables. The watch committee had the power to appoint and dismiss the constables, and to frame regulations governing them, although the common law powers of the office of constable were preserved.

There rapidly emerged a wide range of differences between the borough forces. The largest city forces—Manchester, Bristol, Birmingham and Liverpool—had chief or head constables who were figures of power and importance in their forces and in the local community. At the other extreme, in the smallest forces, most obviously those with only one or two men, the office of chief constable was indistinguishable from that of constable.

> "The 'chief constable,' in any case, held no exceptional position comparable with that of the county man: he was simply the constable who held the highest rank in the force, and his status depended on the numbers under him."[13]

The locus of control in the nineteenth century between borough chief constables and watch committees has been much debated of late. The standard view,[14] supported recently by Lustgarten, holds that in the nineteenth century "the subordination of the police to elected representatives in the boroughs was part of common understanding."[15] This view has been challenged in recent years by Brogden[16] in the specific case of the Liverpool head constable, and Jefferson and Grimshaw.[17] These authors argue that the doctrine of constabulary independence was already in being for borough chief officers, and offer a reinterpretation of some of the examples of watch committee instructions to chief officers which

Critchley proposed as support for the subordination view. The Jefferson and Grimshaw argument about the 1880 Birmingham case is an example of the rather forced nature of their attempted reinterpretation. Following clashes about the chief constable's policies concerning the prosecution of drunks and of "improper" music-hall performances, the Watch Committee passed a resolution that he should not take proceedings "likely to affect a number of ratepayers, or to provoke public comment" without first informing them of his intentions. The chief constable refused to comply unless instructed to by the Home Secretary and the justices. The Home Secretary would not intervene directly, but referred the chief constable to the Municipal Corporations Act which gave the Watch Committee power to make regulations "for preventing neglect or abuse, and for rendering constables efficient in the discharge of their duties," and to dismiss any constable "whom they shall think negligent in the discharge of his duty, or otherwise unfit for the same." In the end, the chief constable gave way, after the Council resolved that it was not desirable to retain a chief officer who was "not subordinate to or not in harmony with" the Watch Committee and threatened him with a requirement to resign. The plain-as-pikestaff interpretation of this is that it demonstrates that watch committees *were* seen as empowered to give chief constables lawful orders about law enforcement priorities. Jefferson and Grimshaw's contrary reading is somewhat tenuously stretched. They claim first that the chief constable's compliance with the Watch Committee's directions does not mean he accepted the *idea* that he lacked independent power to decide on law enforcement. But surely the point is that irrespective of what ideas the chief constable may or may not have entertained (and who is to know?), his ideas did not prevail. Further, they argue that all the Watch Committee claimed was the right to be *informed* of the chief's intentions, not to direct them. But they evidently wanted to be informed of his intentions in order to control them, to be able to ensure that they were "subordinate to" and "in harmony with" the Watch Committee's views (as the Council resolutions put it). I would submit that the orthodox view is correct in holding that in the nineteenth century it *was* generally accepted that watch committees *did* have the power to instruct their chief officers on law enforcement policy. The revisionist reinterpretations establish no more than the obvious limitation that watch committees could only give *lawful* orders, and that especially in the case of experienced heads of large forces (as in Liverpool) the chief constable commanded a certain respect based on professional expertise, but that this was not necessarily deferred to.

In the counties, however, the office of chief constable was not only labelled as such from the outset, but had much of the autonomy of his present-day heirs. The County Police Act of 1839 was a permissive measure, empowering, but not requiring, magistrates in quarter sessions to establish forces for counties (or parts of them). From the outset the county constabularies were under greater Home Office regulation, and also more autonomous of *all* outside influences, than borough forces. The Home Secretary maintained the right to decide whether or not a force should be established, and to approve its size, rules, rates of pay, and the appointment of the chief constable. Guidelines for the selection of chief constables for county forces were issued by the Home Secretary, Lord Normanby, under the 1839 Act, and continued to be enforced until the 1919 Desborough Committee's recommendations superseded them. But "once in post the county chief constable was an autocrat over whom the justices had no power other than the ultimate sanction of dismissal . . . Thus he fulfilled many of the duties which in the borough were assigned to the watch committee."[18] These included appointments, discipline and law enforcement policy. This remained the position without substantial alteration down to the 1964 Police Act. The 1856 County and Borough Police Act, which introduced the Home Office grant and the Inspectorate, the 1888 Local Government Act which established Standing Joint Committees consisting 50 per cent. of elected councillors and 50 per cent. of justices, and the 1919 Police Act which implemented the Desborough Committee's recommendations following the police strikes, all enhanced the role of central government in regulating common basic standards. While they reduced police autonomy *vis-à-vis* central government, they did not substantially diminish the independence of the county chief from *local* electoral control.

This difference in legal status between county and borough chiefs of police is reflected in their social calibre. The county chiefs were drawn from the same landed gentry backgrounds as the justices who appointed them (and so were the elected members who formed the Standing Joint Committees together with the Justices after 1888). It was this congruence of background and outlook with the local elite which made the autonomy of the county chief unproblematic.[19] In recent historical research on the social origins of chief constables, David Wall has noted that three-quarters of the county chiefs in office in 1905 are included in contemporary directories of elites, *e.g. Who's Who* or *Kelly's*

Handbook of Official and Titled Classes.[20] This was because of *who* they were rather than *what* they were (unlike the 50 per cent. of present-day chiefs who also find themselves in these exalted pages).

> "The inclusion of county chief constables in such director-ies was by virtue of their background rather than their occupation. The county chief constableship became a popular occupation for the younger sons of the landed gentry in the same way that the army and the cloth had done."[21]

This same social cachet which integrated county chiefs with the local elite, cut them off from their men. Together with their experience as army officers this enhanced their image as autocrats.

By contrast only 5 per cent. of the borough chiefs in office in 1905 feature in the elite directories, and these were usually the heads of the very large city forces, whose origins were more exalted than those of their subordinates (albeit usually they were recruited from professional rather than military careers). But the majority of borough chiefs were men who had worked their way up the police ranks, and came from the same working (or at most lower-middle) class backgrounds as their subordinates. A common pattern was for boroughs to recruit their chiefs from the middle ranks of larger forces—usually the Met.

The Desborough Committee in 1919 examined the case for a fully professional police service with internally recruited chiefs. It recommended a movement towards this:

> "No person without previous police experience should be appointed as chief constable in any force unless he possesses some exceptional qualification or experience which specially fits him for the post, or there is no other candidate from the police service who is considered sufficiently well-qualified." (para. 139).

This was embodied in Regulation 9 of the rules which the 1919 Police Act empowered the Home Secretary to make governing the pay, conditions of service and appointments of the police. But the effect of the regulation was circumvented by the county forces. They either appointed men of the traditional type with colonial police backgrounds, or ex-military men to Assistant Chief Const-able posts (not covered by Reg. 9) to give them the "police experience" required. The result was that while in 1908 it was found that only three of the 44 English county chief constables had risen through the ranks (the rest being ex-army officers or colonial policemen), by 1939 this had only increased to four of the then 42

English county chiefs.[22] By contrast, only 15 of the 123 borough chiefs in 1908, and six of the 117 in 1939 had *not* risen through the ranks.

During and after the Second World War, the policy of only recruiting chief constables who *had* served as police throughout their careers became effective (*Postwar Committee on the Reconstruction of the Police Service*). However, county forces were able to stave off the full effects of this until the early 1970s, because of the legacy of the short-lived Trenchard scheme in the 1930s which provided for direct entry of (mainly middle-class) graduates to the Hendon Police College as "officer material" with automatic promotion to Inspector.

> "In 1965, the Commissioner, Deputy Commissioner, 4 Assistant Commissioners in the metropolitan Police, 19 county chief constables, 6 borough chief constables, the Chief Inspector of the Constabulary and three of his colleagues were all trained at Hendon."[23]

What is clear is that down to the 1964 Police Act there remained a substantial divide in legal and social status between county chief constables and their borough namesakes (with the partial exception of the largest city forces). While the latter were upwardly mobile career police officers from humble origins, the former were firmly parts of the county social elite. Moreover, they were extremely well-established parts of the local elite. Usually appointed in their 30s, it was common for them to die in office after extremely long periods as chief constable. The Surrey Constabulary, for example, was not unusual in having only two chiefs during its first 80 years: its first chief constable retired in 1899 at the age of 86, after 48 years in office, followed by his successor who retired in 1930.[24] Such longevity was matched by a few borough forces: Chester City, for example, which had only four chief constables in the whole 113 years of its existence (1836–1949), or Oxford City which also had only four chief officers from 1869 (when Charles Head, a Metropolitan Inspector became its "Superintendent") to 1968, when it was amalgamated into Thames Valley.[25] Evidently there would be much more scope for such chief officers to stamp a personal style of leadership upon their forces than would be usual today, and the potential for autocratic command is clear.

One final, most important aspect of the development of the office of chief constable before 1964 was the evolution of effective representative machinery. A Chief Constable's Association was founded in 1896 for city and borough chiefs, and a County Chief

Constables' Conference in 1920. The present Association of Chief Police Officers was formed in 1948 by the merger of the earlier bodies. It includes deputy and assistant chiefs, the Metropolitan ranks from Commander upwards, and the City of London Commissioner and Assistant Commissioner. The vehicle for these bodies to influence (and be influenced by) central government has been the Central Conference of Chief Constables, dating back to the First World War, under the chairmanship of the Home Secretary or a senior Home Office official. These meet two or three times a year. In addition there are district conferences which meet at least quarterly, also dating back to 1918. These are conduits both for the formation of a collective voice, and communication with the Home Office.

(ii) *The Office of Chief Constable Since 1964*

The statutory basis of the office of chief constable now, and of its relationship with local and central government, is the Police Act of 1964, together with the case law this has generated. The Act largely implemented the recommendations of the 1962 Report of the Royal Commission on the Police, which had been established in the wake of a series of cases raising concern about the accountability of the police generally and chief officers in particular.[26] The Royal Commission was faced by two conflicting and cogent lines of argument. The first was the view (articulated most explicitly by the Association of Municipal Corporations) that local police authorities should be (and watch committees were) able to issue instructions on policy matters in the same way as to other local officials (but not in individual cases of law enforcement). On the other hand, several representative bodies of professional legal opinion (the Law Society, the Inns of Court Conservative and Unionist Society, and Professor E. C. S. Wade who was consulted as an expert witness) all argued for a centrally controlled force, under parliamentary supervision, both on grounds of efficiency and accountability. This view was accepted in the dissenting memorandum by Professor Goodhart. Interestingly, it was also supported by the *New Statesman*, now the champion of the ACPO/police state conspiracy theory. An article by C. H. Rolph saw the report as

> "22 pages by Dr. Goodhart, with a preface seven times as long by a faintly admiring syndicate of diplomats."[27]

The majority of chief constables rejected the case for national control, but also reasserted the notion of constabulary independence from local control. A few chief constables (notably Eric St. Johnston of Lancashire), as well as the Police Federation, went along with the arguments for nationalisation, or at least regionalisation.

In the end, as C. H. Rolph's comments intimate, the Commissioner's Report, and the ensuing Act was a diplomatic compromise, the "tripartite" system of control by chief officers, Home Office and local police authorities. The latter were essentially a hybrid of the old watch and standing joint committees, consisting of two-thirds elected councillors, and one-third J.P.s. As critics remarked at the time (notably Geoffrey Marshall) the boundaries of function, responsibility and power between the points of the triangle were ill-defined and contained the seeds of future conflict once the political and social consensus about policing broke down, as it did increasingly after the late 1960s. There have been several excellent recent statements of the statutory position and case law, so this can be summarised briefly.[28]

The main duty of the police authority is to maintain "an adequate and efficient" force for its area. (s.4(1)). It is responsible for providing buildings, vehicles and other equipment, "as may be required for police purposes of the area." (ss.4(3), 4(4)). Subject to the approval of the Home Secretary, it also appoints, and "in the interests of efficiency" may dismiss, the chief constable, his deputy and assistants. (ss.4(2), 5(1), 5(4), 6(4), 6(5)). Again with the Home Secretary's approval, the police authority determines the establishment of the force. (s.4(2)). It controls force revenue and expenditure, although it can be required to pay sums necessary to give effect to regulations issued by the Home Secretary, or a court order, or to implement statutory changes. (s.8(1), s.8(4)). Central government meets 50 per cent. of policing costs directly, and also contributes to the local 50 per cent. through rate support grant. The chief constable is obliged to make an annual report to the police authority, and the authority may ask for further reports on any matter connected with the policing of the area. (s.12). But the chief constable may refuse such a report if it appears to him not to be in the public interest, or not to be "needed for the discharge of the functions of the police authority." In the event of such disagreement, the Home Secretary decides what should be done.

This apparently substantial list of functions begins to evaporate when the allocation of powers and duties to the chief constable and the Home Secretary is considered. The role of the chief constable is described almost parenthetically in the Act.

"The police force maintained for a police area under s.1 of this Act shall be under the direction and control of the chief constable appointed under s.4(2) of this Act." (s.5(1)).

Geoffrey Marshall argued in 1965 that this "merely describes the existing situation."[29] As seen above, this meant that chief constables, arguably, would be obliged to follow the lawful instructions of the police authority. But Lustgarten's critique of this interpretation of the Act seems more convincing. He argues, first, that when establishing other local government services (*e.g.* Education Act 1944; Social Services Act 1970) the terminology "direction and control" is not used to describe the function of the director. The other Acts establish a special local authority (*e.g.* education) or instruct the local authority to establish a special committee (*e.g.* social services), who are responsible for providing the service, to which end they are required to appoint a chief officer who is clearly subordinate to them. This argument by itself is not totally convincing. The main difference in the structure of the statutes is the terminology "direction and control," the meaning of which is precisely what is at issue.

However, Lustgarten's interpretation is further supported by a consideration of the case law. It must be stressed at once that, as is common ground between Marshall and Lustgarten, no case since the Act (and arguably none before it) *directly* has in point the issue of whether a chief constable has to follow lawful instructions from a police authority. The doctrine of constabulary independence has emerged in case law without ever being centrally at issue. *Obiter* on *obiter*. Of the pre-Act cases, the most often cited is *Fisher* v. *Oldham*.[30] As Marshall, Lustgarten and numerous other commentators have argued, this only establishes that constables and police authorities do not have a master/servant relationship for the specific question of vicarious liability in tort (on which the 1964 Act in substance reverses the effect of *Fisher* by explicitly making chief constables vicariously liable for their subordinates' torts in section 48(1) and exposing the police fund controlled by the police authority to the obligation to pay damages). This limited decision about the absence of a specific master/servant relationship in the tort sense, has come to stand as authority in later cases for the broader constitutional doctrine of constabulary independence from any instructions about law-enforcement methods and policy.

The most influential and often cited, post-1964 Act, judicial statement of the independence doctrine is that by Lord Denning in the first *ex p. Blackburn* case.[31] Mr. Blackburn was seeking an order of mandamus directing the Metropolitan Commissioner to reverse a policy of not enforcing the law on gaming. The Court of Appeal[32] found that the police have a public duty to enforce the law, which the courts could, if necessary, compel them to perform. But within this they have a broad discretion about methods and priorities. The courts would only countermand this if it was a policy of complete non-enforcement of a law, amounting to a chief officer "failing in his duty to enforce the law," *e.g.* by a directive saying no one would be prosecuted for thefts worth less than £100.

In the course of this judgment remarks were made about the independence of chief constables.

> "No minister of the Crown can tell him that he must or must not keep observation on this place or that; or that he must or must not prosecute this man or that one, nor can any police authority tell him so . . . he is not the servant of anyone save of the law itself. The responsibility for law enforcement lies on him. He is answerable to the law and to the law alone."[33]

With respect to this particular passage, Lustgarten has remarked "seldom have so many errors of law and logic been compressed into one paragraph."[34] He counts no fewer than six separate fallacies in Lord Denning's remarks. Whether or not he is correct, however, it is clear in any event that the remarks are strictly *obiter*.[35] The relationship between a chief officer, and either a police authority or the Home Secretary was simply not at issue in this case (or any of the later *Blackburn* cases). Nonetheless, these remarks have been used as authority for later judgments in the same vein, *e.g.* by Lord Denning himself in the *C.E.G.B.* case, where he cited, his own earlier words to support the proposition that "it is of the first importance that the police should decide on their own responsibility what action should be taken in any particular situation."[36] In the *C.E.G.B.* case the Board applied for an order of mandamus, after being prevented by protestors from carrying out a survey which they were statutorily empowered to conduct. The chief constable had refused to take action to remove the protestors, claiming no breach of the peace had occurred or was threatened. The court's sympathies clearly seem to have been with the Board, rather than the chief, and they found that the conduct of the protestors in unlawfully obstructing the Board's survey was itself a breach of the peace. However, the Court of Appeal did not grant mandamus. In Lord Denning's argument, this was on the grounds of constabulary independence: "The decision of the chief constable not to intervene in this case was a police decision with which I think the courts should not interfere,"[37] citing his own words in *Blackburn* as authority. However, it is not clear that this view is the basis of the judgment. Lord Lawton uses another argument, and Lord Templeman seems to concur with it. Lord Lawton argued that the application for mandamus

> "showed a misconception of the powers of chief constables. They command their forces but they cannot give an officer under command an order to do acts which can only lawfully be done if the officer himself with reasonable cause suspects that a breach of the peace has occurred or is imminently likely to occur or an arrestable offence has been committed. In July 1981 the Chief Constable of Devon and Cornwall could have, and probably did, order some of his constables to watch what was going on in the field . . . but what he could not do was to give unqualified orders to his officers."[38]

In other words, no one, whether a senior officer, police authority, or court, can order a constable to exercise a power which can only be exercised lawfully if certain factual conditions precedent are satisfied, and this can only be ascertained by the constable on the spot. If this is the ground of the judgment then it too does not really establish independence of constables from being given lawful instructions by police authorities, an issue not directly in question in any event.

The same applies to the more recent case *R. v. Oxford, ex p. Levey.*[39] Mr. Levey lost substantial amounts of jewellery in a robbery by thieves who escaped when the pursuing police car was called back by the Force control room after entering Toxteth. The pursuers had informed the control room of this, in compliance with a Force Order. The order to call off the chase was given by the control room inspector after the police car "encountered a group of some 50 youths armed with bricks, iron bars and pieces of metal" and "one of these youths threw a house-brick at and hit P.C. Bark's car." Mr. Levey sought (i) a declaration that it was *ultra vires* for the chief constable to adopt a policy whereby an area was deemed to be a "no-go" area; (ii) a declaration that it was *ultra vires* for the chief constable to call off the chase when the police car entered Toxteth; (iii) an order of mandamus directing the chief constable to rescind any order or decision to treat Toxteth or any part of the city as a "no-go" area, which would be counter to his statutory and common law duties; (iv) damages for breach of statutory duty. Mr. Levey failed in his action, the decision turning on the specific facts. It was found that the order to call off the chase was motivated primarily by concern for the safety of the pursuing officer. The obligation to inform the control room when entering Toxteth did not amount to a "no-go" policy, as remarks made by some P.C.s to Mr. Levey wrongly implied. Arguably such a policy *would* amount to the total abdication from the duty to enforce the law with which the courts have consistently said they would interfere. The policy to inform the control room was intended to ensure that any law enforcement activities in the sensitive area of Toxteth could take full account of the current situation there. This was a matter about the appropriate *methods* for enforcing the law, a choice over which "chief constables have the widest possible discretion."[40] So the judgment amounts to confirmation of the view that chief constables will not be told by the courts *how* to enforce the law, provided they do not totally abdicate from their duty to do so. Once again, however, while the constabulary independence doctrine is bolstered, the relationship specifically with police authorities was not at issue.

The recent *Northumbria* case[41] *did* concern the powers of police authorities. However, it involved all three parties to the tripartite relation, so consideration will be postponed until after looking at the Home Secretary's powers under the 1964 Act.

The cases considered so far do establish a strong judicial tradition of support for the doctrine of "constabulary independence." Arguably, as Marshall claims, the statements containing this are *obiter*, at any rate as concerns the chief constable/police authority relationship which was never directly at issue. Nonetheless, Lustgarten is surely right that however deficient its initial basis, the doctrine of constabulary independence

> "has ... embedded itself in the lore and learning of both judges and police, and it is inconceivable that, without parliamentary intervention, the courts would resile from the position they have reached."[42]

The third party to the tripartite system, the Home Secretary, has also grown in power, together with chief constables, at the expense of local police authorities, at any rate as compared with pre-1964 watch committees. The Royal Commission and the 1964 Act clearly *intended* to tilt the balance towards the centre. The history of legislation concerning police organisation and accountability reflects a perennially repeated clash of rhetorics, re-emerging in the debates around the 1829, 1835, 1839, 1856, 1888, 1919, and 1964 Acts. On the one hand, there is a clear Benthamite vision of a rationally structured, bureaucratic police organisation, controlled by, and accountable to, the centre. On the other side, there is a chorus of opposition to this, invoking fear of the trampling of hallowed British liberties by a foreign-inspired Leviathan. At each turn, the Benthamites have had much of their way, as evidenced by the very fact of the passage of the legislation. But the libertarian fears result in compromises and concessions from the clear centralist form. Since 1964 the Benthamite vision has had undisputed sway in practice, while, paradoxically, explicit support for it has faded away to such a degree that Lustgarten can remark

"The one point that commands near-universal agreement is that a national police force is undesirable."[43]

The Royal Commission Report was clearly impressed by the Goodhart centralising line. This is most evident in the way they firmly refuted the main bulwark of the localist position: the fear of a centralist and totalitarian "police state."[44] The reasons for rejecting the central control argument are much more tenuous and amount to no more than respect for tradition, and the importance of local ties and identity for policing. The latter point was in fact recognised by the advocates of nationalisation, and various attempts to preserve local links were incorporated in their schemes for change.[45] The accountability argument was stressed by the advocates of centralisation[46] rather than the localists. The description of the benefits of local police authorities by the Commission[47] sees them not so much as a means of accountability but only as consultative devices, and as administrative dogs-bodies. What the Commission seems to be saying, almost explicitly, is that the argument for central control is basically sound, but that it would be better to provide the means while maintaining a semblance of local accountability, than to come clean on the issue. With hindsight, is that too cynical an interpretation of its concluding comment on the matter, where they speak of proceeding by

"accelerating the pace at which the police service moves towards greater unity, rather than by any abrupt and radical change which might not be readily understood."[48]

The means for beefing up central control were two-fold. First, the role of Home Secretary as arbiter in conflicts between police authorities and chief constables. More fundamentally, the Commission wanted the Home Secretary to be made statutorily responsible for the efficiency of the police.[49] This formulation was objected to by the Home Secretary during the Parliamentary debates, on the ground that it would give responsibility without power (an argument which had been anticipated in Professor Goodhart's dissenting memorandum.[50] Instead, it might be argued, he has ended up with power without responsibility. The 1964 Act specifies the general duty of the Home Secretary as being to

> "exercise his powers... in such manner and to such extent as appears to him to be best calculated to promote the efficiency of the police." (s.28).

For this purpose he is given a variety of powers:

(i) to require a police authority to exercise their power under Part 1 of this Act to call upon the chief constable to retire in the interests of efficiency, (s.29(1));

(ii) to require a report from a chief constable on any matter connected with the policing of any area, and to receive an annual report, (s.30);

(iii) the power to make grants of expenses, (s.31), and related to this, the power to appoint the Inspectorate to monitor and advise on efficiency, (s.38);

(iv) the power to establish special inquiries into the policing of local areas, (s.32);

(v) the power to make regulations concerning all aspects of the government, administration and conditions of service of police forces, (s.33) and concerning standards of equipment, (s.36) (and of course the continuing practice of issuing circulars);

(vi) the power to provide a wide array of central services, (s.41), a power which was to prove crucial in the recent *Northumbria* case.

Outside the 16 very long sections (ss.28–43) detailing the Secretary of State's functions and powers, others crop up elsewhere in the Act. Of potentially great importance in the context of a national policing operation such as occurred during the miners' strike of 1984–1985, sections 13 and 14 on collaboration and mutual aid arrangements give the Home Secretary the clear power to direct that such agreements be made if necessary (s.13(5)), to order a force to receive or provide reinforcements (s.14(2)), and to arbitrate on inter-force disputes about the allocation of the financial burden of such co-operation (s.13(3), s.14(4)).

In the event, these powers were never used. Instead, the most extensive mutual aid operation to date, in the 1984 miners' strike, was co-ordinated by the National Reporting Centre under the control of the President of ACPO, implicitly to the satisfaction of the Home Secretary or presumably he *would* have invoked his powers.[51] The accountability implications are significant. Had the operation been directed by the Home Secretary under his Police Act powers, he would have been answerable to Parliament for their exercise. As it was, no one was.

Several recent developments accentuate this centralising trend clearly evident in the 1964 legislation. The statutory requirement to establish consultative arrangements in each police area, which section 106 of the Police and Criminal Evidence Act 1984 introduces, at first sight appears an exception. But whatever the virtues of these arrangements, the form they took was uniformly shaped by Home Office Circular 54/1982.[52] Paradoxically this move to local consultation reveals the way that nominally advisory Home Office Circulars are interpreted as binding.

The Local Government Act 1985 which abolished the six Metropolitan County Councils considerably increased the statutory powers and the *de facto* influence of the Home Secretary. The rate-capping powers of central government allow it to determine the budget, and manpower levels of the Metropolitan Forces, which means the Home Secretary in effect

> "now directly controls the financial resources for nearly half of the entire police strength in England and Wales."[53]

A further consequence of the new Joint Boards which replaced the former Metropolitan police authorities is to increase the likelihood of a "hung" Board, with the magistrates thus having the last say.

> "In the Metropolitan areas the tripartite structure must be viewed as little more than a legal fiction... The 1985 Local Government Act represents the most significant and overt shift in responsibility for the police service, from local to central government, since the passage of the 1964 Police Act."[54]

The point is underlined in the highly significant recent case of *R. v. Secretary of State for the Home Department, ex p. Northumbria Police Authority*.[55] This concerned Home Office Circular 40/1986 which stated that in pursuance of the Home Secretary's 1981 announcement to make available baton rounds and CS gas to chief officers of police "for use in the last resort," it was proposed that such requirements would be met from a central store. This would extend to "cases where a chief officer has been unable to obtain his police authority's agreement to purchase," subject to endorsement by H.M. Inspectorate of Constabulary. The Divisional Court upheld the circular by accepting that the Home Secretary had the power to supply equipment without the police authority's permission under the Royal Prerogative. But it rejected the view that he was also empowered to do this under section 41 of the Police Act which permitted him to supply equipment "for promoting the efficiency of the police." To do this when the police authority objected would be incompatible with its own responsibility for efficiency under section 4(1). The Court of Appeal confirmed the Royal Prerogative argument. But it also held that the power to supply common services under section 41, and the general requirement to use his powers so as to promote the efficiency of the police—section 28—entitled him to provide such services, including riot equipment, even without the police authority's consent. What this seems to amount to is that if the local and the national view of "efficiency" conflict, the Act gives priority to the interpretation by central government. In any event, this same conclusion would be available as a result of the Royal Prerogative powers.

What seems abundantly clear is that in the law in the books as well as the law in action, if there is disagreement about policing policy between local police authorities and the chief constable or central government, the latter parts of the supposed tripartite structure regularly prevail. With regard to the police authority/ chief constable relationship, this is legitimated by the doctrine of constabulary independence.

But what if chief constables and the central government disagree? What becomes of constabulary independence then? The answer is, we don't know. We don't know because, unlike the many well-publicised cases of conflict between chief constables and local authorities,[56] clashes between chief constables and central government have not surfaced. To find out why, we must consider more closely who chief constables are, a question to which my recent empirical research has been addressed.

(iii) *Who Are the Chief Constables? A Social Profile*

The position of chief constables is now quite different from either the county or borough chiefs of the past. County chiefs then had a local elite position stemming from background rather than office. They elevated the standing of the office, rather than vice versa. Borough chiefs (with the possible exception of the very largest cities) were men of humble origins who had worked their way up to gain membership in the local municipal elite.[57] They were not especially prominent locally, and certainly not actors on a national stage.

Today's chief constable typically comes from a relatively humble background, not very different from the men and women he commands, or the general population he is responsible for policing. But he has worked himself up into a professional elite body, which is an important if unusual and unsung part of the national power elite.

Both terms "national" and "elite" may be questioned. In the letter of introduction to chief constables which I sent out last year seeking an interview, I said I was interested in them as "an elite group with considerable power and influence." One chief I interviewed questioned my use of the word elite. He could not see this word as appropriate to describe a group of people many of whom came from ordinary working-class backgrounds. While these origins distinguish chief constables from most groups traditionally thought of as elites, I would maintain the term is appropriate.

Following Weber, most sociologists would analyse position in the social stratification hierarchy in terms of three dimensions: economic class, social status or prestige, and political power. On all three chief constables now rank high.

(a) *Economic.* They command very large resources. In 1983/ 1984 the net expenditure of police forces ranged from a low of £16.3m (Dyfed-Powys) to a high for the Met. of £667.1m, and in the provinces £131.5m. (G.M.P.). Chief constables also command large salaries, ranging around £40,000 p.a. (depending on the size of their forces).

(b) *Status.* Perhaps the clearest index of the rise in chief constables' social standing is their move up the New Year's Honours lists of recent years. Last year Sir Philip Knights, former chief of West Midlands, became the first chief constable to be given a peerage. This year, one chief constable and one former chief (now an H.M.I.) were knighted, and this seems to be an annual pattern.

(c) *Power.* The review of the legal position showed that chief constables are given the direction and control of their forces, and power to determine policing methods and priorities in their areas. This gives them at any rate formal power of an extensive kind. Police forces range in size from 934 (Dyfed-Powys), to the largest provincial force (G.M.P.) 6,943, and the Met. with 27,165. The populations over which they police range from 440,000 (Gwent) to the largest provincial force population, 2,647,000 (West Midlands), and 7,202,000 for the Met.

If they are in these terms an elite group of substantial importance, are they a *national* power elite? Or just 43 separate elite individuals with the same title? In his sociological classic *The Power Elite* C. Wright Mills specifies three conditions for saying that a number of separate elites at the top of different institutions may be considered as a unitary power elite.[58]

(1) *Psychological similarity and social intermingling.*

Are they men of similar origin, education, career, style of life? Is there "considerable traffic of personnel" between the institutions? Does this lead to a convergence of outlook?

(2) *Structural blending of commanding position and common interests.*

Do the institutions and the commanding positions have similar interests, problems, structural pressures?

(3) *Unity of a more explicit co-ordination.*

Do the common outlook, background, interests sometimes coalesce into united action?

The last of these can only be considered in terms of specific historical episodes, but seems confirmed by the 1984 miners' strike, and the complex, co-ordinated policing operation conducted despite lack of central coercive power by the National Reporting Centre. The second criterion is whether common interests override the inter-force and inter-personal rivalries found in any job. Since 1964 many structural differences between forces, particularly the county/borough divide have disappeared or narrowed. The first question requires systematic social research on the demography and perspectives of a group. It is the answer to this question which I have been addressing.

The research was aimed at discovering the demographic characteristics and the policing philosophy of today's chief constables. The views and background of a few chiefs (or perhaps more accurately, one chief) receive widespread media attention and are well-known. But I wanted to determine whether there was a characteristic outlook and background, or substantial variations, and if so, how these would be characterised and explained. To this end, I set out to interview all 43 chief constables in office in England and Wales, about their careers, background and views on a wide range of policing issues. I will not elaborate here on the process of gaining access and setting up these interviews. Suffice to say that I was successful in obtaining the agreement of ACPO and the Home Office to approach individual chief officers. Despite dire warnings from cognoscenti I received an overwhelmingly positive amount of co-operation, and in most cases a warm, occasionally eager, welcome.[59] Four chiefs immediately refused to be interviewed when approached. One other agreed initially, but then declined following widespread controversy about some much publicised remarks of his. To date I have completed interviews with 38 chiefs. I have two more arranged in the near future, having succeeded in negotiating co-operation from two erstwhile refusals. I therefore hope to end up with at least 40 completed interviews. The data not only constitute a representative sample but a virtual census. The interviews lasted for an average of one-and-a-half hours, none appreciably less, and some considerably more. With one exception they were taped. The result is a high pile of transcripts, which since many of the questions were open-ended, is a long and laborious process to analyse. I have fully analysed so far only the demographic parts of the interview. The opinions are still in the process of being analysed, so any conclusions I give about these are tentative and subject to revision.

The background of chief constables

Table 1 shows that the social backgrounds of chief constables are not wildly divergent from police officers in general, nor the population at large. The majority (55.3 per cent.) had fathers whose work careers were spent mainly in skilled manual jobs, with 68.4 per cent. having fathers who were in manual jobs for most of their careers. The majority of the rest (21 per cent. overall) were in routine non-manual jobs. However nearly half (45 per cent.) of their fathers experienced occupational mobility during their own careers, and by the time the chiefs were 18, only 50 per cent. remained in manual work. About a third had fathers who ended up in managerial or professional positions (31.5 per cent. and 2.5 per cent. respectively).

This experience of upward social mobility is a characteristic of the police in general.[60] But it is far more marked amongst chief officers. Not only have they themselves moved up into the Registrar General's Class II. Their initial pre-police occupations were predominantly non-manual (51 per cent. overall, with 29 per cent. having no previous job). Their own adult children exhibit even more marked mobility (allowing for the distortions of parental pride). None are in manual occupations, and over two-thirds are in professional or managerial ones.

Comparing this with the sample of the Federated ranks in an earlier study in terms of father's occupation at age 18, Table 1 shows that the chiefs differed slightly but not enormously in the direction of having higher status fathers. But the difference is not marked, and is the result of the chiefs' father's own occupational mobility.

The proportion of chief constables with police fathers (13 per cent.) is the same as in the Federated ranks (14 per cent.). But 37 per cent. mentioned some police relative as an influence on joining. Interestingly 17 per cent. of their children have followed their footsteps into the police (18 per cent. have at least one child in the police, and there are a few three-generation police families).

The conclusion is clear: the chief constables of today are drawn predominantly from skilled working-class backgrounds, and have a family tradition very much marked by upward social mobility, over three generations. Chief constables can fairly be characterised as a "working-class elite."

This is reflected in their educational experiences, shown in Table 2. The chiefs show a remarkable level of educational achievement compared to the norm for their class of origin, and to the general police level. I found in an earlier study that

> "policemen...have done rather better educationally than other children from manual or lower level backgrounds."

Twenty per cent. of lower grade non-manual and skilled manual children born in the late 1930s went to grammar or independent schools but half of the lower-ranked police in that study had done so. But of current chief constables, Table 2 shows 85.1 per cent. had. Moreover, my earlier study showed that while the Federated ranks had done better than normal for their class of origin in terms of type of school attended, they did not do well in terms of school-leaving qualifications. But this is not true of chief constables. Only 13 per cent. of chief constables left school with no qualifications, compared with 28.6 per cent. of the lower ranks. Most chief constables left with some "O" levels or school certificate passes.

In the 1962 Royal Commission, anxiety was expressed that there was "no recent instance of a university graduate entering the service" (para. 308). This has been partly rectified because 12 per cent. of the current intake of recruits are graduates, and 4.45 per cent. of all police are.[61] But the chief constables are from earlier generations, and none entered the police with a degree. However, over a quarter acquired degrees during their service. Half of these degrees were obtained through the Bramshill Scholarship scheme, whereby the most successful students on the Special Course at Bramshill go to University on police scholarships. The majority of the other degrees were either London externals or Open University degrees, with a few gained by force secondments. In addition, to these degrees, several chief constables have university diplomas, usually in criminology or management.

All this confirms the image of chief constables derived from looking at their social origins. They are predominantly drawn from the upwardly mobile, meritocratically achieving, skilled working class.

Orientation to work

Most of the chiefs were set on a police career from a relatively young age. Although 71 per cent. had worked outside the force before joining, only five had worked for more than two years at anything else. 90 per cent. had experience of military service, but of these the overwhelming majority (85 per cent.) had only done National Service.

Career histories

84 per cent. of the chiefs had joined by the age of 22, and all before the age of 25, as Table 3 shows. However, my earlier study showed that of the same generation in the Federated ranks, over one-third joined *after* the age of 25. Most of the current chief constables (68 per cent.) joined before 1954, and only one later than 1960. Their reasons for joining are predominantly an attraction to the job itself: 54 per cent. gave purely non-instrumental reasons, 30 per cent. mixed, with only 16 per cent. instrumental. This is unusual in their generation. My earlier research found that of recruits joining before 1960, 41 per cent. gave non-instrumental, and 30 per cent. instrumental reasons. Furthermore, while the main instrumental reason mentioned by the lower ranks was security, for the chief constable it was more likely to be the attraction of a career. (Though only two thought they would end up as a chief constable).

Most of the chiefs were overwhelmingly satisfied with their careers. All said they were, and 76 per cent. said they would rejoin if starting all over again.[62]

Thus most of the chiefs had looked to policing for an intrinsically interesting career, and had found what they were looking for.

Experiences in the job

Most police officers are "locals" not "cosmopolitans" in the sociological jargon. They have spent most if not all of their lives in the force area where they work. This is decidedly not true of chief constables. Indeed this is explicit policy. Regulations prevent a person serving more than two of the three ACPO ranks in the same force.

Consequently all chiefs will have served in at least one other force during their careers. In fact only four have served in only one other force, *i.e.* the minimal movement necessary. As Table 4 shows 50 per cent. have served in two others, and 40 per cent. in three or more others. Most will have experience of a mixture of city and county forces. Nine have only worked in city forces, but only three have only county experience although most forces are county ones. Interestingly, as many as 40 per cent. have served in the Met. (usually as the Force they initially joined and worked most of their careers in). It still seems to be the pattern, as in the early history of provincial city policy, that the Met. provides their senior officers!

Almost all will have had experience of at least one of the command courses at the Police Staff College, Bramshill. Only two of the present chiefs have not been on the Senior Command Course. 16 per cent. have been on the Special Course for potential high-flyers amongst constables, which since it only started in 1962, is a high proportion of those chiefs young enough to be eligible for it. In addition to these national elite training courses several (16 per cent.) have been on the Royal College of Defence Studies Course, an invitations-only one-year course primarily for senior military officers, diplomats and civil servants.

In terms of careers and training, chief constables, unlike their subordinates, are decidedly (and by design) "cosmopolitans" not "locals." By the time they reach ACPO rank they will have developed a network of national contacts and experiences.

Most will have had a variety of work experience within their forces. It is a commonly held myth that specialist detectives are unlikely to reach the top. In fact, 34 per cent. of my sample have been detectives for more than half of their careers. But the majority had a mixed bag of operational experience, albeit predominantly in uniform territorial patrol work.

For most, promotion was rapid, at any rate after the first hurdle of promotion to sergeant, which took seven years on average. The average time for all other promotions was two–three years. The average age of appointment as chief constable was 50. The youngest appointment was 42, and the oldest 56. Only four were appointed chief constable before 45, and most were appointed in their late 40s. They had been chief constables for somewhere between a few months and 12 years, and on average had been in post for five years. The longevity in service of earlier generations has disappeared.

53 per cent. had been appointed chief constable while being deputy in another force, and 24 per cent. had been promoted from deputy in the same force. Three had been chief constables in smaller forces, three had held ACPO rank in the Met. when appointed, and two had been respectively Commandant and Deputy Commandant at Bramshill.

What conclusions can be drawn from the demographic profile of chief constables? It seems that their origins, education, occupational socialisation, and career patterns indicate that they do satisfy Mills' first criterion of a unitary elite. They overwhelmingly come from a similar background, the upwardly mobile, educationally successful, skilled working class. They had similar (though atypical) education experiences; had similar initial approaches to the police, and were singled out comparatively early on for rapid advancement. They will have got to know each other through moving between forces, and passing through the Police Staff College, and other shared training experiences. They will have been exposed to the same nationally designed curriculum for senior officers. If this is not enough, none will have been appointed chief constable unless they have first been approved by the Home Office as suitable to be on the short-list interviewed by the Police Authority, and after selection their appointment must be formally approved by the Home Secretary.[63]

Small wonder there are no publicly aired disputes between chief constables and central government. The chances of a rogue appointment being made are clearly miniscule.

In the interview material, the orientation to central rather than local government comes through fairly consistently. While most chiefs wish to cultivate good relations with their police authorities, and indeed believe they enjoy them, at best this means they will seek to persuade them to accept their views if disagreements arise, not that they will accept the authority's approach. This comes out clearly, for example, in a question I asked about the use of plastic bullets. Most chief constables would use them if necessary, even in the face of police authority opposition, although they would prefer to carry them along by persuasion. The following approach is typical:

"A lot depends on the circumstances. To start with I wouldn't be concerned about the police authority. If it came down to my professional judgment. It all depends, the scenario is not always the same . . . If you do have your elected members at the scene . . . your community relations council, there is nothing like them seeing what the situation is . . . If not, what you're going to do is make the decision, go ahead, use it, and then provide the evidence afterwards."

This indicates that while consensus is preferred, when the buck has to stop the decision is the chief constable's regardless of the police authority's views.

This is not the attitude taken towards the Home Office. While many rail at this, often bitterly, it is recognised that the Home Office issues many regulations which in effect have to be obeyed. Even its nominally advisory circulars can be ignored only at the chief constable's peril. While disagreements may be strongly argued, this time when the buck stops, it is normally the chief who backs down. Again a typical quote:

"We would all stand and fight our corner to the death if we felt that we were right and they (the Home Office) were wrong, and they were trying to manipulate us or instruct us, but on the other hand one would wish certainly to not be too far out of step with the thinking of the Home Office, who of course are influenced by the government of the day."

For all the pride that chief constables express in their independence, and all the testimony they pay to the value attached to good relations with local authorities, the overall sense I have is that their professional colleagues—and it is ACPO and the HMI that are seen as their peers—are the prime reference group. The Home Office is often resented, and its authority may not be respected. But at the end of the day it has power, as well as the legitimacy of an electoral mandate. The local authority is not seen in this light. Preferably it can be educated to understand the professional point of view. But if not it is that professional judgment which counts. To an extent this picture is overdrawn and oversimplified. There are individual variations, and some chiefs are more fiercely independent, and more locally oriented, than others. But in the main the prime reference group is the national professional one, and the Home Office is accepted as boss, however resentfully.

Conclusion

In a sense my conclusion confirms the conspiracy theory with which I began. Chief constables are a national power elite of considerable significance, though I do not think ACPO itself is their unequivocally supported mouthpiece in the way the Duncan Campbell thesis implies. But I believe the influence is predominantly government over chiefs, rather than the reverse. The main two examples offered by the counter-thesis are:

(1) Robert Mark's account in his autobiography of how he and ACPO succeeded in making Michael Foot as Employment Secretary back down over a proposed change in picketing law. But the power here derived not from ACPO *per se*, but the threat to "go public" over an issue where populist sentiment would back the police, and the result would damage Labour electorally.[64]

(2) The Tactical Options Manual, developed by ACPO without parliamentary or public knowledge or discussion. But here (as with the more robust approach to public order generally) the police were responding to government anxiety about public disorder after 1972 and 1981, and often rather reluctantly.[65]

The issue is hard to resolve finally, because of the general lack of profound disagreement on crunch issues between central government (especially a Conservative one?) and chief constables. What if this did come? What if a Labour Government implemented the policy to give local authorities clear operational control of policy? Some chiefs no doubt would resign, as did Robert Mark over the 1976 Police Act establishing the Police Complaints Board. But those (the majority I suspect) who remained in post would simply have to go along with the new arrangements, however reluctantly, as they have done with such central initiatives (unwelcome in many forces) as consultative committees, lay visitors and the procedures of the Police and Criminal Evidence Act.

If my conclusions are correct, the implication is that what the Inns of Court Conservative and Unionist Society, Professor Goodhart and others forecast in 1962 has come about. Rejecting a *de iure* national police force, we have ended up with the substance of one. But without the structure of accountability for it which the explicit proposals embodied. You cannot have accountability for something that is not supposed to be there.

Arguably attempts to relocalise control are like pushing a stream uphill. The key impetus for central influence has come not so much over routine crime, law enforcement or order maintenance, though the pressures are there too in the name both of efficiency, and of fairness as uniformity. The main sources of central control have been in the course of national labour disputes and other serious public disorder. This is not only true of the last 15 years. Jane Morgan's recent study of the police and labour disputes in 1900–1939 demonstrates the covert nationalisation of control of public order policing occurring already in the first three decades of this century.[66]

My final submission is that this trend cannot really be reversed. Only by recognising it and accepting it can some accountability over national policies be achieved. Partly this would be to Parliament. But beyond that, John Alderson's suggestion during the miners' strike should be seriously considered: "a national (emergency) police committee" comprising the Home Secretary, representatives of local police authorities, ACPO and arguably the Police Federation.[67] This should not only be an emergency committee, but be responsible for reviewing and formulating national policies and guidelines for policing. (These would also be discussed in Parliament of course, though detailed work would be done by the Committee.)

It is unlikely, however, that such a proposal would be politically feasible, any more than local control, in the present climate. Why should the Government change a position which gives it power without responsibility, a most unroyal prerogative?

Table 1: Social Origins and Mobility of Chief Constables

Father's Class When Son 18 (%)

I	II	IIIN	IIIM	IV	V	NA
2.6	31.5	15.7	44.7	2.6	2.6	—

N=38

Father's Class Earlier (%)

I	II	IIIN	IIIM	IV	V	NA
—	5.3	21	55.3	5.3	7.8	5.3

Own Pre-Police Jobs (%)

I	II	IIIN	IIIM	IV	V	None
11	8	32	21	—	—	29

N=38

Adult Children's Jobs (%)

I	II	IIIN	IIIM	IV	V	NA	Police
16.9	52.1	12.7	—	—	—	1	16.9

N=71

Mobile Fathers: 45%   Police Fathers: 13%   Police Family: 37%

Federated
Ranks (Reiner 1978)
N=168

Father's Class When 18 (%)

I	II	IIIN	IIIM	IV	V	NA	Police
2.9	14.9	16.7	36.9	19.1	3.6	6.5	14

Table 2: Education of Chiefs

School	Elementary	Secondary	Comprehensive	Technical	Grammar	Private
Chiefs N=38	7.9	5.2	—	5.2	78.9	5.2
Federated Ranks N=168	34		6.5	7.7	45.9	6

Age left School	Elementary	Secondary	Comprehensive	Technical	Grammar
Chiefs	14	15	16	17	18
Chiefs	7.9	7.9	42.1	15.8	23.7
Federated Ranks	19.6	14.9	45.8	11.9	7.7

School Leaving Qualification	None	School Cert.	'O'	'A'	CSE
Chiefs	13.1	50	23.7	15.8	—
Federated Ranks	28.6	—	54.8	4.2	12.5

Degrees %	Chiefs	Deputy Chiefs	Assistant Chiefs	Current Recruits	All Police
	26	40	37	12	4.45
	N=43	N=43	N=89		

Table 3: Career

Date Joined
%
N=38

-1949	1950-4	1955-9	1960-
22	46	30	3

Aged Joined
%
N=38

19	20	21	22	24	25
5	30	30	19	5	3

When Serjeant
%

-5 years	6/7 years	8/9 years	10+ years
26	29	37	8

Age When Chief

-45	46-50	50+
4	17	17

Present Age

46-9	50-4	55-59	60+
3	12	18	5

Years As Chief

-3	4/5	6-9	10+
12	13	7	6

Table 4: Work Experience

No. of Previous Forces

1	2	3	4	5
4	19	12	3	3

Types of Forces

County only	City only	Mix	Met.
3	9	26	15

Specialist or Uniform

CID	CID=Uniform	Uniform
13	4	21

National Courses

Senior Command Course	Other Command Course	Special	Royal College of Defence Studies
36	34	6	6

Previous Post When Appointed Chief

Deputy Chief Elsewhere	Deputy Chief Same Force	Chief in Other Force	ACPO in Met.	Other
20	10	3	3	2

NOTES

[1] *New Statesman* May 23, 1986, pp. 3–4.

[2] *cf.* also Duncan Campbell's programme on ACPO in his celebrated *Secret Society* BBC2 series, and his accompanying article "Policing: A Power in the Land" *New Statesman* May 8, 1987, pp. 11–12.

[3] Freeman, M.D.A. (1984) "Law and Order in 1984" *Current Legal Problems* (1984), London: Stevens, pp. 175–231.

[4] Para. 102, p. 34.

[5] Reiner, R. *The Politics of the Police* (1985) Brighton: Wheatsheaf.

[6] Reiner, R. "Who Are The Police?" (1982), *Political Quarterly*, 53:2, April–June, pp. 165–180.

[7] *New Statesman*, May 8, 1987, p. 11.

[8] Reiner, *op. cit.*, p. 174.

[9] pp. 157–181.

[10] The Metropolitan and City of London chiefs have the title Commissioner, and hold neither the offices of "constable" nor "chief constable," as defined by the Police Act 1964. *cf.* Lustgarten, 1986, p. 34. Their everyday role is, however, substantially the same as provincial chief constables, and they belong to ACPO, despite the differences in constitutional position.

[11] *cf.* Critchley 1978, p. 125.

[12] Lustgarten, L. *The Governance of Police*, (1986) London: Sweet and Maxwell, pp. 36–37.

[13] Critchley, T.A. *A History of the Police in England and Wales*, (1978), London: Constable, p. 125.

[14] Found for example in Critchley 1978, pp. 131–133 and Marshall, 1965 pp. 28–29.

[15] Lustgarten, *op. cit.* p. 39.

[16] Brogden, M. *The Police: Autonomy and Consent*, (1982), London: Academic Press, p. 62.

[17] Jefferson, T. and Grimshaw, R. *Controlling the Constable*, London: Muller, pp. 41–44.

[18] Critchley, *op. cit.* p. 124.

[19] Steedman, C. *Policing the Victorian Community*, (1984), London: Routledge.

[20] Wall, D. "Chief Constables: A Changing Elite" in Mawby, R. (ed.) *Policing Britain*, Plymouth Polytechnic: Department of Social and Political Studies, pp. 84–100.

[21] *Ibid.* p. 87.

[22] *Ibid.* p. 93.

[23] *Ibid.* p. 95.

[24] Critchley, *op. cit.* p. 142.

[25] Ross, G. *Oxford City Police 1869–1968* (1979), Oxford: Oxford Publishing Co., pp. 35–36.

[26] Marshall, G., Critchley, *op. cit.* Chap. 9; Reiner 1985: 48–51; Oliver: "Police Accountability Revisited" in Butler, D. and Halsey, A.H. (eds.) *Policy and Politics* London: Macmillan, Chap. 2.

[27] *New Statesman*, June 8, 1962.

[28] Lustgarten: *The Governance of Police* (1986), London: Sweet and Maxwell; Lambert: *Police Powers and Accountability*, (1986), London: Croom Helm, Chap. 2; Leigh, L. *Police Powers in England and Wales* (2nd ed.) (1985), London: Butterworths, Chap. 1; Clayton, R. and Tomlinson, H. *Civil Actions Against the Police* (1987), London: Sweet and Maxwell, Chaps. 1 and 13.

[29] Marshall, G. *Police and Government*, (1965), London: Methuen, p. 98.

[30] [1930] 2 K.B. 364.

[31] [1968] 2 Q.B. 118.

[32] *Per* Lord Denning, *ibid.* at 136.

[33] [1968] 2 Q.B. 118 at 135–136.

[34] *Op. cit.* pp. 64–65.

[35] Marshall, G. "Police Accountability Revisited" in Butler, D. and Halsey, A.H. (eds.) *Policy and Politics* (1978), London: Macmillan, pp. 58, 59.

[36] *R.* v. *Chief Constable of the Devon and Cornwall Constabulary, ex p. C.E.G.B.* [1981] 3 All E.R. 826 at 833.

[37] *Ibid.* at p. 833.

[38] *Ibid.* at p. 835.

[39] *The Times*, November 1, 1986 and *Police* December 1986, 16–18.

[40] *Per* Sir John Donaldson M.R.

[41] See below, note 55.

[42] *Op. cit.* p. 67.

[43] *Op. cit.* p. 177. But for some recent support for centralisation *cf.* Zellick; 1986: p. 19.

[44] pp. 45–46.

[45] *e.g.* paras. 121, 122.

[46] *e.g.* the Inns of Court Conservative and Unionist Society: para. 122, p. 42.

[47] Para. 144, para. 146.

[48] Para. 150, p. 50.

[49] Para. 230, p. 72.

[50] Critchley *op. cit.* 286.

[51] Loveday, B. *The Role and Effectiveness of the Merseyside Police Committee* (1985), Merseyside County Council, pp. 131–132. "Central Co-ordination, Police Authorities and the Miners' Strike," (1986), *Political Quarterly*, 57:1, January–March, pp. 60–61.

[52] Morgan, R. "Police Consultative Groups: The Implications for the Governance of the Police (1986) *Political Quarterly* 57:1, January–March, pp. 83–87. Morgan and Maggs: *Setting the P.A.C.E. Police-Community Consultation Arrangements in England and Wales* (1985) University of Bath: Centre for the Study of Social Policy.

[53] Loveday, B. "The Joint Boards," *Policing* (1987), 3:3, Autumn, pp. 196–213.

[54] *Ibid.* pp. 211–212.

[55] *The Times* November 19, 1987, *The Independent* November 19, 1987.

[56] *e.g.* Loveday 1985. *op cit.* n. 51.

[57] Wall, *op. cit.* p. 98.

[58] Mills, C.W. *The Power Elite* (1956), New York: Oxford University Press, pp. 18–20.

[59] The details will be elaborated in a forthcoming book to be published by Oxford University Press.

[60] Reiner, R. *The Blue-Coated Worker*, (1978), Cambridge: Cambridge University Press, p. 150.

[61] H.M.I. Report 1985.

[62] This is a level that compares with professionals, and is far more than the norm for police 51 per cent.: Reiner 1978, p. 173.

[63] Police Act 1964, s.4(2).

[64] In the way that American police have acted as a powerful lobby by mobilising "law and order" sentiment. (Reiner 1980).

[65] Reiner, R. *The Politics of the Police* (1985), Brighton: Wheatsheaf, pp. 71, 72.

[66] Morgan, J. *Conflict and Order: The Police and Labour Disputes in England and Wales 1900–39* (1987), Oxford: Oxford University Press.

[67] *The Guardian* September 13, 1984, p. 16.

Labour Courts: Some Comparative Perspectives

BOB HEPPLE

The Lifting of a Taboo

Edmund Burke once said that most policy decisions involve choosing between the disagreeable and the intolerable. Some of our leading labour lawyers now find the activities of the common law courts so intolerable that they are willing to contemplate the disagreeable vision of a British labour court.

Lord Wedderburn[1] has recently said that "if labour law is to escape from the clutches of common law thinking and procedures, the compass seems to point in a direction in which few instinctively wish to travel. That is (dare one say it?) towards labour courts." Lord McCarthy agrees "that attempts to restrict the influence of common law norms may not be possible without the creation of new and separate institutions," and says that "if we go down that road we have to face the fact that at the apex of such a structure there would need to be some kind of labour court. Those blessed with long memories or faint hearts, or both, will protest: he wants to dig up the NIRC! I can only reply that if this proves to be the only way to ensure that the will of Parliament prevails, then I for one am prepared to face the prospect."[2]

It is clear, however, that Wedderburn and McCarthy are not advocating, as Sir Pat Lowry did,[3] some kind of "son of NIRC" or a Donaldson-court in which the judges aim to tell the public who is "right" in an industrial dispute.[4] They want a new kind of judiciary who will assert and develop an autonomous labour law freed from the property-based concepts, procedures and habits of the common law. The overall dimensions of this new labour law have not yet been defined but might include a new concept of the

169

employment relationship,[5] which breaks free from the prerogatives of the proprietor to organise and distribute work and the
status of subordination of the worker. Above all, it would be
distinguished by its collective character and its avoidance of
legally-imposed solutions.[6]

Against this vision of an autonomous labour law administered
by a variety of specialised bodies, including a labour court, stands
the dominant political philosophy of our time, which sees the
common law principles of contract and tort, administered by the
common law courts, as the best way of meeting "the needs of a
changing economy" so as to allow flexibility to employers.
Graham Mather argues that the privatisation of employment
protection law (*e.g.* through the growth of self-employment)
"casts doubt on the suitability of statute law to bear the brunt of
regulation." He believes that alongside the individualisation of the
labour market, the "common law approach works . . . because it
can accommodate a healthy differentiation in individual terms and
conditions." He suspects that "the common law is too deeply
entrenched in the bosom of the judges, and our social institutions,
to be excluded by a few strokes of the draftsman's pen. The NIRC
was a foreign body in the juridical corpus, which promptly began
to show rejection symptoms. Re-establishing a Labour Court
system would be to build upon some increasingly far-fetched
fictions."[7]

The outcome of the General Election in June 1987 means that
Britain is not going to have new labour courts in the immediate
future. Indeed, even had there been a Labour government we may
not have embarked on the path towards autonomous labour
courts. But the debate opened up by Lord Wedderburn indicates,
as he says, that "the topic must lose its taboo."[8] Scholars can and
should seek to explain why we do not have an autonomous labour
court and why, possibly, we shall never have one.

One approach to this question is through comparative law.
Labour courts exist in a number of Western European countries.
They are remarkable chiefly for their diversity, in terms of
jurisdiction, composition and procedure and in their relationship
to the ordinary courts. In another group of countries, such as Italy
and the Netherlands, both individual and collective disputes are
dealt with exclusively by the ordinary courts, and there appears to
be no pressure in those countries for a system of specialised labour
courts.

In this paper, I shall endeavour first to describe the special
characteristics of labour courts in France, Belgium, Sweden and
Germany that distinguish them from the ordinary courts, with a

few comparative remarks about the British industrial tribunals. Secondly, I shall examine the major arguments in favour of labour courts from the viewpoint of experience in those countries in comparison with countries where there are no labour courts. These are arguments based on tripartism, expertise and autonomy. Finally, I shall make some general observations, in the light of this comparison, about the prospects in Britain.

What are labour courts?

In the traditional morphology of procedures for the settlement of labour disputes adjudication is distinguished from arbitration[9] but one searches in vain for a clear modern account of the features of labour courts which differentiate them from ordinary courts. In this context, by "ordinary" courts I mean those which exercise general jurisdiction in civil disputes under a particular legal system. One may attempt to draw out the divergences between these ordinary courts and special labour courts by examining a number of general features of adjudication as a form of dispute settlement.

(1) *The Judge Applies the Law*

This is true of both ordinary courts and special labour courts. The law may have its source in legislation, or in a collective agreement or in an individual contract of employment. In France these are all called "judicial conflicts" whether tried in the *conseils de prudhommes* or in the ordinary courts.[10] The distinction between these legal disputes over rights, and economic disputes over interests arising in the course of collective bargaining over the terms to be embodied in a collective agreement was introduced in the Weimar Republic, when special *Schligtungs* [arbitration] boards were established and it became necessary to mark off their jurisdiction from that of the labour courts. The distinction made by Jacobi, a leading labour lawyer of that time, was that disputes over rights were to be decided by "legal judgment" according to the legal order, while disputes over interests were to be settled by adjustment according to the interests of the parties.[11] Disputes over interests involved non-justiciable issues: the legal system laid down no rules as to their outcome and they were therefore outside the scope of any kind of court. Conciliation, mediation and arbitration were regarded as the principal means for their settlement. In disputes of rights about the existence, validity or interpretation of a collective agreement or individual contract of employment, on the other hand, it was assumed that there was some "correct" or "legal" solution which a court could discover.

This distinction was adopted in Denmark, Norway and Sweden, where it is closely linked to the idea that disputes of right should be resolved by a court and not by industrial action.

However, the distinction in itself gives no clue as to why some disputes of right are dealt with in ordinary courts and some in special labour courts. In Sweden, for example, the competence of the Labour Court is limited to disputes between the parties to a collective agreement or the conditions of an employee who is a member of a trade union, while disputes between an unorganised employee and his employer go to an (ordinary) District Court in the first instance with an appeal to the Labour Court. In other words, the jurisdiction is determined by whether the interests of collective parties may be directly affected. In the United Kingdom, disputes of rights arising under a number of statutes are within the exclusive jurisdiction of industrial tribunals while disputes of rights arising under individual contracts of employment are dealt with by the ordinary courts. In France, too, there is a fragmentation of courts dealing with disputes of rights, while in Italy and the Netherlands all disputes of rights are within the competence of the ordinary courts. Only in Germany do we find all labour disputes of rights being dealt with in the labour courts.

If both ordinary courts and special labour courts apply the law, is the distinction perhaps to be found in the extent to which considerations of industrial "equity" and legal precedents are taken into account in the decision-making process? In France, according to Blanc-Jouvan, "labour court judges use strictly legal methods of reasoning, that is, they apply the law and resolve a dispute in compliance with existing statutory provisions or contractual clauses. Like any other judge, they do not ignore legal provisions to meet the alleged requirements of natural justice or of the public interest."[12] In Sweden, according to Schmidt, the first president of the Labour Court "consistently took the view that the court should apply strict principles of law. Administration of justice was not a matter of arriving at a compromise as in conciliation." To Schmidt's knowledge (in 1971) only two decisions of the Labour Court could be characterised as based on considerations of equity calling for a compromise solution.[13] Moreover, he observed that the Labour Court was even less flexible than the Supreme Court in its approach to precedent.[14]

There is, perhaps, a parallel with the British Employment Appeal Tribunal which at one time developed a set of "guidelines" as to the interpretation of what constituted "equity and the substantial merits of the case" in unfair dismissal cases, only to have the Court of Appeal reassert that the tribunal should act as an "industrial jury" virtually unconstrained by precedent.[15]

By way of contrast, one may consider the way in which the Italian *pretori* have utilised "political mediation, rather than strictly legal adjudication" in their decisions.[16] The *pretori* are generally young and are more sympathetic to workers than one finds in labour court judges in other countries. The national average of decisions in favour of the worker by the *pretori* (who are career judges) is three to one, compared to about four to one against the worker in the British industrial tribunals, in which the trade union member dissents in less than 4 per cent. of cases. There is a long-standing conflict between these *pretori* and the *Corte di Cassazione* which tends to be more cautious in its judgments than the *pretori* particularly in respect of collective action.[17] But the lesson is clear, that "equity" or sympathy for the worker (albeit a paternalistic one) is not the monopoly of labour courts. It has far more to do with the age, background and training of the judiciary and the social, legal and political climate in which they operate than with the existence of a separate labour court, a point to which I shall return when discussing the composition of labour courts.

(2) *Disputes are Bipolar*

By this is meant that litigation is organised as a contest between two or more specific parties and is decided on a "winner-take-all" basis. Related to this are the features of a lawsuit as a self-contained episode, initiated and controlled by the parties and in which the direct impact of the judgment is on the parties alone.[18] In this model of adjudication, the judge is a neutral umpire who finds the facts and applies the law. The judge deals only with those issues which the parties wish to raise. The court's concern is to resolve private disputes about individual transactions. The dispute is about a completed set of events. Did they occur? Who was at "fault?" The remedies are usually financial, the transfer of money payments from one party to another. They rarely involve prospective relief or the performance of an act at the suit of workers, like reinstatement.

How far do lawsuits in special labour courts diverge from this model of the traditional civil court? First, let us consider the parties. In some labour court countries, a fundamental distinction is drawn between individual and collective disputes. The prime example is France, in which a dispute is regarded as individual if its object concerns only one employer and one employee, without affecting a group or collectivity on either side. In other words, it is a dispute of rights which have their source in the individual employment relationship. It is usually initiated by the employee because his subordinate position puts him or her in greater need of legal remedies. A dispute retains its character as an individual one even though several individuals have similar claims arising from the same circumstances. On the other hand, a dispute is treated as a collective one when it has its origin in the rights or interests of a group of workers and is likely to affect the situation of all members of the group. In other words, it may be a dispute of rights or of interests, but a collective group (organised or unorganised) is effectively a party to the dispute. It remains collective even if the workers are opposed by only a single employer. The jurisdiction of the *conseils de prudhommes* is limited to individual labour disputes. In this sense, the French labour courts are no different from any other court concerned with bipolar disputes.

However, in practice the distinction has proved to be extremely ambiguous and difficult to apply. So far as subject-matter is concerned, a dispute may involve both the violation of an individual right and a collective interest (*e.g.* selection of workers for redundancy which turns on the application of a custom or practice that is directly applicable to individuals through their contracts of employment). So far as the nature of the parties is concerned, it seems that the characterisation as individual or collective depends very much on the way in which the parties see their dispute. If several individuals institute simultaneous proceedings, even if these are consolidated the dispute remains individual so long as the merits of each are considered separately and not as part of a collective group. On the other hand, art. L135–4 of the Labour Code while allowing individuals to initiate actions also permits organisations whose collective interests may be affected to intervene in the proceedings. According to Blanc-Jouvan,[19] parties often prefer to classify the dispute as "individual" because of the existence of more satisfactory procedures for settlement of such disputes than there are for collective ones. Better still, wherever possible they classify the dispute as both individual and collective so allowing them to choose the procedure they regard as most suitable and even to use both procedures simultaneously or successively.

In Sweden, by way of contrast, collective rights and interests occupy the dominant position in the proceedings of the Labour Court. So far as subject-matter is concerned, it has already been pointed out that this relates to disputes over a collective agreement, disputes covered by the Joint Regulation of Working Life Act and other disputes between an employer or employers' organisation and a trade union or its members. Disputes between an unorganised worker and his employer, on the other hand, go in the first instance to an (ordinary) District Court. So far as the parties to Labour Court proceedings are concerned, the right of representation belongs to the collective parties. An individual member first has to show that his or her union has refused to bring the claim before the member is allowed to do this himself or herself. A union has the right to represent its member as defendant and the union answers for the member who does not himself or herself defend the case. A plaintiff who brings an action against a member is obliged to join the union as a party. Linked to these rules about collective representation is another, that a claim may not be tried until collective negotiations under the agreed or statutory procedures have been exhausted.

What are the justifications for the union's right of representation in Sweden? Put another way, how can one draw a line between the union's authority to represent the member and the member's independent right by virtue of his or her contract of employment? Schmidt[20] explains the union's right of representation as the logical corollary of its power to conclude legally enforceable collective agreements which bind the member. The union must represent the member in order to ensure that the agreement is properly applied in a way which does not have adverse repercussions for other members. This apparently simple principle has, however, given rise to thorny problems as to how far the union can control or compromise the vested rights of individual members. The Act on the Joint Regulation of Working Life of 1976 strengthened the individual's position, by allowing the member extended time limits in which to claim after the time limit applicable to the union has expired.[21] Moreover, when a member's rights under statute (*e.g.* the Paid Holidays Act) or an individual contract (*e.g.* for an amount additional to that laid down in the collective agreement) are in issue, the union must have authorisation from the individual before disposing of his or her claim.

In Germany, the labour courts deal with all labour disputes, whether individual or collective (with the sole exception of criminal matters). But the very different structure of German labour law from Swedish labour law has the result that the union does not "own" the grievance. Individual plaintiffs may appear in the lower tier of the German labour court without representation, as they do in British industrial tribunals. In both Germany and Britain, the parties may choose to be represented by their associations and this is done by a somewhat higher proportion of West German litigants than British ones.[22]

One sees, therefore, that it is possible to structure the jurisdiction of and access to a labour court in ways which are either similar to or divergent from the traditional bipolar model. Both jurisdiction and access must reflect the organic structure of the particular system of labour law. When one compares non-labour court countries, one is equally impressed with the fact that the bipolar model is not an essential feature of litigation. Compare Italy and the United States, for example.

In Italy, the only disputes falling under the jurisdiction of the ordinary courts are those concerning "private subordinate relationships." Although they may involve the interpretation of a collective agreement, the court's decision is binding only for the single case and judicial interpretations may differ from case to case. The claim has to be brought by individuals although these may be identical and may affect a collective group. On the other hand, in the United States, the bipolar model has declined in public law litigation, for example relating to job discrimination, in the federal courts. This is typified, above all, by the class action. Under this procedure a group of individual plaintiffs (the class) who have similar complaints against a common defendant may join together to pursue their claims. The group is represented by one or more plaintiffs who sue on their own behalf and on behalf of the group. This not only gives the plaintiffs a sense of emotional solidarity when suing powerful corporations, but it also enables them to share the costs. Furthermore, it eases the burden of proof. For example, in discrimination cases, proof of the pattern or practice of discrimination is eased by admitting evidence of discrimination against any member of the class and there is wide scope for discovery of documents and other information. Any member of the class can intervene. It is not necessary for each member of the class to prove his loss—there is a wide range of techniques including class-wide calculation of damages. Other features of this new kind of public law litigation in the United States, are the willingness of the federal courts to depart from the "winner-takes-all" approach, to fashion equitable remedies such as the mandatory injunction requiring affirmative action. The court's decree sets out to change future behaviour, and the American judges have become involved in drafting the decree, in the negotiations before its terms are finalised and in supervising compliance on a continuing basis.[23]

The point of these comparisons is that a departure from the bipolar model is not a peculiarity of labour courts. In the right circumstances, even ordinary courts can develop a more "collective" approach, one which draws in parties other than the immediate litigants, which is not purely adjudicative but is also predictive, which fashions remedies on flexible lines, and negotiates rather than imposes that remedy.

(3) *Accessible, Informal and Speedy Procedures*

There can be no doubt that one of the principal motives for setting up special courts to deal with labour matters has been the belief that these will be more accessible, informal, cheap and expeditious than ordinary courts. Yet one finds that the rather shallow criticism of "legalism" is made of labour courts in most countries— and even of grievance arbitration under collective agreements in the United States[24]. In France, the growth of legalism is said to be associated with the complexity of the substantive law, and delay is due to insufficient courts.[25] In Britain, "legalism" covers a multitude of sins, including the way in which tribunals interpret and apply employment legislation, the degree of formality in the physical arrangements of the tribunal room and the taking of evidence, and the use of adversarial techniques. While industrial tribunals are usually more relaxed and informal than say, a county court, they are far closer to an ordinary court in procedural matters than to a round table conciliation session or an investigative arbitration.

The point is that labour courts differ in procedural respects from ordinary courts only in degree rather than in kind. Once a labour court or tribunal is established as part of the legal system it will have to interpret highly complex statute law in a legal fashion.[26] The adoption of an adversarial or investigative approach—the choice between the "verbal pugilism" of cross-examining advocates[27] and the probing questions of the judge—depends not on the specialist nature of a labour court but on the legal traditions of a particular country. That is why in the countries surveyed in this paper, the investigative approach is usual in labour courts. A similar approach is used in the ordinary courts in those countries, although more opportunities for conciliation and court-imposed mediation are frequently made available in labour courts.

For example in the German labour courts, the first oral pleas are made before the Chairman, at a session designed to achieve a settlement. In the British adversarial system, by comparison, it was thought to be inappropriate to compromise the Chairman's position as "neutral umpire" in this way, and so ACAS has the independent task of attempting to achieve a conciliated settlement. At the hearing itself, the German labour courts rely far more on written briefs than do the British industrial tribunals. This is possible because legal and other forms of representation are more common in the German labour courts than in industrial tribunals—a curious fact when one remembers that, ostensibly at least, the British system claims to be "adversarial" and so has to rely upon adequate representation! A crucial difference between the German and British approaches is that it is the judge, in Germany, who takes the initiative in structuring the issues and arguments; the judge tends to be the most active participant in the courtroom, asking questions of fact and law.[28]

In Italy and the Netherlands, an investigative (or, if you prefer, inquisitorial) type procedure is used by the ordinary courts when dealing with the adjudication of labour disputes. In Italy, the proceedings before the *pretori* are designed to increase speed, informality and accessibility and differ in many important respects from other civil proceedings, but all of this is done within the ordinary system of courts. In the Netherlands, the ordinary *kantonrechters* handle labour cases alongside others and use similar procedures. Despite some criticisms of delay and formality (no more severe than those of British industrial tribunals) there is no pressure in the Netherlands for specialist labour courts.

One must conclude that, although the establishment of labour courts may provide the occasion for an improvement in judicial proceedings there is nothing inherent in specialisation which leads to this improvement. One has but to read the current consultation papers in the Lord Chancellor's Civil Justice Review to see that an inquisitorial, informal, speedy and efficient system can be proposed within the context of the ordinary courts.[29]

(4) *Expert and Specialist Jurisdiction*

One is therefore left with two features which do seem to distinguish labour courts from the ordinary courts. This is their composition and their specialisation in labour disputes. The French *conseils de prudhommes* represent the classic model of "judgment by peers." The *conseillers* are elected (since 1979 by proportional representation) representatives of employers and employees. In other labour court countries the composition is tripartite rather than bipartite, and the industrial expertise is provided in different ways. In Sweden, there are "official" members, chosen for their judicial experience or "specialised knowledge of conditions on the labour market" as well as employer and worker members. In Germany and Belgium there is a career judge with lay judges nominated by the organisations of employers and employees, differing from the British industrial tribunals in the crucial respect that the chairman is generally a life-long specialist in labour law and not, as in Britain, a practitioner who usually has had no previous experience of labour law and industrial relations. By way of comparison with all these labour courts, the judges in the ordinary courts are professional lawyers (in the civil law systems usually career judges) who sit without lay members, although they may in some cases call on expert assessors to assist them.

To conclude, one is bound to say that the only features which clearly demarcate labour courts from the ordinary courts are their expertise and specialisation. Why, then, have some countries chosen to develop such expertise and specialisation in special courts while others have been content to leave this to ordinary courts?

Why Labour Courts?

Three main reasons may be considered.

(1) *Tripartism*

The first labour court—the *conseil de prudhommes* set up by Napoleon I on the petition of the manufacturers of Lyon in 1806—was, in the words of Marcel David,[30] "closer to disciplinary committees than to an arbitral court of some kind." It was made up of manufacturers and foremen. The nature of the *conseils* was transformed under the Second Republic, by a decree of May 27, 1848 which stated that all people exercising a profession, including labourers, could vote and stand in the elections. The principle of parity between manufacturers and all workers in the *conseils* represented a "conquest" for the republicans and workers.[31] Bipartism has remained an essential feature of the French system of labour courts. Decisions are taken by majority vote, and third-party intervention, in the form of a professional judge from the local *tribunal d'instance*, occurs only when there is a deadlock, which is said to be rare in practice. Blanc-Jouvan comments[32] that the "threat of intervention of a professional judge motivates the lay judges to impartiality and objectivity. In other words it is the fear of tripartism that makes bipartism successful or that permits it to operate." Tripartism is advocated in France only by the legal profession and has been successfully resisted by those who believe that it would work to the disadvantage of workers.

The position is different in other labour court countries. The principle of tripartism in special labour courts owes its origin to the historical circumstances in Germany at the time when the persecution of socialists under the Anti-Socialist Act 1875 to 1890 came to an end. The industrial courts (*Gewerberichte*) were set up in 1890, and the commercial courts (*Kaufmannsgerichte*) in 1904. These were tripartite labour courts composed of a professional judge (or in the commercial court a higher civil servant) and lay members, one from the employers' side and the other from the employee's side. These courts had only limited competence. When the first full-scale labour courts were established in 1926, the tripartite structure was retained, at all three levels, the lower *Arbeitsgericht*, the appellate *Landesarbeitsgericht*, and the supreme *Reichsarbeitsgericht*. But, in the *Reichsarbeitsgericht*, which was one division of the Supreme Court, the professional judges were in the majority (three judges and two lay members). This ensured that the professional judges were able to carry on the legal tradition in all important questions.[33] In his celebrated critique of the *Social Ideal of the Supreme Labour Court*,[34] Kahn-Freund, then a judge of the Berlin labour court, described the prevailing attitude of the *Reichsarbeitsgericht* as one of hostility to strikes and the institutions of collective labour law and of admiration for a "petty bourgeois ideal of economic peace" which failed to understand the political idea of labour law.

In the Federal Republic of Germany, the Weimar model of tripartism has been retained. Tripartism, with various minor modifications, was also introduced into Britain in the Munitions Tribunals during the First World War,[35] and revived in the industrial tribunals since 1964. It has also flourished in Sweden since the Labour Court was established in 1928. In Belgium, which started with a bipartite system modelled on the French *conseils de prudhommes*, tripartism is now a pillar of the labour tribunals and labour courts set up since 1970. Indeed, in the majority of countries where they exist, labour courts are tripartite.[36] This may be contrasted with the unipartite character of ordinary courts where, at first instance, a professional judge usually sits alone.

The attractions of tripartism in labour courts have been

differently portrayed at various times. In Imperial Germany, the establishment of tripartite labour courts at a time when unions were not even recognised by employers in the textile and metal industries and the employers still claimed autocratic power to lay down the works rules, had a "strong psychological influence upon the workers: for the first time they were recognised by the state as equal partners in the employment relationship."[37] It was part of a pattern of state "help" for workers, initiated by the Bismarckian reform of welfare provisions, designed to incorporate workers in the state apparatus. It could also be represented as a major inroad on the "class justice" of the ordinary courts whose anti-union and anti-strike decisions were highly unpopular with German (male) workers who had been enfranchised in 1871.

In Sweden in 1928, as in Britain in 1964, tripartism was an important part of the growth of a form of corporatism. In these countries, as in Germany and Belgium, the employer and worker members are nominated by the employers' organisations and trade unions. In practice, these nominations are almost invariably accepted by the appointing Minister. This not only binds these organisations to the state, but also confers on them a considerable power of patronage over their own members. This may be contrasted with the bipartite French system in which the *conseillers* are elected, since 1979 by a system of proportional representation (similar to that adopted in 1947 for the election of members of *comités d'enterprise*) by all workers aged 16 or older. This open, accessible and democratic method appears to result in far more representative panels than are found in British industrial tribunals, where, as the study by Dickens and her colleagues shows,[38] the union panel is dominated by white male non-manual workers and trade union officials aged over 45, and the employer panel is also notable for its absence of production-related experience and for the age of its members.

The method of selection does not, however, appear to affect one other remarkable feature of both bipartite and tripartite labour courts. This is the high degree of unanimity achieved in all countries between members from employer, worker and legal backgrounds. In France, despite the underlying idea that the worker and employer *conseillers* represent opposing interest groups, in 95 per cent. of disputes a majority emerges among judges who traditionally are divided on class and ideological grounds.[39] In the tripartite British system, 96 per cent. of tribunal decisions are unanimous. In Germany and Belgium dissents are not announced but a similar degree of unanimity appears to exist. In Sweden, there was a relatively high degree of dissent by worker members in the first years, but this later declined and steadied at around 20 per cent. of all decisions.

The major reason for this is the tradition of judicial impartiality and objectivity and the collegiate atmosphere of the court in which mutual control is exercised by the judges. Even in a bipartite setting, the desire for compromise and for a common interpretation of legal standards motivates the judges towards agreement. In tripartite courts, the professional judge may be able to exert a decisive influence over the lay judges because of his or her legal knowledge, greater experience (the lay members sit far less often), and training in the finding and evaluation of facts. In France, at the end of the nineteenth century, the unions attempted to impose a *mandat impératif* on the worker *conseillers* obliging them always to vote in favour of the worker. Blanc-Jouvan records that this met with such resistance that it actually produced the opposite effect of strengthening the attitude of impartiality among the judges. The *mandat impératif* was expressly outlawed by a decree of December 22, 1958.[40]

(2) *Expertise*

Another justification for specialist labour courts is their expertise in industrial relations and in handling employee grievances. This is supposed to follow from their bipartite or tripartite constitution. In the tripartite courts a mixture of legal and industrial expertise is expected. Historically, it was the knowledge of "custom and practice" which was all-important. For example, in Italy the tripartite *Collegi dei Probiviri*, which operated between 1893 and 1928, laid the foundations of labour law by deciding cases according to principles of equity, that is without the observance of strict rules of law.[41] However, as custom has become less important and statute law and general principles of civil law have come to the centre of the stage in disputes of rights, more importance has been attached to legal expertise. The view of the Franks Committee in England (1957, para. 55) that "objectivity in the treatment of cases and the proper sifting of facts are most often secured by having a legally-qualified chairman" has been shared in other systems. A major difference between Britain and other European countries, however, is in the selection and training of the legal members of labour courts.

In Germany, for example, the professional judges are appointed after passing two state examinations in law, including a period of training in labour matters. They are appointed for life after a probationary period. The appointments procedure varies in different states, but in several this involves some form of consultation with representatives of unions and employers. In practice, the president of the appellate labour court has a strong influence and takes account of the applicant's knowledge and experience in labour law. It is, of course, possible to achieve a degree of specialised knowledge and experience in labour law even where ordinary courts are used. For example, in Milan about one-third of the *pretori* hear labour disputes exclusively. A similar use of specialist labour sections in the *Tribunale* can be found in other large Italian cities, but "there are many complaints... that the best judges are not assigned to these sections" and many young judges, although well-trained in labour law, prefer assignment to the civil section where more complex issues of law tend to arise.[42] A bland diet of factual disputes is unlikely to attract those lawyers who have a predeliction for fine points of law, and that is not altogether a bad thing in courts which aim to avoid technicality in dealing with the problems of ordinary employers and workers.

One of the peculiarities of the British tribunals is that in constituting a particular tribunal no attempt is made to allocate lay members to cases where their background and experience would be most relevant. Thus, as Dickens points out, a school teacher and the director of an engineering company may sit on a case about the dismissal of a farm labourer, shop assistant or construction worker. This could not happen in France where, according to the Law of January 18, 1979, each *conseil de prudhommes* must have five sections, devoted respectively to industry, commerce, agriculture, miscellaneous occupations and *cadres* (upper-level supervisory, technical and managerial employees) and the *conseillers* are elected by employers and workers of the relevant section. In Sweden, where a case has significance for a particular bargaining area only, the Labour Court will be made up of representatives whose area of bargaining the dispute mainly concerns. The absence of special expertise in the customs of the particular industry may, perhaps, help to explain the great reluctance of British tribunals to "second-guess" management decisions.

(3) *Autonomy*

The reason most recently advanced by Wedderburn[43] and McCarthy[44] for pointing us towards a Labour Court is the quest for an autonomous labour law which "promotes collective bargaining and is freed from the contract of service."[45] The arguments have been well canvassed by Wedderburn and need not be repeated here. The kind of "exclusivity of jurisdiction" which such a British Labour Court would require, has been attained in Germany, Sweden and Belgium. In Germany, as we have seen, this is a broad jurisdiction over individual and collective disputes of rights and apart from the possible intervention of the Constitutional Court where a constitutional right is involved it is relatively immune from control by other courts. In Sweden there is the possibility of a new trial being ordered by the Supreme Court on grounds of gross error of law or other special circumstances, but this does not seem to have inhibited the autonomous development of principles by the Labour Court. In Belgium, too, *cassation* (review by the *Cour de Cassation*) seems to be rare.

This may be compared with the fragmentation of courts dealing with labour disputes in France and the important role which the Court of Cassation has played, at various times, in shaping French labour law. The substantive jurisdiction of the *conseils de prudhommes* does not extend to all kinds of individual labour disputes, and the coverage of the courts although widened since 1979 is not comprehensive in territorial and occupational terms. In these cases, the action must be heard by a *tribunal d'instance*, or where the employer-defendant is in commerce, before a commercial court. Even more serious is the absence of an appellate labour court. Appeals must be brought before the ordinary courts (courts of appeal and the "Social Chamber" of the *Cour de Cassation*). About 10 per cent. of cases are subject to such appeals and since they are the more important ones, they carry most weight as precedents. Blanc-Jouvan concludes that it is the "*Cour de Cassation* that plays the decisive role in the formation of law in labour matters."[46]

As Wedderburn has argued,[47] the central issue is not whether the labour court is technically a part of the ordinary hierarchy of courts—witness the ability of the *Cour de Cassation* in France to assert the "autonomy of labour law in respect of the civil law of contracts and obligations,"[48] and that of the Italian *Corte di Cassazione*[49] and the Netherlands *Hoge Raad*[50] to widen the boundaries of lawful strikes—but above all that of the composition of the court and the extent to which its attempts to develop an autonomous labour law can be protected from the common law judiciary.

An agenda for Britain?

It would be an abuse of the comparative method to find in any of the foreign models discussed in this paper a "model" for Britain. Graham Mather is surely right to describe the NIRC as just such a "foreign body," one whose descendants would find in the Britain of the late 1980s an inhospitable climate. But a comparison of the process by which labour courts have evolved or been imposed in other countries can help us to understand the tensions in this country between labour law and the general legal system. Such conflicts have been the very essence of the development of the English legal system, as is shown by the struggles between the King's courts and the medieval manorial courts, and between the common law courts and the courts of equity.

At present, the three major pressures for separate labour courts staffed by a new judiciary face powerful resistance. Tripartism is not yet dead, but it is in a state of suspended animation. In the industrial tribunals the system of nomination by the C.B.I. and certain other employers' bodies, and by the T.U.C. and the Managerial, Professional and Staff Liaison Group, has failed to produce a good spread of lay members in terms of age, sex, industry, and occupation. Only 31 of the 2,128 panel members (in 1987) came from ethnic minorities. Only 441 (21 per cent.) were women. Most are aged 45 or over. More important, the lay members tend to exert relatively small influence over decision-making and, in the main jurisdiction of unfair dismissal have accepted a consensus view which upholds most managerial prerogatives. Unlike the Swedish Labour Court, in British industrial tribunals tripartism does not rest on the strength of the collective parties.

The pressure for specialisation and the development of expertise in labour law has also come up against strong opposition, particularly from the legal profession. Chairmen of industrial tribunals tend to come from social and professional backgrounds which make them unsympathetic to the parties who appear before them. On appointment they often lack specific expertise and training in employment law and lack experience in industrial relations. They are strongly influenced by the habits learned in the common law courts. Although some recent steps have been taken to improve their training, including bringing the tribunals within the scope of the Judicial Studies Board, resources for this task are severely limited. The proposals by the C.R.E. for a specialist discrimination division to hear all discrimination cases have not been accepted, and even the E.O.C.'s more limited suggestion that all discrimination cases should be heard by a chairman and members specially trained and experienced in them is not followed in all regions. The common lawyer thinks of himself as a "generalist" who can absorb any special area of fact-finding and law with relative ease.

The arguments for an autonomous labour law, administered by a specialised judiciary with exclusive jurisdiction, meet their strongest opposition in the neo-laissez-faire philosophy which views the common law of contract and tort, administered by the ordinary courts, as the natural partner of an individualised economic order. When Sir John Donaldson is said to have proposed that industrial tribunals could be expanded "to become in effect general purpose local labour courts" embracing arbitration functions as well as more strictly judicial tasks,[51] and wrote that "there is nothing an arbitrator can do which a specialised labour court cannot do better,"[52] he was not envisaging a labour court based on collectivist principles but one which would be highly individualistic in the common law tradition.

The decisive factor in the making of labour law is the powerfulness of the opponents of change.[53] From this perspective, it seems that the common law tradition will remain dominant in British labour law. Sir John Wood has said that "the legal system is likely to win, indeed it will win," and that "if in winning it sticks rigidly to its traditional ways this will be to many a misfortune."[54] Those who espouse the cause of an autonomous labour law will have to exercise all their ingenuity to avert that misfortune. They may do so in a great variety of ways. These include improving the procedures of industrial tribunals and the recruitment and training of chairmen and lay members; and the development of new forms of voluntary arbitration and greater use of the voluntary jurisdiction of the C.A.C. One may also build upon the pressures within the legal system for change, such as the growing support for class actions, which could be a vital way forward in discrimination cases. The reform and improvement of adjudication in labour disputes has to proceed in the context of the reform of civil procedure in general.

APPENDIX

Notes on Foreign Labour Courts

Procedures for the resolution of disputes over *rights* in the labour-management context generally fall into one of the following three types:

(1) Labour courts

(2) Ordinary courts

(3) Arbitration.

Some examples are given below.

(1) Labour Courts

(a) *France*

The *conseils de prudhommes* are essentially bipartite, the *conseillers* being elected representatives of employers and employees in equal numbers. Each chamber is presided over by a president elected alternately, for a year at a time, by employer and employee members. Decisions are by majority vote; in the event of a tie (said to be rare), a professional judge from the local *tribunal d'instance* participates and has a casting vote. Unions complain that the employee members often compromise their position in the face of employer opposition and accept the predominantly conservative views of the regular judiciary. The *conseils* deal with all disputes concerning individuals arising from a contract of employment. In practice they tend to interpret collective agreements, since these have a normative effect on individual contracts. Unions have a right to intervene, with the consent of an employee, where such a question of interpretation arises; unions may also join in the proceedings where there is possible prejudice to the collective group it represents. Appeals (where the amount claimed is over a prescribed sum) and requests for judicial review go to the ordinary courts—the social chamber of the *cours d'appel* and social division of the *Cour de Cassation*. The *conseil* is required to go through a conciliation procedure; the conciliators may be the very persons who later adjudicate and some commentators say this encourages settlements by giving parties a chance to evaluate their chances of winning or losing. If the case is not settled at conciliation or withdrawn it goes forward to a full hearing. The case may be investigated before hearing by two *conseillers*, one employer and one employee, specially appointed as investigators, who may make inquiries at the place of work, thus easing the burden of proof for the employee. Their recommendations may be accepted by the full *conseil* consisting of two employer and two employee members, without a formal hearing. This investigatory process is used only for complicated cases where the full *conseil* might otherwise spend a long time establishing the facts. Van Noorden[55] reports that legalism is regarded as being as much a problem in France as in Britain, largely because of the complexity of the substantive law, and there is much delay in the system (up to two years). Legal aid is available; legal representation is the norm among employers but is not common among employees who tend to come from small non-unionised enterprises. The *conseils* generally have power only to recommend but not to order reinstatement. Only in cases of *délégués syndicaux* and *délégués du personnel* can reinstatement be ordered with a criminal sanction for non-compliance, but such orders are rare.

(b) *Belgium*

Before 1970 there was a multiplicity of courts, commissions and arbitral bodies concerned with labour and social security adjudication. A Royal Commission was set up in 1958 to propose a simpler, speedier and less costly process. The Commission was opposed to completely autonomous labour tribunals. After much discussion in parliamentary committees and political consultations, a compromise was found. The labour tribunals would enjoy wide autonomy *within* the judicial system. The system, since 1970, consists of two tiers. The lower tier is a labour tribunal (*arbeidsrechtbank*) in each of the 26 judicial arondissements, with separate chambers for blue-collar and white-collar workers. The tribunal for each case consists of a career judge (*beropsrechter/juge professionel*) as chairman, and two "social judges" (*rechters in soziale zaken/juges sociaux*) appointed by the Minister of Labour, one on the nomination of representative trade unions, one on the nomination of representative employers' organisations. The social judges are appointed for three years, subject to renewal, and sit on a part-time basis. Each judge has an equal vote, and in practice most decisions are unanimous. The tribunals' jurisdiction covers all "social law" including

(a) all individual disputes in connection with employment contracts and training (in practice most concern termination of employment);

(b) disputes about compensation for accidents at work and industrial diseases;

(c) social security of workers and the self-employed;

(d) disputes concerning works councils and safety committees;

(e) disputes about administrative sanctions in social matters.

Prosecutions for "social criminal law" (*e.g.* social security fraud, offences by foreign workers without permits, health and safety offences) are heard in the criminal courts. (As much as 80 per cent. of Belgian social law carries criminal sanctions). The upper tier is a labour court (*Arbeidshof/La Cour*), similarly composed to the tribunal, which sits in five centres. Appeals go to this court on questions of fact and law. In practice about 20–25 per cent. of decisions are the subject of appeals. There are limited possibilities for judicial review on grounds of gross error of law to the *Cour de Cassation*. Since the tribunals and court are part of the judicial system, hearings take place in ordinary court buildings and the lawyers (including the social judges) wear robes. The procedure is inquisitorial. The tribunal or court receives a full *dossier*, prepared by the parties (with the assistance of the *auditeur* in social security cases, see below). Most parties are legally represented (workers by trade union lawyers—70 per cent. of workers are unionised, and non-unionised workers usually engage a lawyer of their own). At every tribunal and court there is an *auditeur*, an independent public officer, whose functions include:

(i) undertaking preliminary investigation to help the claimant in social security cases (*e.g.* to obtain the workers' social security records which might otherwise be inaccessible to the worker because of the "privatised" institutions responsible for social security;

(ii) prosecuting in social criminal cases;

(iii) advising the tribunal or court;

(iv) instituting appeals or review where the tribunal has acted contrary to law.

(c) *Sweden*

The Labour Court (*Arbetsdomstolen*) began its activities on January 1, 1929. This was seen to be a logical necessity following the incorporation of collective agreements into the legal system by the Act on Collective Agreements of 1928. It was widely believed that the ordinary courts were unsuited to the task of judging disputes over collective agreements. Since its inception the Court has been tripartite in character. Under the Act on Litigation in Labour Disputes of 1974 (which replaced the Law of 1928) the court consists of (1) the officials; (2) the employer members; and (3) the employee members. For trials, seven people normally sit in Court: a chairman, two other officials, two employer members and two employee members. The chairman and vice-chairman have to be legally trained and have judicial experience. The other official members must have "specialised knowledge of conditions on the labour market." The employer members are appointed on the recommendation of employers' organisations and the employee members on the recommendation of the trade unions. In the period 1929–1974, officials dissented in 6 per cent., employer members in 12 per cent. and union members in 15 per cent. of all decisions. The number of employee dissents dropped sharply to about 10 per cent. in the mid-1960s, but in the 1970s steadied at just under 20 per cent.[56] Under the 1974 Act a case goes exclusively to the Labour Court when the dispute concerns the relationship between parties to a collective agreement or relates to conditions of service of an employee who is a member of a trade union. A dispute between an unorganised employee and his employer goes to an (ordinary) District Court in the first instance, but with an appeal to the Labour Court. The decisions of the Labour Court are final. A new trial may be ordered by the Supreme Court but only in the event of "gross error" or similar special circumstances. Arbitration remains as an alternative procedure which can be agreed upon either in a particular dispute or for future disputes generally. It appears that most disputants *prefer* the Labour Court to arbitration. This is because of the Court's close links with the employers' organisations and trade unions, as well as the fact that its procedures are at least as speedy and inexpensive as arbitration, and the parties do not have to risk a dispute about the appointment of arbitrators. The collective organisations dominate the procedures of the Court. They have the right to represent members in all kinds of dispute. Should a union refuse to prosecute a member's case, the member may do so him/herself. A plaintiff who brings an action against a union member must also join the union as a party. A claim may not be tried until negotiations have taken place in accordance with the procedure laid down in the Act on the Joint Regulation of Working Life or in a procedural agreement which may be substituted for the Act's rules. The court can grant prohibitory or mandatory injunctions but only if this is of "substantial importance" to one of the parties. Declaratory judgments can be sought in cases which are of importance as precedents. The procedure is relatively simple. The plaintiff's written application and the defendant's reply are exchanged after which one or more oral hearings are held. There is an informal pre-trial hearing to facilitate last-minute settlements. Decisions are often reasoned in considerable detail, but in a language comprehensible to those who are not legally trained. The decisions of the Court have played an important part in shaping the basic principles of Swedish labour law.

(d) *Federal Republic of Germany*

The labour courts are tripartite, each panel of the local *Arbeitsgerichte* and appellate *Landesarbeitsgerichte* consisting of two lay judges appointed by the Minister of Labour on nomination of employers' and trade union bodies, and one professional judge. The Federal Labour Court (*Bundesarbeitsgericht*) has multiple divisions, each with two laymen (who act as impartial judges) and three professional judges. The professional judges make their career in these courts soon after graduation, and enjoy life tenure after a four-year probationary period. A nomination for labour court judgeship has to be approved by a tripartite committee. The courts have exclusive jurisdiction over both individual and collective disputes. Reinstatement of unfairly dismissed employees is rare. The courts have a statutory obligation to seek settlements by compromise, throughout the proceedings. The first oral pleas are made before the chairman, sitting without laymen for this purpose, at a session designed to achieve a settlement. The chairman discusses all aspects of the case with the parties "under free consideration of all the circumstances." S/he has broad discretionary power to develop the facts but may not investigate anyone under oath at this stage. If conciliation fails, about three months usually elapses before the full hearing (only about 10 per cent. of cases go to final decision). About 45 per cent. of these decisions are appealed against on fact or law. According to Blankenburg and Rogowski (1985), 50 per cent. of all plaintiffs win their cases in final judgments at trial level (compared to 27–30 per cent. in industrial tribunals). The procedure requires both parties to formulate their evidence and arguments in written briefs, which are studied by the judge who chairs the case and are sent to the opposing side for a written response. In this way a file is built up based on written exchanges. The judge takes the initiative in structuring the issues and arguments; the judge tends to be the most active participant in the courtroom, asking questions of fact and of law, and during the hearing may (repeatedly) propose terms for settlement shifting his role from judge to mediator or arbitrator. The lay members tend to play a smaller role both in court and in chambers than the professional chairman.

(2) Ordinary Courts

(a) *Italy*

Labour disputes fall under the ordinary civil courts in Italy because article 102 of the Constitution forbids special courts. There are no significant demands for special labour courts, according to Treu[57] because "the ordinary civil courts, and in particular the *pretori* (usually young and more open-minded judges) have been seen to handle efficiently and competently the growing number of often very delicate labour disputes...." The *pretori* (career-judges) have general first instance jurisdiction in all labour disputes in the private sector and these disputes are customarily assigned to one or more *pretori* in each local office (*e.g.* in Milan about one-third of the *pretori* hear labour disputes exclusively). Appeals on fact or law involving a minimum amount are heard by the *tribunale* (a panel of three professional judges), with a further appeal on questions of law only to the Supreme Court (*Corte di Cassazione*). The proceedings before the *pretori* are designed to increase speed, informality and accessibility and differ significantly from ordinary civil proceedings. In theory, the maximum allowable period between submission and decision is 60 to 70 days; in practice, very few offices have enough judges to achieve this. The *pretori* have extensive investigative powers and may gather evidence independently of the parties, *e.g.* they can call additional witnesses, order "free interrogation" of the parties, order inspection of the workplace and ask for written or oral representations from union representatives. Oral evidence prevails over written evidence. Labour cases are exempt from the usual taxes imposed in other cases. The parties have to pay their attorney's fees and costs are generally awarded against the loser. The worker usually has legal assistance from a trade union. There are tripartite conciliation commissions which seek to achieve the settlement *inter alia* of rights disputes under collective agreements, and settlements under this procedure can be enforced immediately by decree of the *pretori*.

(b) *Netherlands*

All civil disputes concerning the contract of employment, collective agreements and strikes are dealt with in the ordinary courts.
There are no labour courts or administrative boards, although in
the case of termination of employment the Director of the District
Labour Office has to decide whether or not to consent to
termination by the employer, a role which in practice is the
functional equivalent of the conciliation role of ACAS. There are
62 lower courts (*kantongerechten*), 19 district courts (*arondisse-
mentsrechtbanken*), five courts of appeal (*gerechtshoven*), and the
Supreme Court (*Hoge Raad*). A lower court judge sits alone as the
court of first instance in all disputes connected with the contract of
employment or collective agreements, irrespective of the amount
of the claim. There is an appeal to the district court, consisting of
three professional judges. Decisions of all courts are subject to
cassation (judicial review only on grounds of gross error of law).
The *Hoge Raad* has, through *cassation*, established important
rules in labour law by providing guidelines (*e.g.* the liberal
decision of May 30, 1986 on the legality of "political" strikes in the
Netherlands Railways case). Although the judicial procedures
have been criticised on grounds of delay and formality, there is no
evidence of a growth of grievance procedures in collective
agreements to provide an alternative. Nor does there appear to be
any pressure from employers' organisations or trade unions for a
system of labour courts.

(3) Arbitration

Grievance arbitration has been extensively developed in the
United States, where about 95 per cent. of all collective agreements
in the private sector include some provision for arbitration by an
independent third party as the last stage of the agreed grievance
procedure. Only cases that are not settled by negotiation proceed
to arbitration. The employer and union usually have full-time
officers to deal with grievances. They choose the arbitrator, either
from those known to them or from lists submitted by bodies like
the Federal Mediation Service or the American Arbitration
Association (A.A.A.). At the hearing, the employer is generally
represented by a specialist lawyer or a member of the personnel

staff; unions are frequently represented by a specialist lawyer. The employer and union share the arbitrator's fee and the costs of the hearing. The parties agree to accept the arbitrator's decision as final and binding and the award is legally enforceable through the courts. The scope of the arbitration is determined by the parties themselves, through the collective agreement, and usually covers a wide range of grievances in addition to unjust discharge. About one-third of agreements contain procedural rules governing the hearing, and most of the remainder follow the A.A.A. procedural rules. Strict rules of evidence are rarely applied, but according to Aaron[58] most arbitrators "seem to be aware of and to give some consideration to the policies underlying the exclusion of hearsay testimony and the parol evidence rule in judicial proceedings." The arbitrator is under no duty to give reasons for his decisions unless the parties agree that he should do so. Aaron reports[59] that "the increased employment of lawyers in arbitration has also led to the greater use of pre-hearing and post-hearing written arguments (briefs) and of verbatim transcripts of arbitration proceedings." Arbitrators have power in most states to subpoena witnesses, administer oaths and examine witnesses. The procedures are adversarial. The main strengths of the system are (1) its essentially voluntary nature and flexibility, allowing the parties to make it as formal or informal as they wish; (2) the remedies, which almost always include reinstatement with back pay of employees found to have been unjustly discharged. The main weaknesses are (1) workers in enterprises where there is no collective bargaining representative (over 80 per cent. of the U.S. workforce) have no protection against unfair treatment and unjust discharge; (2) even where there is a collective bargaining agent, the individual has less access to procedures than in labour court countries—the union "owns" the grievance and controls the proceedings and individuals or groups in bad favour with the union face many procedural and evidential obstacles in suing either the union or employer or both for breach of the collective agreement or violation of the duty of fair representation; (3) the costs to the parties are relatively high, and there are long delays (an average of 244 days from filing of grievance to award in 1980).

NOTES

[1] "Labour Law: from here to autonomy" (1987) 16 I.L.J. 1 at p. 26.
[2] "Freedom, Democracy and the Role of Trade Unions in a Modern Industrial

Society," Jim Conway Foundation Sixth Annual Memorial Lecture, November 12, 1986, *J.C.F. Trade Union Report*, Vol. 8, No. 1, January 1987, p. 1 at p. 5.

[3] *Financial Times*, October 25, 1986.

[4] Sir John Donaldson, "Lessons from the Industrial Court" (1975) 91 L.Q.R. 181, 192; see Wedderburn (1987) 16 I.L.J. at p. 26.

[5] Hepple, "Restructuring Employment Rights" (1986) 15 I.L.J. 69.

[6] Wedderburn, *op. cit.*, p. 3.

[7] *The Future of Labour Law: Two Views*, Warwick Papers in Industrial Relations, No. 14, May 1987, pp. 1–12. See for a valuable overview of the relationship between substantive law and attitudes to labour courts, Paul Davies and Mark Freedland, "Labour Courts and the Reform of Labour Law," in *In Memoriam Zvi Bar Niv: Collection of Essays on Labour Law*, Israel 1987, pp. 41–72. They point out that labour courts are "inimical to the labour policies shaping current legislation" (at p. 72).

[8] Wedderburn (1987) 16 I.L.J. at p. 28.

[9] See, *e.g.* I.L.O., *Conciliation and Arbitration Procedures in Labour Disputes: a comparative study*, Geneva, 1980, pp. 15, 151. The classic study by the I.L.O., *Labour Courts*, Studies and Reports, Series A No. 40, Geneva 1938 pp. 17–18, also contains a definition of the distinctions between arbitration and adjudication.

[10] X. Blanc-Jouvan, in B. Aaron (ed.) *Labour Courts and Grievance Settlement in Western Europe*, Los Angeles, 1971, p. 8 (hereafter, *Labour Courts*).

[11] *Grundlehren des Arbeitsrechts* (1927) pp. 148 *et seq.*, discussed by Ramm in Aaron (ed.) *Labour Courts*, p. 94.

[12] *Op. cit.*, pp. 33–34.

[13] *Op. cit.*, p. 202.

[14] *Op. cit.*, p. 203.

[15] See generally, S. Anderman *The Law of Unfair Dismissal*, London, 1985, pp. 107–117.

[16] T. Treu, "Italy" in *International Encyclopedia for Comparative Labour Law and Industrial Relations*, p. 95.

[17] Giugni in Aaron (ed.) *Labour Courts* pp. 278–280.

[18] The terminology used here is based on that employed by A. Chayes, "The role of the judge in public law litigation" (1976) 89 Harv.L.Rev. 1261.

[19] *Op. cit.*, p. 12.

[20] *Law and Industrial Relations in Sweden*, Stockholm, 1977, p. 57.

[21] Act on the Joint Regulation of Working Life 1976, s.68.

[22] E. Blankenburg and R. Rogowski, *West German Labour Courts and the British Tribunal System: a socio-legal comparison*, University of Wisconsin-Madison Working Paper, 1985, Table 6.

[23] A. Chayes, (1976) 89 Harv.L.Rev. 1281, 1298 describes the decree as "a complex ongoing regime of performance rather than a simple, one-shot, one-way transfer."

[24] See, *e.g.* George Nicolau, "Can the Labor Arbitration Process be simplified?" in *Arbitration 1986: Current and Expanding Roles*. Proceedings of the 39th Annual Meeting of the National Academy of Arbitrators, Washington D.C., B.N.A. 1987 69–92, who concludes, however, that "much of the complexity and waste of effort that has crept into the arbitration process is a result of external considerations that have little, if anything, to do with the system itself" (at p. 92).

[25] S. Van Noorden, "French labour courts and unfair dismissal law" (1980) *Employment Gazette*, 1098–1102.

[26] See generally, R. Munday, "Tribunal Lore: Legalism and the Industrial Tribunals" (1981) 10 I.L.J. 146–159.

[27] The expression used by Lord Devlin. *The Judge*, Oxford, O.U.P., 1981, p. 58.

[28] Blankenburg and Rogowski, *op. cit.*

[29] See, *e.g. Civil Justice Review*, Consultation Paper No. 6, General Issues, L.C.D., 1987, esp. Chap. 5; Consultation Paper No. 2, *Small Claims in County Courts*, L.C.D., 1986, esp. Chap. 4.

[30] M. David, "L'évolution historique des conseils de prudhommes en France" *Droit Social* (1974) special ed. (ed. G. Lyon-Caen) 10, 12.

[31] T. Ramm, in B. Hepple (ed.) *The Making of Labour Law in Europe*, London, 1986, p. 271.

[32] In Aaron (ed.), *Labour Courts*, p. 71.

[33] Ramm in Aaron (ed.), *Labour Courts*, pp. 85–86.

[34] Translated by Jon Clark in *Labour Law and Politics in the Weimar Republic, Selected German Writings of Otto Kahn-Freund*, Oxford, 1981.

[35] G. R. Rubin, "The origins of industrial tribunals: munitions tribunals during the First World War" (1977) 6 I.L.J. 149.

[36] B. Aaron, "Labour Courts and Organs of Arbitration," Chap. 16 in B. Hepple (ed.) *International Encyclopedia of Comparative Law*, vol. XV, p. 5.

[37] Ramm in Aaron (ed.), *Labour Courts*, p. 84.

[38] L. Dickens *et al.*, *Dismissed: Unfair Dismissal and the Industrial Tribunal System*, Oxford, 1985, p. 57.

[39] Blanc-Jouvan in Aaron (ed.), *Labour Courts*, p. 22.

[40] Blanc-Jouvan in Aaron (ed.), *Labour Courts*, p. 22, n. 12.

[41] Giugni in Aaron (ed.), *Labour Courts*, p. 250.

[42] Giugni, in Aaron (ed.), *Labour Courts*, p. 260.

[43] See n. 1.

[44] See n. 2.

[45] Hepple (1986) 15 I.L.J. 83.

[46] Blanc-Jouvan in Aaron (ed.), *Labour Courts*, p. 39.

[47] *Op. cit.*, p. 27.

[48] See the example given by Wedderburn, *op. cit.*, pp. 11–12.

[49] *Public Prosecutor* v. *Ardizzone* Case No. 165/1983, Constitutional Court of Italy, noted by Wedderburn (1983) 12 I.L.J. 253.

[50] *N.V. Nederlandse Spoorwegen*, May 30, 1986, *Nederlandse Jurisprudentie* 1986, n. 688.

[51] *The Guardian*, November 30, 1983, based on a leaked memorandum from the Department of Employment.

[52] (1985) 91 L.Q.R. 181.

[53] See generally for this thesis, Hepple in *The Making of Labour Law in Europe*, London, 1986, Introduction, esp. at pp. 4–5.

[54] Sir John Wood, "The British Arbitrator—a Question of Style" in *Arbitration 1986: Current and Expanding Roles*, (ed. W. Gershenfeld), Bureau of National Affairs Inc., Washington, 1987, 8, 17.

[55] (1980) *Employment Gazette*, 1098–1102; see too B. Napier, "The French Labour Courts—an Institution in Transition," (1979) 42 M. & R. 270–284.

[56] F. Schmidt, *Law and Industrial Relations in Sweden*, Stockholm, 1977, p. 40.

[57] "Italy," in *International Encyclopedia For Labour Law and Industrial Relations*, 1977.

[58] Chap. 16, Vol. XV, *International Encyclopedia of Comparative Law*, 1986, p. 71.

[59] *Ibid.*

Floating Charges: Recent Developments Under Israeli Law

JOSHUA WEISMAN*

Introduction

When compared with other types of security devices the floating charge probably ranks as one of the most sophisticated security interests. This inventive security of English law, the product of courts of equity about a century ago, has spread from England to other common law countries, where it can also be found in statutory form.

The distinction of the floating charge lies in the fact that it is well tailored to the needs of the parties who use it. The less developed forms of security interests are characterised by the fact that they go beyond what is needed for the securing of an obligation. The more primitive a security device is, the more it incorporates elements which are not really required for security purposes. A good example is the "mortgage." A mortgage takes the form of a sale of an asset which belongs to the debtor subject to his right to repurchase it. Actually the debtor has no wish to sell his property to the creditor, nor is the creditor interested in purchasing the debtor's property. The transaction of sale is being used to attain a much more limited purpose, that of guaranteeing the satisfaction of the debtor's obligation.

Higher up the scale of security devices is the "pledge" which unlike the "mortgage" does not involve transfer of ownership, but only transfer of possession of an asset belonging to the debtor. Again, the parties to a pledge have no interest in the creation of a "bailment." What they seek is only the securing of an obligation.

The "sale" in a mortgage, and the "bailment" in a pledge grant the creditor more than is necessary for the creation of a security,

197

and this demonstrates how unrefined these two forms of security devices are.

A more developed security device is the "hypothecation," which involves neither transfer of title, nor transfer of possession. A specific asset of the debtor is earmarked to serve the purpose of satisfying the creditor's right in case of non-fulfilment by the debtor.

The "floating charge" goes one step further still in that the creation of the security requires no transfer of title or possession, nor the earmarking of any specific asset of the debtor. The debtor's estate, in general, is made to guarantee the satisfaction of the creditor's right.

The ingenuity of this form of security is founded on two principles. First, that the floating charge applies not only to assets which the debtor owned at the time when the security was created but also to assets which the debtor might subsequently acquire ("after-acquired property"). To Continental legal thinking this was a daring notion. The traditional Continental attitude is that the asset subject to a right of property must be in existence when the right is created.

The second principle upon which the floating charge is founded is that the creation of this security does not deprive the debtor of the freedom to deal with the encumbered property, free of the floating charge, by granting rights in specific assets, *e.g.* by sale or mortgage. This freedom to continue to deal with the property after the creation of the floating charge lasts until "crystallization" of the floating charge takes place, at which stage the property becomes frozen in the hands of the debtor, who is not permitted any longer to enter into any transaction in relation to the property comprised in the floating charge. Crystallisation takes place, *e.g.* upon appointment of a receiver.[1]

Thus, the floating charge has the distinction of being a pure security, with no foreign elements involved in its creation, and limiting to the minimum the burden on the debtor.

The statutory formulation of the floating charge under Israeli law is as follows:

> "Floating charge" means a charge on all or part of the assets and undertaking for the time being of the Company, in the varying condition in which they happen to be from time to time, but subject to the power of the Company to create specific mortgages or charges on all or any part thereof.[2]

Under Israeli statutory law the floating charge was made available to debtors who are companies or co-operative societies.[3]

The main use of a floating charge is with regard to transient inventory. In such cases it is impracticable to charge the constantly changing inventory as a specific charge. In the framework of a floating charge no new security agreements are required whenever the debtor's assets change hands. However, the floating charge is not limited to inventory only. It may also comprise machines, equipment, real property, etc.

Recent developments

(A) The freedom of the debtor who granted a floating charge to execute overreaching transactions with regard to specific assets caused concern among the creditors secured by floating charges. To overcome this concern it became customary to include in floating charge agreements a proviso under which the debtor undertook not to execute such transactions without the consent of the holder of the floating charge. The Supreme Court had an opportunity to express its view on the effect such a proviso had on third parties who acquired rights in specific assets of the debtor.[4] The court held that a third party was bound by the restriction imposed on the debtor only if he was aware of the existence of such a restriction. In addition the court held that upon registration of such a restriction in the office of the companies registrar third parties became affected by constructive notice.[5]

Following this decision an amendment to the Companies Ordinance was introduced by the Knesset, adopting the opinion of the court.[6]

(B) Three further Supreme Court decisions are relevant to this development. In the first decision[7] the court responded to the question whether a floating charge in which the debtor was deprived of the right to execute transactions with regard to specific assets was still a floating charge. The court answered this question in the affirmative, but did not elaborate the reasons for this position. Indeed one may wonder in what sense such a floating charge is still floating if no specific item of the debtor's property can be sold or charged without the consent of the holder of the floating charge. A possible answer to this question is that the fluctuating nature of such a floating charge expresses itself in the application of the floating charge to after-acquired property, and in the subordination of the assets comprised in the floating charge to levies by other creditors of the debtor (including unsecured creditors). Even if this reply is not totally satisfactory[8] there is no doubt that the attitude of the Israeli legislature was that a floating charge subject to an undertaking by the debtor not to execute transactions with regard to specific assets was still a floating charge. This attitude is clearly expressed in the above mentioned amendment of the Companies Ordinance, which adopted the *Electrogenics* decision by the Supreme Court.[9]

The second decision was with regard to the question whether constructive notice through registration in the companies registry also affected good faith purchasers of inventory items of the company creating the floating charge. The court held that the need to facilitate commercial transactions required that constructive notice should not affect such purchasers. To expect purchasers of inventory items (as distinct from assets not regularly sold by the debtor, *e.g.* vehicles belonging to the business, office equipment, accounts receivable) to check the companies registry before every purchase would create an impracticable situation. Consequently such purchasers are not affected by a registered provision in a floating charge agreement restricting the debtor's freedom to execute transactions with regard to the property which is comprised in the floating charge.

The third decision dealt with the question whether a floating charge agreement which prohibited the debtor from granting specific charges without the consent of the holder of the floating charge was nevertheless effective against a mortgagee who financed the purchase of the mortgaged property (a purchase-money-security-interest). Following English precedents the Supreme Court held that the mortgage was valid and had priority over the floating charge.[11] Such preference was not detrimental to the floating charge holder, or to other prior secured creditors, since the purchase-money-security-interest did not deprive previous creditors of any assets that were available to them. On the contrary, it added an asset to the property of the debtor.

The cumulative effect of the developments in the Israeli law of floating charges described above was:

(1) A restriction in a floating charge agreement on the debtor's freedom to execute transactions with regard to specific assets comprised in the floating charge is effective, if properly registered in the companies registry. Such restriction is not incompatible with the nature of a floating charge as conceived by the Israeli legislature.

(2) The restriction mentioned in paragraph 1 is subject to two exceptions:

(a) a sale to a good faith purchaser of inventory (*i.e.* merchandise regularly sold by the debtor in the course of his business);

(b) a purchase-money-security-interest, granted by the debtor.

A floating charge on non-corporate assets

As mentioned above, the floating charge type of security is, under Israeli statute law, available to debtors who are companies or co-operatives.[12] The question has recently arisen whether this type of security should not be extended to individuals so that non-corporate assets could also be made subject to a floating charge. The assumption was that if this was desirable statutory amendment would be necessary since under present statute law such an extension of the floating charge was impossible. Presumably, this assumption was based on the understanding that although the Pledges Law, 1967, seems to have adopted the position that there is no *numerus clausus* of security devices, in practice one cannot, relying on the freedom of contract, create new security devices, or extend existing security devices beyond the boundaries laid down by statute. According to section 2(*b*) of the Pledges Law, 1967, a security interest can be created regardless of the device employed: "The provisions of this law shall apply to every transaction, however designated, the intention of which is to charge property as security for an obligation." This freedom is largely illusory, however, since the statute continues (in section 4) that in order for a security interest to be effective against third parties, certain measures must be taken, as enumerated in the law, to give notice of its existence. The open-list rule governing the creation of a security interest has thus been drained of substance by the adoption of a closed-list rule with respect to the obligation to give notice. The general tenor of these measures is incompatible with a security over undetermined fluctuating assets, which can become subordinate to subsequently created rights of third parties. Consequently, a commission was appointed by the Minister of Justice to look into the question whether the present Pledges Law should be amended so as to enable the creation of a floating charge on non-corporate assets. The final conclusion of the committee was that such an amendment was not to be recommended.[13] The following reasons were put forward for and against such a change of the law.

1. *Considerations in Favour of Extending Floating Charges to Non-corporate Assets*

(a) *The acceptance by Israeli law of real rights in after-acquired property*

Israeli law does not, in principle, rule out the possibility of granting real rights in future assets. The Sale Law, 1968, has been interpreted as providing for the sale of future assets.[14] A legal system of this nature will be more inclined to recognise a security interest in future assets than a legal system which negates the sale of future assets.

Furthermore, and with special reference to security interests in future assets, Israeli law explicitly recognises in several statutes the possibility of creating such securities. Apart from the clear example of floating charges by a company or a co-operative society we can refer to the Short Term Crop Loans (Security) Ordinance of 1935, which allows for the creation of a security interest in an expected harvest or any other forthcoming agricultural produce as a guarantee of credit for a period not to exceed one year. It is additionally possible to cite the Co-operative Societies Ordinance of 1933 (Art. 26), which enables a member of a co-operative society to create a security interest in future harvests and agricultural produce to the benefit of his society. The Transfer of Obligations Law, 1969, also facilitates the charge of future obligations (s.1), and the Patents Law, 1967, provides for a security interest in future income from a patent (s.89).

Given this position of Israeli law, it is possible to argue that the principle allowing the charge of future assets should be given general application instead of the present regime which provides security interests in future assets only under specified circumstances.

(b) *Present situation discriminates against non-corporate debtors*

Denying a non-corporate debtor the possibility of creating a floating charge on his assets unjustly discriminates against him in comparison to corporate debtors. Furthermore, the current state of the law encourages a negative phenomenon of incorporation for the sole purpose of obtaining credit against a floating charge. This could be undesirable to the debtor for taxation reasons, as well as the administrative burden inherent in the existence of a company, such as bookkeeping, accountant's auditing, etc. The present inequality in the competition for credit should be amended to enable all debtors to create the same security interests.

(c) *Acceptance by other countries*

In the past there has been a reluctance to allow a debtor to create security interests in future assets. Today, however, the tendency is to utilise this important source of transient assets in order to obtain credit. For example, it is possible to create security interests in future assets, regardless of the nature of the debtor, in most of the United States, and in Ontario, Canada. Although in England a non-corporate debtor cannot effect a floating charge, it has recently been recommended that a debtor who constitutes a natural personality be permitted to create such charges.[15] In those countries, such as France, where the traditional reluctance to allow a charge of future assets still exists, it has been weakened by the recognition of a great number of exceptions to the rule.

Recognition by the Israeli legislature of the possibility of creating security interests in future assets would therefore not be exceptional; on the contrary, it would constitute an adaptation of the law to present needs, as acknowledged in advanced countries.

2. *Consideration against floating charges on non-corporate assets*

(a) *Difficulties with floating charges by non-corporate debtors*

Initially, the argument that Israeli law should allow non-corporate debtors what it allows companies or co-operative societies seems just; however, upon further examination it is rendered less convincing. The value of a charge of inventory, as currently effected through floating chrges, is contingent upon the ability of the creditor closely to follow the course of business of the debtor in order to ensure that he is not divesting himself of his assets. In the absence of effective supervision of the debtor's transactions, the holder of the floating charge may be subject to the danger that his security will prove valueless upon its realisation. Supervision of the debtor's business is both possible and practical when (1) the law requires bookkeeping under the audit of an accountant; (2) the loan is of a considerable sum; and (3) the debtor's business is of substantial scope. Only then will the bother and expense of the monitoring prove worthwhile. A businessman who has not yet formed a company is usually of small stature, and the credibility of his bookkeeping might be questionable, as he is not required by law to have it audited. Jackson and Kronman have recently commented on the necessary relationship between the charge of future assets and the expense incurred by the creditor's supervision of the debtor's business, stating that monitoring may prove uneconomical for creditors with small claims.[16]

Doubt was voiced in expert testimony before the Commission regarding the expected usage of security interests in future assets by banking institutions, should such a charge be rendered available to non-corporate debtors. It was explained that without proper bookkeeping, and in the absence of any possibility of continuous monitoring of the state of the borrower's assets, creditors will not tend to extend credit against a floating charge. It was stressed that even when reasonable mechanisms of supervision are available, as in floating charges effected by companies, creditors are careful not to rely solely upon this charge. Even less should it be expected that increased credit will become available to non-corporate debtors in exchange for floating charges. It therefore appears unrealistic to expect that security interests in future assets will play a substantial role in the mobilisation of credit when offered by a non-corporate debtor, as the means of supervision available to the lender are very flimsy.

(b) *Acceptance by other countries not because of the merits*

The argument that "everyone does so" as a reason for acting in a certain way often arouses objection because of our yearning to be original and our reluctance to imitate others; nevertheless, it is considerably persuasive. The fact that the legislatures of various states have contemplated a particular legal problem and reached a uniform solution should not be dismissed lightly. One should therefore not disparage the argument that security interests on future assets should be allowed because it is provided for in the legal systems of other countries. Nonetheless, the weight of this argument is not to be overrated. Its real strength lies in the reasons for the adoption of the institution of security interests in future assets, examination of which will determine the extent of persuasiveness to be attributed to the practice of given states.

Foremost among the countries recognising the possibility of security interests in future assets is the United States, which consolidated this legal institution in great detail in section 9 of the Uniform Commercial Code. Examination of the explanations accompanying the Uniform Commercial Code, however, reveals that the formulation of section 9 was not motivated by a wilful endeavour toward the charge of future assets, but rather by *ex post facto* resignation with the undesirable situation already existing in American law, which was difficult to challenge. Comment 2 of the official interpretation of the Uniform Commercial Code, 1972, section 9–204 reads:

> The widespread nineteenth century prejudice against the floating charge was based on a feeling, often inarticulate in the opinions, that a commercial borrower should not be allowed to encumber all his assets, present and future, and that for the protection not only of the borrower but of his other creditors a cushion of free assets should be preserved. *That inarticulate premise has much to recommend it. This article decisively rejects it not on the ground that it was wrong in policy but on the ground that it was not effective....* This article, in expressly validating the floating charge, merely recognizes an existing state of things. [author's emphasis].

A well-known authority on security interests in the United States, similarly writes that section 9 of the U.C.C. was enacted not because of the advantages involved in the charge of future assets, but because of the need to reconcile with the legal reality that had evolved in American law. Advocates of section 9 rely "not so much on the merits or the positive excellence of the floating lien as on an argument of *fait accompli.*"[17] Similar arguments are raised in the report of the Cork Commission in England, where the question of security interests in future assets has only recently been examined. The Commission referred to the demand that corporate debtors be divested of the right to create floating charges, due to the preference which they grant to secured creditors as opposed to the regular creditors of the company. Rather than justify the institution of the floating charge, the report states that "the floating charge has become so fundamental a part of the financial structure of the United Kingdom that its abolition cannot be contemplated."[18]

Contrary to the United States and England, in Israel we do not face a situation in which security interests in future assets have already become established practice, thereby leaving the legislature little choice but to reconcile with and regulate it. Hence, one must pose the question whether it would be worthwhile to incorporate general recognition of security interests in future assets by non-corporate debtors into Israeli law. It is accordingly necessary to acknowledge that the aforementioned countries acted out of resignation when formalising the institution of security interests in future assets by non-corporate debtors. Moreover, the states that actually do so are few. The recommendation of the Cork Commission that security interests in future assets be made available to non-corporate debtors has yet to be realised. The fact that the English institution of the floating charge, which was adopted in many countries (Israel among them), was strictly confined to corporate debtors is indeed illustrative.[19] Throughout Europe, security interests in future assets are usually viewed as fraudulent as against the debtor's other creditors. A charge of future assets is recognised on the Continent only as an exception, and in explicitly specified circumstances.[20] In sum, much reservation exists regarding security interests in future assets. Those countries that do recognise this institution have done so out of resignation with established reality, rather than out of appreciation of the benefits which it extends.

(c) *Lack of demand*

Abiding by the policy that superfluous legislation should be avoided the commission inquired to what extent there was a real need for a floating charge by non-corporate debtors. Examination of this question has failed to yield any clear evidence of such a demand. No requests were forthcoming from any sector of credit consumers to introduce security interests in future assets in addition to those presently available. Experts invited to testify before the Commission did not provide any clear appraisal of whether this is to be considered a void in the Israeli legal system, or whether a desire for such floating charges indeed exists among non-corporate borrowers. Although it was claimed that it was unreasonable to force the incorporation of a debtor for the sole purpose of enjoying the benefits of credit in exchange for a floating charge, the Commission was not presented with any evidence clearly indicating a substantial phenomenon of incorporation for the primary purpose of creating floating charges. Moreover, the Transfer of Obligations Law, 1969, enables a non-corporate debtor to create security interests in future obligations. No argument was raised before the Commission that this option has been widely utilised, which might perhaps justify its extension to other types of future assets in addition to future obligations. On the contrary, there was evidence that little use had been made of future obligations as security.

It should be noted in this context that although the floating charge applies to the general future assets of a company, its recipients apparently prefer to realise the charge by acting against the rights of the company towards clients with outstanding debts rather than against corporeal assets held by the company. In other words, creditors in possession of a floating charge prefer future obligations as collateral, rather than tangible property.[21] Since the charge of future obligations by non-corporate debtors is provided for by present Israeli law, practically speaking, it is possible to take advantage of the essential benefits to be had from security interests in future assets without any need for additional legislation to that end.

In any case, there is no evidence that the present limitation on the charge of future assets by a non-corporate debtor to future obligations has caused any substantial inconvenience in the credit market, or that an actual demand exists on the part of the borrowers to extend this framework to include future inventory as well as obligations.

(d) *Extensive legislation will be required to remedy negative side effects*

The ramifications of making the floating charge available to non-corporate debtors might be such that manifold amendments of the law would then be required to take care of these ramifications. This is a price one would be willing to pay if convinced of the need to extend the floating charge to non-corporate debtors. However, the greater the doubts regarding the justification of such an extension of the floating charge the less justified seems the price involved. These ramifications include:

(i) *Impairment of the position of regular debtors and subjugation of debtor's future.* It is expected that, as a matter of routine, banking institutions will insist that a general charge on future assets be added to the specific securities supplied by their clients as collateral for loans. Inasmuch as such a charge could only be to his benefit, it is unlikely that a professional lender would relinquish the use of this legal instrument. Consequently, in the case of bankruptcy the majority of the bankrupt's assets would be subordinated to secured creditors, while the regular, unsecured creditors (such as claimants in torts, small suppliers, employees owed wages, public authorities owed taxes, etc.) would not receive anything. This is not mere conjecture, but rather the reality in states which recognise the possibility of creating security interests in future assets.[22] The phenomenon will be particularly grave should a practice develop according to which a customer will be required to charge all of his future property in order to finance the purchase of consumer goods.[23] In England, practice has indicated that the liquidation of companies that have granted floating charges usually leaves nothing for the regular, unsecured creditors. The floating charge has accordingly been the target of substantial criticism there.[24] In the United States as well, these two negative ramifications of security interests on future assets have been noted, *i.e.* the limitation of the possibility that regular creditors will be paid in time of bankruptcy and the subjugation of the debtor's entire future in order to secure a present debt.[25] In Israel it must be expected that a charge on future assets will be accompanied by an undertaking that the debtor will not transfer ownership of the charged asset without the consent of the creditor, even when such transfer is subject to the charge.[26] This will increase the element of subjugation inherent in security interests in future assets. Attempts have been made to deal with these problems through special legislation. For example, there are laws that list types of creditors that are to be given priority over the creditors possessing security interests on future assets, and laws negating the application of security interests in future assets on consumer goods. A proposal has also been made that a certain percentage of the value of assets subject to securities be set aside for the benefit of regular, unsecured creditors in time of bankruptcy.[27]

(ii) *Floating charge holder monopolising debtor's future credit.* A debtor who provides a lender with a charge on his future assets is in essence granting him a monopoloy in the event that the debtor will require additional loans. The debtor will not be free to offer any of his assets as collateral to another creditor. The first lender will retain the monopoly until the debtor pays his debt in full. When the charge is given in order to secure future debts the debtor's release is likely to encounter particular difficulties. Such monopolies, a side effect of security interests in future assets, require legislative intervention in order to mitigate their ramifications. This problem has been partially dealt with in the United States by giving priority to a subsequent creditor when the debtor purchased the asset that he pledged to that creditor by means of a loan given by him.[28] Subsequent creditors whose funds did not finance the purchase of the debtor's assets will, however, be unable to enjoy priority. Other conceivable legislative solutions include (1) guarantee of the debtor's right to terminate the security at any time before the agreed date by an early payment of his debt, and (2) the right to release specific assets from the charge should their value substantially exceed the amount of the debt which they secure.

(iii) *Floating charges by individuals and the doctrine of "reputed ownership."* Recognition of security interests in future assets by non-corporate debtors will require legislation to amend the Bankruptcy Ordinance regarding reputed ownership. At present, the general creditors of the bankrupt can be satisfied out of movable property in the possession of the bankrupt for occupational purposes, when he is reputed to be the owner of such property, even though a third party may have property rights in such assets. Security interests in future assets, whose primary purpose is the transient inventory assets of the debtor (who is the reputed owner thereof), will be frustrated if the doctrine of reputed ownership remains in effect, inasmuch as it would enable all of the bankrupt's creditors to be satisfied out of the inventory of the bankrupt although subject to the security interest. With regard to floating charges, this doctrine was indeed rendered inapplicable in liquidation of companies.

Many of the problems listed above can, perhaps, be rectified by legislative activity but, given the lack of demand for the extension of floating charges to non-corporate debtors, and the other difficulties involved with such an extension, one wonders whether the allocation of scarce resources and considerable effort for drafting the many amendments that would be required would be justified.

Conclusion

After having weighed the reasons for and against introducing floating charges on non-corporate assets, as described above, the conclusion reached by the commission was to recommend no change in the present law. This recommendation was adopted by the Minister of Justice, with the result that floating charges under Israeli law continue to be available only to companies and co-operatives, but not to individuals.

NOTES

* This article is based on a faculty seminar held at University College and on a report written by the author when acting as chairman of the Pledges Law Revision Committee, in Israel (21 *Is.L.Rev.* 129 (1986)).

[1] On the question of what the other causes for crystallisation are see: R. R. Pennington, "Loans to Companies: The Development of the Law," *Company Law in Change: Current Legal Problems* (1987) P. 91, at pp. 107 *et seq.*

[2] Article One of the Companies Ordinance. Although the article does not explicitly mention sale, judicial interpretation has left no doubt as to its inclusion. See *Bank Leumi Ltd.* v. *Anglo-Palestine Bank* (1972) 26 (ii) P.D. 468–473.

[3] The Companies Ordinance (N.V.), 1983, 37 *Dinei Medinat Israel* (N.V.) 761, articles 1, 164, 166.

[4] *Electrogenics Ltd.* v. *Elsint Ltd.*, C.A. 471/73, 29 P.D. (1) 121.

[5] The mere filing of the floating charge agreement does not achieve constructive notice. It is only the separate registration of the restriction which gives rise to constructive notice.

[6] Amendment No. 17, of 1980, of the Companies Ordinance.

[7] *Credit Bank* v. *Receiver of D.T.P. Co.* C.A. 288/68 22 P.D. (2) 529.

[8] A security which applies to after-acquired property is not, because of that, equivalent to a floating charge. Further, the subordination of a floating charge to levies by other creditors is not, in itself, an essential feature of the floating charge. Such subordination can be excluded from a floating charge by an agreement that an attempt to levy by any creditor will bring about the crystallisation of the floating charge.

[9] *Supra.* n. 4.

[10] *Rosenstreich* v. *Hevra Eretz-Israel Leautomobilim Ltd.*, C.A. 716/72, 27 P.D. (2) 709.

[11] *Bank Leumi Ltd.* v. *Bank Eretz Israel Britania*, C.A. 603/71, 26 P.D. (2) 468.

[12] *Supra* n. 3.

[13] The members of the commission were: Ephraim Avramson, Gideon Ben-Dov, Haim Crown, Davida Lachman-Messer, Varda Losthoiz, Avraham Lozowick, Tana Shpanitz and Shimon Weiss. The secretary of the commission was Rivka Levi and the present author served as its chairman. The recommendation of the commission was reached by a vote 6–3.

[14] *Yekutiel* v. *Bergman* (1975) 29 (ii) P.D. 757,.765; see Zeltner, *Sale Law*, 1968 in *Commentary on Laws Relating to Contracts*, G. Tedeschi, ed. (Jerusalem, 1972, in Hebrew), section 2.

[15] Insolvency Law and Practice, 1982, Cmnd. 8558 (1982), p. 354 (known as the Cork Commission); Report on Consumer Credit, 1971, Cmnd. 4596, (1971), (known as the Crowther Report), Article 5.6.5.

[16] Jackson and Kronman, "Secured Financing and Priorities among Creditors" 1979) 88 *Yale L.J.* 1143, 1158.

[17] G. Gilmore, *Security Interests in Personal Property* (Boston, Little, Brown, 1965) vol. 1, p. 360.

[18] Cork Commission Report, *op. cit. supra* n. 15 at 345–346.

[19] A. S. Abel, "Has Article 9 Scuttled the Floating Charges?" in Ziegel and Foster, *Aspects of Comparative Commercial Law* (Dobbs Ferry, Oceana, 1969) 410, 413.

[20] Cork Commission Report, *op. cit. supra* n. 15, at 344–345.

[21] Mr. Lev, presenting the banker's perspective, testified that regarding floating charges, he attributes greater importance to debts owed to his clients, rather than merchandise which they may possess. Merchandise necessitates a search for a buyer, while the former type of security does not.

[22] A. Schwartz, "Security Assets and Bankruptcy Priorities: A Review of Current Theories" (1981) 10 J. Leg. Studies 1, 4–5.

[23] R. H. McLaren, *Secured Transactions in Personal Property in Canada* Toronto, 1980, s.5.02.

[24] Cork Commission Report, *op. cit. supra* n. 14, at 4, 32, 34.

[25] G. Gilmore, *op. cit. supra* n. 17, at 360.

[26] This is the lesson that may be learned from the Israeli experience with floating charges. A practice has developed according to which such charges are rendered conditional upon an undertaking by the debtor not to transfer any of his assets in the absence of the creditor's consent, with the exception of inventory assets transferred in the ordinary course of business.

[27] Cork Commission Report, *op. cit. supra* n. 15, at 345–346.

[28] "Purchase Money Security Interest," see Gilmore, *op. cit. supra* n. 17, at 349–350; Jackson and Kronman, *op. cit. supra* n. 16 at 1167.

The Soviet Procuracy under Gorbachev

HIROSHI ODA

The Procuracy in the Soviet Union and East European countries is unique in that the procurators are empowered to monitor the activities of administrative agencies and officials from a legal point of view. The Soviet Constitution provides that the Procurator-General and the procurators subordinated to him exercise supreme supervision over the activities of ministries, state committees, agencies, enterprises, and government officials.[1]

Traditionally, this power of general supervision has been regarded as the primary function of Soviet Procuracy. In addition, the Procuracy plays a major role in criminal procedure. Procurators take part in the investigation of crimes, supervise the activities of other investigative agencies, approve arrest warrants and indictments, and take part in trials. They are also charged with supervising places of detention and penitentiary institutions. A controversial function exercised by the Procuracy is that of "judicial supervision." Procurators are expected to supervise the legality of civil and criminal proceedings and rectify any illegality by way of appeal or supervisory procedure. Since their role is not limited to criminal procedure, they are called procurators instead of public prosecutors.

Generally, in Civil Law countries, public prosecutors exercise broad powers, and are often more powerful than the judges. This was true with Japanese public prosecutors before the Second World War. Owing to their close links with the Ministry of Justice, which was empowered to appoint judges, public prosecutors held a much more prestigious position than judges. Talented judges were often recruited to work as public prosecutors. Vested with a vast power, Soviet procurators are even more powerful than the public prosecutors in other countries with Civil Law tradition. While the position of the Procurator-General accompanied the membership of the C.P.S.U. Central Committee, which signifies the prestige of

213

an agency, since 1961, the Chairman of the U.S.S.R. Supreme Court became a member only in 1976.[2]

In order to find out the reason why the Soviet procurators were given the power to monitor the activities of the administration, one has to look into its history—back to the eighteenth century. The prototype of the Soviet Procuracy can be traced back to the reign of Peter the Great. In 1722, he established the post of the Procurator-General and some senior procurators in order to ensure that his orders were implemented strictly by his subordinates. Thus, Russian procurators started not as prosecutors, but as officials supervising the administrative apparatus. In 1864, a large-scale judicial reform took place in Russia. This was truly a progressive reform, reputed to be the most advanced in the Western world at that time. By this reform, the procurators were deprived of the power to supervise the administrative apparatus and their power came to be limited to criminal procedure.[3]

The position of procurators was abolished by the October Revolution in 1917. However, five years after the Revolution, the Procuracy, modelled after the eighteenth-century Russian system, was reintroduced. The plan to restore the Procuracy met vigorous opposition from among the Bolsheviks. It was only with the personal interference of Lenin—he actually persuaded his colleagues to reconsider the draft which had once been disapproved—that the Statute on Procuratorial Supervision was enacted. The Soviet regime was in need of an agency which was capable of overseeing the activities of local governments and lower echelons of the administration. This agency had to be politically reliable, which meant that they had to be staffed with members of the Communist Party and not Mensheviks or Socialist Revolutionaries. In order to ensure that the agency was staffed with reliable personnel, the officials had to be appointed from above and not elected by citizens, as was the case with judges. With this background, the old procuratorial system with officials appointed from above and acting as the eyes of the Tsar emerged as the best system.

It should be added that there was a proposal to establish a system of administrative courts. This was supported by the Liberal Democrats who remained in Russia after the Revolution. However, this proposal was not accepted, partly because it was supported by the liberals—members of the bourgeoisie, and partly because supervision of the administrative apparatus was considered to be a concern of the state, and should not be left to the initiative of private individuals.[4]

Since the enactment of the Statute on Procuratorial Supervision in 1922, there were three major changes in the law. First, in 1933, the all-union Procuracy was established. Then in 1955, a new Statute on Procuratorial Supervision was enacted. Third, after the adoption of the U.S.S.R. Constitution in 1977, a new law on the Procuracy was enacted in 1979. Apart from the establishment of the U.S.S.R. Procuracy in 1933, the organisation and the power of the Procuracy have remained almost unchanged since 1922. However, it should not be overlooked that legislative change concerning the Procuracy has always come at the time of political change. 1922 was one year after the New Economic Policy was launched. 1933 signifies the consolidation of Stalin's rule. The Statute of 1955 was one of the first pieces of legislation which underwent revision after the death of Stalin. The 1977 law—the present law—is a direct outcome of the new Constitution. Finally, in June 1987, amidst Gorbachev's reforms, the power of the Procuracy has been expanded. This indicates the significance attached to the Procuracy by political leaders.

In order to discuss the recent developments involving the Procuracy, it is necessary to give an overview of the structure and the role of the Procuracy. The following data are based upon a survey and computer analysis of the career patterns of 274 senior procurators conducted by the present author.

The law provides that procurators must have received a legal education, have to be over 25, and have to be morally and politically sound.[5] Although a legal education was not a statutory requirement until 1979, the Procuracy has been staffed with highly-qualified officials from the beginning. While a majority of judges had not received legal education in the 1920's, the overwhelming majority of procurators and other officials of the Procuracy had had a legal education. The general educational level of the procurators was much higher than that of the judges in the 1920s. At present, with the exception of some elderly procurators, almost all procurators and investigators attached to the Procuracy have received some form of advanced legal education.[6]

The primary institutions which provide higher legal education in the U.S.S.R. are the law faculties of the state universities and juridical institutes. There are 48 state universities which provide legal education and four juridical institutes.[7] Out of 274 senior procurators whose career is known, 147 graduated from state universities while 82 came from juridical institutes. Among the universities and juridical institutes, Sverdrovsk and Khar'kov Juridical Institutes have produced more senior procurators than the remaining two institutes: 25 and 22 respectively.

The Procuracy has very close links with the Communist Party of the Soviet Union (hereafter C.P.S.U.). The recruitment of personnel is carefully arranged by the Procuracy in co-ordination with party organisations and educational institutions. Thus, the former Procurator General, R. A. Rudenko had been seconded from a local party organisation to work in the Procuracy.[8] This is not an isolated case. The late deputy Procurator-General was also seconded from the party.[9]

Recruitment to the Procuracy starts before a candidate enters university or juridical institute. This is through the system of *abitur*. The Procuracy, in co-ordination with party and komsomol organisations, educational institutions, trade union organisations, etc., selects suitable candidates for possible entry into the Procuracy and recommends them to the universities and juridical institutes. The overall number of these *abiturients* is controlled by the U.S.S.R. Procuracy.[10] Other law-enforcement agencies such as the courts and the Ministry of Internal Affairs also have such a system.[11] In 1986, 1,200 *abiturients* who were recommended by the Procuracy were accepted as first-year students of law faculties and juridical institutes.[12] People who are recommended by the Procuracy to these legal institutions are chosen from among young people who are politically reliable and with good academic records, young workers who are politically active and are ardent workers—"vanguards of production," and demobilised youth who have distinct military and political ability. Upon the request of the U.S.S.R. Procuracy, the Ministry of Higher and Intermediate Special Education issued an instruction to higher educational institutions to accept, outside fixed quota, those who have been demobilised and wish to work in the Procuracy, provided that they are recommended by the Procuracy.[13] Local procuracies are expected to keep close contact with those *abiturients* and assist them in their education and training.

This system is sometimes abused by officials of the Procuracy by recommending children of influential persons or accepting bribes for recommendation.[14] In 1983, it was revealed that the Procuracy of Krasnodal Region had arranged illegal entry of 30 students in the law faculty of Kuban State University.[15] More recently, incidents of abuse of power, "protectionism" and even bribery were revealed in Moscow and other law faculties as well as Sverdrovsk Juridical Institute.[16] The procurator of Kemerovskaia province and the head and a procurator of the department for cadres of the province were dismissed for recommending children of influential officials to a juridical institute.[17]

The procurators and other staff are reviewed periodically by attestation. At each level of the Procuracy, an attestation commission is formed with the participation of a representative of the C.P.S.U.[18] Those who are found by the attestation commission to be unsuitable for their positions are dismissed or transferred.[19] Usually the secretary of the party organisation within the Procuracy takes part in attestation, but in some cases, representatives of the local party organisation, and even the Central Committee department are present in attestation proceedings.

The personnel of the Procuracy do not necessarily come directly from universities and juridical institutes. Out of 274 senior procurators, 21 procurators have had experience in other agencies (Table 1). These agencies include: the courts, the Ministry of Internal Affairs, the Ministry of Justice and its subordinate organisations, and the trade unions. There were altogether 10 procurators who had formerly worked in the court. There was even a case where a president of the provincial court became a procurator of a province. There are also transfers from the Procuracy to the courts and other agencies. The current Chairman of the U.S.S.R. Supreme Court once worked in the Procuracy before being transferred to the Ministry of Justice. A first deputy procurator of a republic later became a vice-chairman of the republican supreme court.[20] The newly-appointed chairman of the Ukrainian K.G.B. was once a procurator.[21]

Personnel exchange between the Procuracy and the courts and other agencies symbolises the peculiarity of the interrelations between these agencies. In the Soviet Union, there is a concept of law-enforcement agencies, which covers not only the Procuracy, the Ministry of Internal Affairs, and the K.G.B., but also extends to the courts. These agencies are expected to pursue a common goal—"liquidation of violations of law." As the C.P.S.U. Politbureau decision of October 2, 1986 pointed out, "the Procuracy, police, courts, and other law enforcement agencies are required to serve as examples of the observance of law, at the same time, earnestly reveal anti-social phenomena and conduct the struggle against crime and other violations of law without compromise."[22]

Soviet courts do not passively hand out sentences on the merits of the cases. They are required to follow a common criminal policy which is set by the political leadership. For instance, in the recent campaign against alcoholism, the courts were required, *inter alia*, to ensure that violations concerning alcoholic beverages were punished accordingly and offenders who committed crimes while intoxicated receive aggravated punishment. The courts were recommended to see to it that alcoholics be sent to compulsory treatment and remove the cause of alcohol abuse in individual cases by way of a special decision of the court.[23] The Procuracy, in turn, is expected to supervise the courts so that judgments strictly coincide with the policy set by the political leaders. In a resolution of the Presidium of the Supreme Soviet of February 1987, the Procuracy, the police, and the court of a certain province were jointly blamed for the failure in "preventing drunkenness and ensuring the inevitability of punishment for violating the law."[24]

Law-enforcement agencies are required to co-ordinate their activities in order to achieve their common goal. A co-ordination committee of the law-enforcement agencies is organised from the all-union level down to the district level.[25] A co-ordinative meeting takes place twice a year at the all-union level, while it is convened every three to four months at the province and regional level.[26] Representatives of the C.P.S.U. invariably take part in the meeting.

At the provincial level, co-ordination meetings discuss the situation concerning crimes in the locality, work out annual plans of the province for combatting crime, and make specific recommendations concerning criminal policy.[27] The plans and recommendations are sent to the lower-level cities and districts, where annual plans and measures for the cities and districts are worked out. The plans and measures at each level are confirmed by party organisations beforehand.

In July 1984, a co-ordination meeting of law-enforcement agencies of the union republics took place. The meeting was chaired by the U.S.S.R. Procurator-General: the Chairman of the Supreme Court, the Minister of Internal Affairs of the U.S.S.R., and the Minister of Justice took part. Representatives of the C.P.S.U. were present and the deputy head of the administrative organs department of the Central Committee gave a speech on the topic—the struggle against social parasites and vagrants. At the meeting, it was pointed out that law-enforcement agencies had been slow in performing the tasks given by the party and the government—struggle against parasites and vagrants. Some provincial courts were criticised for not clarifying the sources of income of those who were brought to trial as parasites. City and provincial procuracies were blamed for not reacting to these shortcomings on the part of the courts.[28]

In practice, co-ordination meetings often become a formality. "Departmentalism" of each agency makes co-ordination of activities difficult. Recommendations of such conferences are sometimes superficial and are without specific proposals. Some procurators are passive and inactive in the conference and leave the steering of the meeting to the representatives of party organisations.[29]

As is the case with all other institutions in the U.S.S.R., the activities of the Procuracy are closely monitored by the C.P.S.U.[30] The administrative organs department attached to the C.P.S.U. Central Committee is responsible for supervising the Procuracy. At the local level, local party organisations as well as party organisations organised within the procuracies keep a close eye on the Procuracy in order to ensure that nothing goes on without the knowledge of the C.P.S.U. As the secretary of the U.S.S.R. Procuracy's party committee has put it, no one is beyond the control of the C.P.S.U.[31]

The appointment of procurators also requires the approval of party organisations. The Constitution and the Law provide that the Procurator-General is to be appointed by the Supreme Soviet, and other procurators are appointed by the superior procuracy.[32] What is not written in the Constitution and the Law is that no appointments to senior positions within the Procuracy, from the Procurator-General down to the district procurator and his deputies, can be made without the approval of the respective party organisations.

Each level of territorial party organisations has a list of positions which require the approval of the party. This list is called the *nomenklatura*. Presumably, procurators of the union republics are on the all-union *nomenklatura* as well as the union republican *nomenklatura*.[33] Archival materials show that provincial procurators are on the union republic and provincial *nomenklaturas*. For instance, the appointment of a provincial procurator—who is the head of the provincial Procuracy—has to be approved by the party organisations at the union republic level as well as at the provincial level. The appointment of the procurator of a union republic is made with the approval of the all-union party apparatus and the republican party apparatus.[34]

The percentage of C.P.S.U. members within the Procuracy is very high. The percentage was already high in the 1920's, when there were not so many party members. At present, around 70 per cent. of all personnel in the Procuracy are party members. This figure is very high, considering the fact that this includes young recruits to the Procuracy who have not yet joined the party. Furthermore, out of 274 senior procurators whose career is known, all without exception, were party members. It should be noted that most senior procurators are members of the party committee at the respective level. Thus, the head of the provincial Procuracy is usually a member of the provincial party committee.

Some of them are even members of the party bureau, which is the executive body of local party organisations—a body of a small group of local party elites.[35] The links the Procuracy has with the C.P.S.U. are even closer than has been imagined in the West. The analysis of the careers of senior procurators show that, on average, 30 per cent. of senior procurators have worked in the C.P.S.U. apparatus as full-time party officials (Table 2). The average length of their service was 5.2 years.

At the top level, the former deputy Procurator-General is now the deputy head of the administrative organs department of the C.P.S.U. The former sector head of this department had been transferred to the Procuracy and became a deputy Procurator General. This was S. A. Shishkov, who had worked in the Central Committee apparatus for 15 years, first as an instructor, and later as head of a section supervising the Procuracy, courts, and the Ministry of Justice.[36]

Out of 15 procurators of the union republics, seven have had experience in the party apparatus as department instructors of the all-union apparatus, as heads of the provincial administrative organs department, and in other senior capacities.

It is presumably because of this close link with the C.P.S.U. and the high quality of personnel, including their political reliability, that the Procuracy was entrusted to carry out the anti-crime campaigns since the late 1970s.

The drive towards the "strengthening of socialist legality," which started in the late 1970s placed the Procuracy in the forefront of this political campaign. It should be noted that strengthening socialist legality in this context primarily means strict observance of laws and elimination of crimes. It is not necessarily a concept which is aimed at protecting citizens from the abuses of the state power. Near the end of Brezhnev's rule, social and economic stagnation was evident. Corruption was rampant everywhere and nepotism among senior party officials resulted in gross social injustice. In order to revitalise the economy, a strict state and social discipline was needed. After all, in a system where officials take bribes, embezzle public property, produce sub-standard goods, and where workers pilfer state property to meet their daily needs and indulge in their own "private enterprise," it is inconceivable that the economy could continue growing. Thus, a campaign for strengthening law and order was launched in 1978.

Considering the power given to the Procuracy, it was natural that it was expected to play a major role in this campaign. In early 1979, the Presidium of the Supreme Soviet discussed the activities of the Procuracy and the Ministry of Internal Affairs and gave a rather critical assessment.[37] In the same year, the Central Committee of the C.P.S.U. passed a resolution "On the Improvement of Activities of Protecting Law and Order and Strengthening of The Struggle Against Violations of Law." In this resolution it was pointed out that the 'task of strengthening socialist legality" was not being carried out effectively enough. The Procuracy was required to eliminate shortcomings in the work of lower procuracies, increase responsibility of cadres and strenghthen discipline. As primary areas of responsibility, the Procuracy was recommended to

(1) improve the work on the preservation of social order in the cities;

(2) consistently enforce the campaign against alcoholism;

(3) improve works concerning the prevention of offences by minors;

(4) strengthen the struggle against violations of socialist properties;

(5) activate the struggle against parasites and speculators.[38]

The Procuracy's response to this resolution was rather half-hearted, perhaps because the resolution did not specifically single out the Procuracy for criticism. A leading article in a periodical published by the Procuracy discussed this resolution, but seemed to be shifting the blame to the Ministry of Internal Affairs.[39] The activities of the Procuracy did not seem to have changed significantly in the remaining three years of Brezhnev's rule.

Perhaps the only exception was in Georgia. E. Shevarnadze, current Politbureau member and the foreign minister, who was then the first secretary of the Georgian Republic, carried out a large-scale purge of law-enforcement agencies within the Republic. According to the Procurator of the Republic, A. Barabadze, the campaign against negative phenomena started in 1972, *i.e.* the year when Shevarnadze became the first secretary, and was intensified after the Central Committee's resolution.[40] In nearly 40 towns and districts, procurators were sacked for their failure to control "negative phenomena," *i.e.* bribery, extortion, speculation, black-marketeering, report-padding, etc. In one district, the entire staff of the procuracy was removed.[41]

In 1982, Andropov succeeded Brezhnev. He launched a campaign against corruption, which was to be pursued also by his successors Chernenko and Gorbachev. Corruption in the Soviet

Union is a broad concept; it covers all crimes in which government officials are involved or which involve public property. Not only bribery and extortion, but also report-padding, embezzlement and theft of socialist property are included. Since Andropov, Soviet criminal law has undergone various amendments, which resulted in the expansion of criminal sanctions.

In January 1983, the Presidium of the Supreme Soviet discussed the activities of the Procuracy in its regular meeting. Andropov and other members of the Politbureau were present. In the speeches, Andropov and others stressed the necessity of improving the activities of the Procuracy, especially the uncovering of thefts of socialist property, abuses of power by officials and bribery. The Presidium adopted a resolution "On the Activities of the Procuracy" which made it clear that there were "essential shortcomings" in the activities of the Procuracy. The resolution criticised the Procuracy in that the struggle for the strengthening of socialist legality had not progressed, and co-ordination with other law-enforcement agencies concerning prevention of crimes had been poorly organised. Because of departmentalism and local favouritism, the struggle against report-padding was also ineffective. Procurators were not always active in their supervisory functions, failed to eliminate violations of law and were lax in pursuing offenders.

Since the drive for socialist legality had emerged from economic necessity, the resolution pointed out that special attention should be paid to the ensuring of legality in the field of the economy. The strengthening of state, planning, and labour discipline, the protection of socialist property and natural resources were among the most important fields of activity.[42]

While the Procuracy itself was slow in reacting to these criticisms, the C.P.S.U. selected several Central Asian republics as targets of the clean-up. The Procuracy was actively involved in this drive against corruption. It should be noted that the Procuracy, in such a campaign, does not act on its own. Usually, it is the C.P.S.U. leaders in Moscow who single out a target area and carry out a clean-up campaign there. The Procuracy is merely an instrument in this campaign. More often than not, the Procuracy at the republic level becomes an object of this campaign rather than the instrument.

Uzbekistan was one of the union republics which was singled out by the party leadership as being corrupt to the roots. The clean-up campaign had started in 1983 when the long-time party first secretary of Uzbekistan, S. Rashidov, came under sharp criticism from Moscow for having manipulated the cotton harvest figures. A commission attached to the Central Committee, with representatives of the C.P.S.U. administrative organs department, was sent to the republic to conduct an investigation.[43] Large-scale padding of plan results and embezzlement in the cotton sector were uncovered. At the session of the plenum meeting of the republican central committee in June 1984, it was revealed that deception, embezzlement and bribery had been encountered all over the republic. Farms paid bribes to government officials in order to obtain receipts for the delivery of non-existent raw cotton. This payment was embezzled by officials and farm administrators. The heads of major industrial enterprises were found guilty of falsifying production figure achievements. In Tashkent province alone, 1,056 employees of shops, depots and hospitals were dismissed and some of them were brought to trial.

Law-enforcement agencies in the republic were unable to cope with rampant corruption. It was only with the assistance of "central monitoring agencies," *i.e.* on the initiative of Moscow, that measures against corruption were adopted in the republic.[44]

Under Gorbachev, the struggle for state, social, production, and labour discipline has become more intensive. Gorbachev's economic reforms require some breathing space in the political system and have therefore accompanied liberalisation and democratisation to a certain degree. However, at the same time, in order to achieve efficiency and productivity in the economy, strict discipline was needed. Again, the Procuracy was expected to play a significant role.

Already at the Supreme Soviet session of July 1985, which heard the report of the Procurator-General A. M. Rekunkov, V. P. Mironov, a C.P.S.U. Central Committee member and the Chairman of the Legislative Proposals Committee of the Council of Nationalities, criticised the "considerable shortcomings" in the Procuracy's work, especially in the field of the economy. He pointed out that the activities of the Procuracy and other law-enforcement agencies in preventing and combatting crimes did not fully meet the targets set by the Party and the state. There had been serious shortcomings in the work of agencies of inquiry and preliminary investigation in the investigation of crimes and in seeing that persons guilty of crimes did not escape punishment.[45]

In his speech at the 27th Party Congress in early 1986, Gorbachev stressed that any attempt to obtain "unearned" income had to be prevented. He pointed out ruefully that there still were those who do not consider it a crime to steal from their workplaces and do not hesitate to abuse their positions for mercenary crimes. He concluded that the law should be employed in full measure in the struggle against crimes and other violations.[46] He referred to the Procuracy and stated that the role of the Procuracy should be decisively strengthened.[47]

Soon afterwards, a wide-scale campaign against "unearned" income was launched. As the Procurator-General pointed out, the chief source of such income was criminal activity, theft, bribery, speculation, extortion and report-padding.[48] This campaign can be regarded as a continuation and development of the campaign against corruption which was passed under Andropov and Chernenko.

In Georgia, a collegium meeting of the republican Procuracy took place in 1985. At this meeting, the secretary as well as the head of the administrative organs department of the republican communist party and a representative of Moscow—the deputy Procurator-General Shiskov, formerly a section head of the C.P.S.U. administrative organs department—were present.[49] It was reported at the collegium meeting that the activities concerning observance of law in the economic field and the strengthening of state and labour discipline had only slightly increased. In another collegium meeting in February 1986, it was pointed out that corruption was still rampant. Report-padding could be seen in one out of two enterprises; in construction and transportation organisations, it was even worse. However, in most cases, procurators closed their eyes to these gross violations of law. The activities of the Procuracy in combatting the production of substandard goods were ineffective. The preservation of social order had not reached a satisfactory standard, the prevention of crimes was insufficient and serious crimes were unexposed because of poor organisation.[50] If these negative phenomena were to be eliminated, the Party newspaper commented, the economic potential of the republic would be much better.[51]

In the republican central committee plenum which was held in October 1986, the problem of further strengthening socialist legality was discussed. On this occasion, it was reported that a city procurator had been dismissed for serious offences and a district procurator was recommended to leave because of lax supervision and investigative activities.[52]

In Turkmenstan, on the initiative of Moscow, Tashauz Province was singled out for criticism in October 1986.[53] In this province, report-padding, theft of socialist property, embezzlement of state funds, and "other ugly phenomena" had become widespread. Local party organisations often shielded these officials. For flagrant violations of party and state discipline, for closing their eyes to report-padding and deception of the state, and even corruption, top party officials of the province were dismissed and eventually tried by the court.[54]

What was disturbing for the political leaders as well as the Procuracy was that the procuracies of the Central Asian republics have not only been inactive or closed their eyes to corruption, but closed their eyes out of favouritism and even taken bribes. This was bluntly pointed out by Gorbachev in the Central Committee plenum of January 1987.[55]

In one province of Uzbekistan, no less than 398 employees of these agencies were dismissed and brought to trial for bribe-taking, abuse of power and other offences. In another province, the provincial procurator and the head of the internal affairs administration were involved in embezzlement and bribery on a large scale.[56] Even an investigator for especially important cases of the republican Procuracy was found to be involved in fabricating a case against a party official, who had criticised his superior.[57] He was dismissed and arrested for a number of serious crimes. In addition, the former first deputy procurator of Uzbekistan was relieved from his position and expelled from the Party. Also a number of lower staff of the Procuracy were dismissed.[58]

In Turkmenstan, the new first secretary of the republic told the plenum of the republican central committee that attempts of the law-enforcement agencies to bring those guilty of economic crimes to the court had been blocked by corrupt officials. He even implied that the Minister of Internal Affairs and the Procurator were somehow involved in the cover-up.[59] The Party press asserted that the republican Minister of Internal Affairs and the republican procurator should be held responsible for the extremely grave situation.[60]

The U.S.S.R. Procuracy, presumably in co-operation with the Party leaders in Moscow, sent a brigade of investigation to Turkmenstan in November 1986. This brigade was headed by the Deputy Procurator-General S. Shishkov. The brigade uncovered various shortcomings of the Procuracy in the republic. The republic procurator, his deputies, the provincial procurators of Tashauz and other provinces were criticised for delays in reacting to negative phenomena and their indifference to such problems: Hearing the report of Shishkov, the collegium of the U.S.S.R. Procuracy instructed the procurators of Kazakhstan, Kirgiz, and Tazhikstan republics to take certain remedial steps.[61] The procurator of Turkmenstan, Khar'chenko, was dismissed in 1987.[62] A similar brigade was sent to Azerbaidzhan headed by the Deputy Procurator-General V. Naidenov, who also had worked in the Central Committee department.[63]

In October 1986, the Politbureau discussed the activities of law-enforcement agencies. It was decided to restructure the activities of the Procuracy, *militsiia*, courts and other law-enforcement agencies.[64] The Central Committee adopted a resolution following discussions in the Politbureau. According to this resolution, activities aimed at enforcing legality and legal order were still not sufficiently effective and did not meet contemporary demands. In day-to-day activities of state and economic organisations, serious violations of law occur frequently. The struggle against violations of state and social property and other mercenary crimes has faltered. "This explained why groups of thieves and bribetakers were able to operate in the ministries without being detected for so many years."

The resolution recommended the Procuracy and other law-enforcement agencies to eliminate shortcomings, improve leadership, and improve the quality of the cadres.[65]

What was new in this resolution was that not only was inactivity of some procurators blamed, but also improper interference from various quarters in the work of the Procuracy was criticised. The criticism of "local influence" itself is not new: this kind of pressure from the local party and government officials has been common and, from time to time, this practice has been criticised. However, none of these criticisms matched the scale of those under Gorbachev.

In the last three years, there has been a constant flow of articles in the media concerning the vulnerability of the procurators to pressure. In the Soviet Union, under a strict censorship, criticisms are never published without the approval of the C.P.S.U. Therefore, these published criticisms are tantamount to being those of the C.P.S.U. against the Procuracy. A celebrated case occurred in Novosibirsk. An employee of a factory was accused of stealing linoleum. A member of the district Procuracy came to the rescue of this person. The linoleum had actually been "put aside" for the district Procuracy. It was revealed, further, that some years ago, two other members of the Procuracy were accused of building a new home at a wholesale price, *i.e.* abusing their power. However, the district and the provincial procurators, as well as the provincial head of the administrative organs department tried to hush up the incident. The provincial procurator allowed the employees involved to retire and asked the provincial party organisation not to review these "minor offences." After the criticism appeared in Pravda, the provincial procurator and others involved were dismissed.[66] Similar incidents, mostly at provincial and regional levels were reported in *Pravda* and *Izvestiia*.[67]

Confronted with mounting criticisms of the Procuracy in the press, the Procurator-General had to give a press interview and refute the criticism.[68]

However, it is premature to conclude that the Procuracy has become a genuine independent agency—a guardian of law. The revelations are limited to interference by local party or government bosses, and the reason for interference is invariably one of personal interest. Criticism does not extend to political intervention: institutional interference by party organisations is still permissible. In the Central Committee resolution, party organisations were instructed to heighten the level of political guidance *vis-à-vis* the Procuracy. Primary party organisations were asked to increase their role in restructuring the Procuracy. In addition, the responsibility of the local party committees in the selection, placement, and training of cadres was stressed.[69]

Gorbachev's call for restructuring was seriously taken by the Procuracy. An article by the Procurator-General published in February 1987, while acknowledging some "slight improvement" in the activity of the Procuracy admitted that shortcomings were not entirely eliminated. He stated that the work of the Procuracy should be concentrated on especially significant areas, such as the struggle against report-padding and embezzlement of socialist property. He also emphasised the necessity of raising the standards of the procurators and went on to criticise the procurators of some republics.[70]

In response to Gorbachev's call for restructuring, especially the appeal to raise the quality of personnel, there was a fairly large-scale reshuffle of personnel within the Procuracy. As the deputy Procurator-General remarked, "a negative process which had developed in the 1970s, was inevitably reflected in the activities of the Procuracy and investigative agencies." In many (lower) procuracies, the timely transfer and replacement of cadres was not ensured.[71]

Improving the quality of cadres within the Procuracy thus has taken priority. Cadre policy, *i.e.* proper selection, training, and placement of cadre-members became one of the core-elements of "restructuring" the Procuracy.[72] First, aged "veterans" of the Procuracy were advised to retire. Younger personnel were promoted, and the staff of the Procuracy became much younger. Now 25 per cent. of procurators and investigators are under 30.[73] Whereas the average age of becoming a provincial procurator was 46.9 in 1981, it came down to 44.8 in 1987. Second, improvements in the system of *abiture* were stressed in order to ensure that the right people joined the Procuracy. In this regard, a joint meeting of the Ministry of Higher and Intermediate Special Education and law-enforcement agencies took place in late 1986 with the participation of a representative of the C.P.S.U. Central Committee department.[74] Third, attention was drawn to the system of attestation, which periodically reviews the suitability of personnel. It was stressed that when appointing procurators and investigators, the practical, personal and political qualities of the candidate as reflected in his past work should be examined in detail. One procurator commented that "shameless persons who commit immoral offences, drunkards" should not be allowed in the Procuracy.[75] It was recommended that the best way to judge these qualities was to take part in party meetings within the procuracies.[76]

In 1987 alone, at least six out of 15 republican procurators were replaced. Apart from the procurator of Moldavia, who retired without any pressure, all were dismissed for either lax enforcement of their duties or even involvement in violations of law. These included Kirgiz, Turkmenstan, Tazhik, and Lithuania. These republics have actually been targets of the clean-up campaign. The turnover of senior procurators in 1987 was the highest—56—in the last seven years (Table 3).

As if expressing dissatisfaction with the Party leaders of the Procuracy, the Politbureau in its regular meeting in June 1987 discussed measures to enhance the role of the Procuracy. Noting that the Procuracy occupies a significant position within the law-enforcement agencies, the Politbureau pointed out that the effectiveness of supervision over the observance of economic legislation had declined in recent years. The Politbureau stressed that it was necessary to effect a fundamental restructuring of the Procuracy and to improve drastically the form, style and methods of its activity. It was decided to give additional power to the Procuracy.[77]

Following the discussions in the Politbureau, the Central Committee adopted a resolution entitled "On Measures for Increasing the Role of Procuratorial Supervision for The Strengthening of Socialist Legality and Law and Order."[78] The resolution pointed out that the Procuracy, especially at the local level, failed to perform its functions properly. Large-scale thefts of socialist property, bribe-taking, report-padding and other crimes in which a large number of people, including high-ranking officials, were involved, have not always been exposed in a timely fashion. Supervision in the economic field was also lax.

The Central Committee resolution concluded that the power of the Procuracy should be strengthened so that it may cope more effectively with violations of law. Accordingly, the Supreme Soviet approved an amendment to the Law on the Procuracy. Procurators are now given power to be present in the sessions of the Supreme Soviet Presidium as well as the Council of Ministers and also in collegium meetings of ministries and other agencies. Government officials and citizens can be held criminally liable for non-enforcement of the demands of the Procuracy. Protests and representations of the procurators were given suspensive effect.[79] The amendment demonstrates the significance attached to the Procuracy by the C.P.S.U. leaders. In a way, the Procuracy is the sole state agency which the Party leaders can rely on, considering the quality of personnel, its political reliability and the broad power possessed by it. The new power given to the Procuracy further indicates the expectations held by Party leaders in the performance of the Procuracy. However dissatisfied the leaders are, the C.P.S.U. has to rely on the Procuracy to carry out its drive for state and social discipline.

To conclude, Gorbachev's reforms have indeed resulted in the democratisation and liberalisation of the Soviet society to a certain extent. The scope of freedom which the Soviet media is experiencing may be the broadest since the early 1920's. However, it should be noted that Gorbachev's reforms, which grant more discretion to the lower levels of the economy and give some freedom to citizens require, at the same time, stricter discipline.

The Soviet Procuracy is expected to be the primary agency for strengthening law and order in the Soviet society. Through the current restructuring, it is intended that the Procuracy will become an effective instrument of the C.P.S.U. strengthening law and order. Following his predecessors, Gorbachev plans to strengthen the Procuracy by ensuring closer contacts with the party organisations.

Whether the Procuracy can meet this expectation is dubious. The system of the Procuracy is a product of eighteenth century absolutism. An agency designed to oversee all government agencies, enterprises, social organisations, and citizens could have been effective in pre-industrial Russia where the society may be described as under-developed. After all, there was not even a court system at that time. However, the task which the modern Soviet Procuracy is facing is quite different. The struggle against violations of law in the U.S.S.R. is truly a formidable task. As in most industrialised countries, crime is still a serious problem in the U.S.S.R., despite the prediction of Marx. In fact, the scope of criminal offences has increased a considerable extent.

It is almost impossible for a single agency to oversee the

activities of all agencies and organisations, to uncover and prevent crimes, while supervising the courts and investigative agencies and prosecuting offences. A change cannot be brought about merely by streamlining the Procuracy and purging corrupt and incompetent staff. A possible solution would be to shift the burden to other agencies. Instead of the Procuracy being the almost sole guardian of socialist legality, an optimal distribution of functions between the courts, the Procuracy, the Ministry of Internal Affairs, etc., may bring positive results.

To date, however, such a distribution has proved to be a difficult task. The long awaited law on judicial review of administrative decisions was disappointing.[80] The proposals of academics have been watered down considerably. Since the scope of judicial review was narrower than expected, the Procuracy still has to deal with an enormous number of citizens' complaints. There is also a proposal to separate preliminary investigators from the Procuracy.[81] Since a radical restructuring of the Procuracy was proposed in the Politbureau meeting in June, this organisational reform may take place in the near future.

TABLE 1

Current Position	*Positions in other Agencies*
1. Head of Dept., U.S.S.R. Procuracy	People's Judge
2. Head of Directorate, U.S.S.R. Procuracy	"Soviet Work"
3. First Deputy Procurator, Republic	Head of Provincial Dept. of Justice
4. First Deputy Procurator, Republic	Trade Union
5. Deputy Procurator Republic	Head of Provincial Dept. of Justice
6. Deputy Procurator Republic	Deputy Chairman, Provincial Court & Head of the Provincial Dept. of Justice
7. Procurator, Autonomous Republic	Minister of Justice, Autonomous Republic
8. Procurator Province	Deputy Chairman, Provincial Executive Committee
9. Procurator Province	Chairman, Provincial Court

TABLE 1—*cont.*

Current Position	Positions in other Agencies
10. Procurator Province	Chairman, Provincial Court & Head of the Provincial Dept. of Justice
11. Procurator Province	Deputy Chairman, Provincial Court & Head of the Provincial Dept. of Justice
12. Procurator Province	Deputy Head of the Administration of Internal Affairs, City & Judge, Supreme Court of the Republic
13. Procurator Province	People's Judge, Chairman of the People's Court & Deputy Chairman of the Provincial Court
14. Procurator Province	Judge, Provincial Court
15. Procurator Province	Judge, Provincial Court
16. Procurator Province	Secretary of the Provincial Executive Committee & Head of Dept. of Justice
17. Procurator Province	"Soviet Work"
18. Procurator, Autonomous Province	Chairman, City Court & Provincial Dept. of Justice
19. Procurator of a Department, Region	Judge, Chairman of the District Court
20. Procurator, City	Dept. of General Affairs, Council of Ministers
21. Transport Procurator	Judge, Provincial Court

TABLE 2

Current Position	Position held in the C.P.S.U. Apparatus
U.S.S.R. Procuracy (4/12)	
First Deputy Procurator General	Secretary, District Committee
Deputy Procurator General	Section Head, A.O. Dept., U.S.S.R. C.P.S.U.

TABLE 2—cont.

Current Position	Position held in the C.P.S.U. Apparatus

U.S.S.R. Procuracy (4/12)

Head of Directorate Head of Dept.	Party Work Head, A.O. Province & Instructor, A.O. U.S.S.R.

Republican Procuracies

Procurator, Republic (11/18)	Instructor, A.O. U.S.S.R.
Procurator, Republic (11/18)	Head A.O. Province & Instructor, A.O. U.S.S.R.
Procurator, Republic (11/18)	Deputy Head, A.O. Republic (2)
Procurator, Republic (11/18)	Instructor, A.O. Republic
Procurator, Republic (11/18)	Instructor, District Committee & A.O. Republic
Procurator, Republic (11/18)	"Responsible Position", A.O. Republic
Procurator, Republic (11/18)	Party Work (3)
Procurator, Republic (11/18)	Komsomol Work
Deputy Procurator (12/36)	Deputy Head, A.O. Republic (2)
Deputy Procurator (12/36)	Instructor, A.O. Republic (4)
Deputy Procurator (12/36)	Instructor & Head A.O. Province
Deputy Procurator (12/36)	Head A.O., City
Deputy Procurator (12/36)	Instructor A.O. City
Deputy Procurator (12/36)	Part Work (3)

Procuracy, Province

Procurator Province (42/137)	Instructor A.O., Republic (2)
Procurator Province (42/137)	Head, A.O., Province (8)
Procurator Province (42/137)	Deputy Head, A.O. Province (5)
Procurator Province (42/137)	Section Head, A.O. Republic
Procurator Province (42/137)	Instructor, A.O. Province (11)
Procurator Province (42/137)	Instructor, A.O., Region
Procurator Province (42/137)	Head, A.O., City (2)
Procurator Province (42/137)	Assistant to the First Secretary, Province
Procurator Province (42/137)	Secretary, District Committee
Procurator Province (42/137)	Party Work (9)
Procurator Province (42/137)	Komsomol Work

TABLE 3

Year	New Appointments	Above Republican Level
1981	16	2
1982	19	4
1983	48	11
1984	33	13
1985	46	20
1986	40	11
1987	56	21

NOTES

[1] Article 164, the Constitution of the U.S.S.R.
[2] H. Kraus ed., *The Composition of Leading Organs of the C.P.S.U. (1952–1982)*, Munich 1983, pp. 38.43.
[3] F. B. Kaiser, *Die russische Justizreform von 1864*, Leiden, 1972.
[4] For details, see H. Oda, "Judicial Review of the Administration in the Countries of Eastern Europe," *Public Law*, 1984 No. 2, pp. 116–117.
[5] Article 20, the Law on the Procuracy (1979).
[6] *Sotsialisticheskaia zakonnost* (hereafter S.Z.), 1986 No. 1, p. 20.
[7] S.Z., 1987 No. 3, p. 28.
[8] S.Z., 1987 No. 7, p. 30.
[9] S.Z., 1987 No. 6, p. 80.
[10] S.Z., 1985 No. 6, p. 17.
[11] S.Z., 1987 No. 11, p. 19.
[12] S.Z., 87 No. 5, 1987 No. 5, p. 8.
[13] S.Z., 1986 No. 3, p. 7.
[14] S.Z., 1987 No. 11, p. 19.
[15] *Current Digest of Soviet Press* (hereafter C.D.S.P.), vol. 35 (1983), No. 44, pp. 1–2.
[16] S.Z., 1987 No. 3, p. 28.
[17] S.Z., 1987 No. 5, p. 8.
[18] A. M. Rekunkov ed., *Kommentarii k Zakonu o prokurature SSSR*, Moscow 1984, pp. 91–92.
[19] *Ibid.* p. 92.
[20] *Pravda* July 25, 1986.
[21] C.D.S.P., vol. 39 (1987), No. 26, p. 22.
[22] *Pravda*, October 3, 1986.
[23] *Sovetskaia iustitsiia* (hereafter SIu), 1986 No. 22, p. 6.
[24] *Pravda*, February 15, 1987.
[25] Art. 3, the Law on the Procuracy. See also Rekunkov, *supra* pp. 28–29.
[26] S.Z., 1987 No. 3, p. 12.
[27] S.Z., 1983 No. 1, p. 9.
[28] S.Z., 1984 No. 11, p. 7, No. 4, p. 69.
[29] S.Z., 1987 No. 8, p. 24.

[30] For details, see H. Oda, "C.P.S.U. and the Procuracy," in D. Barry *et al* eds., *Law in Gorbachev Era*, Dortrecht 1988.

[31] S.Z., 1986 No. 3, p. 7.

[32] Articles 165 and 166 of the U.S.S.R. Constitution.

[33] Two *nomenklaturas* are translated by the author and published in D. A. Loeber ed., *Ruling Communist Parties and their Status under Law*, Dortrecht, 1986.

[34] Consultation with A. Rozanov, secretary of the Party Committee of the U.S.S.R. Procuracy (June 2, 1987).

[35] A. M. Rekunkov ed., *Sovetskaia prokuratura*, Moscow 1982, pp. 217–227.

[36] S.Z., 1987 No. 6, p. 80. Shishkov died in 1987.

[37] S.Z., 1979 No. 4, pp. 5–7.

[38] *Kommunist*, 1979 No. 14, pp. 3–6.

[39] S.Z., 1979, pp. 3–6.

[40] S.Z., 1984 No. 11, p. 10.

[41] E. Fuller, "A Portrait of Eduard Shevarnadze," *Radio Liberty Research*, R.L. 219/85. See also R.L. 284/80.

[42] S.Z., 1983 No. 3, pp. 2–4.

[43] A. Sheehy, "Major Anti-Corruption Drive in Uzbekistan," *Radio Liberty Research*, R.L. 324/84, pp. 1, 8.

[44] S.Z., 1987 No. 5, pp. 14–15.

[45] *Izvestiia*, July 4, 1985.

[46] M. S. Gorbachev, *Politicheskii doklad TsK KPSS XVII s'ezdu* K.P.S.S., Moscow 1986, pp. 50, 78.

[47] *Supra*, p. 78.

[48] *Izvestiia*, June 2, 1986.

[49] *Zaria vostoka*, September 14, 1985.

[50] *Zaria vostoka*, February 11, 1986.

[51] *Ibid.*

[52] *Zaria vostoka*, October 17, 1986.

[53] B. Brown, "The Anti-Corruption Campaign in Turkmenstan," *Radio Liberty Research*, R.L. 49/87.

[54] C.D.S.P., 1986 No. 43, pp. 1–3.

[55] *Materialy plenuma Tsentral'nogo komiteta KPSS 27–28 ianvaria 1987 g.*, Moscow 1987, pp. 61–62.

[56] Radio Liberty RL/84.

[57] *Pravda*, January 4, 1986.

[58] *Pravda*, July 25, 1986.

[59] Bess, *supra*, p. 3.

[60] C.D.S.P., vol. 38, (1986), No. 43, p. 4.

[61] S.Z., 1987 No. 6, pp. 6–8.

[62] S.Z., 1987 No. 5, p. 6.

[63] S.Z., 1987 No. 4, pp. 14–16.

[64] *Pravda*, October 3, 1987.

[65] S.Z., 1987 No. 2, pp. 3–6.

[66] *Pravda*, November 18, 1986.

[67] See for example, *Izvestiia*, December 2, 1986.

[68] V. Tolz, "Procurator General Rekunkov attacks Journalists who criticize Soviet Justice Apparatus," *Radio Liberty Research*, RL/265/86.

[69] S.Z., 1987 No. 7, p. 5.

[70] S.Z., 1987 No. 2, pp. 7–14.

[71] S.Z., 1987 No. 5, p. 7.

[72] S.Z., 1987 No. 5, p. 25.

[73] S.Z., 1987 No. 5, p. 7.
[74] S.Z., 1987 No. 3, p. 28.
[75] S.Z., 1987 No. 5, pp. 11–12.
[76] S.Z., 1986 No. 5, p. 19.
[77] *Pravda*, June 5, 1987.
[78] Full text in *Pravda*, June 19, 1987.
[79] *Ukaz*, June 16, 1987.
[80] H. Oda, "The New Law on Judicial Review in the U.S.S.R.," paper presented at the International Symposium on *Soviet Law under Gorbachev*, Bridgeport, U.S.A. (November, 1987).
[81] A. M. Iakovlev in *Literaturnaia Gazeta*, September 24, 1986.

Racial Discrimination: The Role of the Civil Law

SIR NICOLAS BROWNE-WILKINSON

The American entertainer, Sammy Davis Junior, was once playing golf. He was asked by another golfer what was his handicap. He replied "I'm a one-eyed Jewish Negro: what's yours?" Under the law both of this country and of the United States he would be entitled to compensation for the handicap due to the loss of one eye if caused by the fault of another, the compensation for such disability running to many thousands of pounds. Would the same be true of the handicap due to his treatment by others as a Jew and a black?

It is now 10 years since Parliament legislated to give such a right of action under the civil law in the Race Relations Act 1976. Previously, the sanctions against racial discrimination had been largely criminal, incitement to racial hatred being a criminal offence. This had proved to be wholly ineffective. Parliament quite deliberately turned to the American experience where the enforcement of Title 7 of the Civil Rights Act, 1964 had proved to be a tempestuous, but very effective, means of changing racially discriminatory behaviour and attitudes. In passing the 1976 Act, I believe that Parliament had a dual purpose. One was purely social and moral: to state publicly that racial discrimination was unacceptable and unlawful in this country. The other was to back up this moral pronouncement with sanctions by giving the person unlawfully discriminated against the right to sue the discriminator. Uniquely, I believe, the Act was conceived as a piece of social engineering designed to change the then current attitudes to racial discrimination. The hope was that in this country, as in the United States, civil actions brought by individuals or groups of individuals, would prove to be an effective legal disincentive to racially discriminatory behaviour.

I want to consider, 10 years on, what has been the fate of

Parliament's attempt to counteract racial discrimination by these means.

The single most striking feature is that, relative to the incidence of racial discrimination in our society, very little use has been made of the Act. For example, in 1984, the total number of applications under the Act appears to have been less than 400. As in previous years, the overwhelming majority (364 cases) related to employment and were therefore brought in Industrial Tribunals. Of the applications in Industrial Tribunals only 158 came to hearing. The claimant was successful in only 29 of those cases, 129 being dismissed. The damages awarded were moderate in the extreme: in only five cases did they exceed £1,000.

Given the extent to which our society is beset by problems of race relations, this very limited recourse to the protection of the Act is most surprising. In my view there are a number of reasons for it. The first (which is inherent in the very nature of the disputes) is the difficulty of proving the existence of discrimination. The state of a man's mind, although as much a question of fact as the state of his stomach, is much more difficult to prove. A blatant discriminator who makes no bones about his motivation is today a rare figure. Far more common is the man who dissimulates his real motives or the man who discriminates unconsciously, for example the man whose attitude is based on stereotypes of what a black is like. Moreover, all the facts which might tend to proof of direct discrimination are within the knowledge of the discriminator. The complainant knows what the alleged discriminator did: only the alleged discriminator knows why he did it. The law has gone some way to meet this difficulty. It is established that if the facts suggest that, in the absence of racial discrimination, the complainant would have got the job or promotion for which he had applied, the inference of racial discrimination should be drawn unless the employer gives a convincing explanation of his reasons for not appointing or promoting the claimant. So, if a black applicant has better qualifications than the other candidates but does not get the promotion, the tribunal should draw the inference that the decision was taken on racial grounds unless the person making that decision goes into the witness box and satisfies the Tribunal that his decision was really made on other grounds.

Proof of indirect discrimination does not raise these problems since it does not involve proof of a man's intentions. However, it raises other problems. Indirect discrimination requires proof of the fact that a requirement or condition imposed by the discriminator bears more heavily on ethnic minorities than on the rest of the population. Except in the most obvious cases, such proof should involve statistical evidence. Further, a detailed analysis of the business of the employer would often be necessary to test a defence that the requirement or condition was justified for other, non-racial, reasons. Such evidence would give rise to complex and lengthy litigation with widespread discovery and major statistical evidence. That is what has happened in the United States where class actions involving such evidence last for years and rival anti-trust litigation in complexity and expense. It is for this reason and because discrimination cases in this country have to be tried in Industrial Tribunals or county courts, that our superior courts have done everything possible to discourage full discovery and statistical evidence in race cases. As a result the proof of indirect discrimination is made very difficult.

The second reason for the lack of use of the Act is related to the first. Given the great difficulties of proof, the need for skilled advocacy, especially good cross-examination, is obvious. Yet, in Industrial Tribunals where the overwhelming majority of cases have to be brought, legal aid is not available. The Commission for Racial Equality supports a number of cases; but its resources are too limited for this to be anywhere near sufficient. In 1984 when less than 400 applications under the Act were made, the Commission received over 1,200 applications for assistance but supported only 231. This means that a would-be complainant under the Act is faced with the task of himself cross-examining the alleged discriminators to demonstrate racially discriminatory motivation—difficult enough for an experienced cross-examiner and a hopeless task for a litigant in person. It is scarcely surprising that the success rate is so low. In the United States the problem of legal representation has been met by the legal profession treating race discrimination as a matter of major public concern. The profession has done many of the cases on a *pro bono* basis. The traditional large law firms seconded trial lawyers, free, to co-operate with the Civil Rights Movement, the legal arm of which was itself made up of highly competent and balanced black lawyers. Nothing corresponding to this has occurred in this country to date.

The third reason for neglect of the Act is the nature of the remedies available. As I have said, the great majority of cases actually brought relate to employment and therefore come before Industrial Tribunals. If the complaint relates to discriminatory failure to employ the complainant at all, the ordinary damages recoverable are very small: moreover, as a result of a decision in the Court of Appeal damages for injury to feelings are even smaller, normally £200 or less. Hence the low level of damages I have mentioned. Therefore the financial inducements to bring a case are very limited. In the case of an employee who is still employed by the alleged discriminator (for example a complaint of failure to promote), the fear must be that the employer will "have it in for you" in the future whatever the outcome of the case. I would think twice before embarking on a venture where the best result, even if successful, would be a very small amount of damages, to be weighed against the downside risk of high probability of failure coupled with the possibility of future victimisation. The Act makes the victimisation of a complainant unlawful: but this is little consolation to a man who has lost his job.

This position is to be contrasted with that in the United States. There the Civil Rights Act has made a major impact as the result of class actions brought on behalf of all employees from the ethnic minorities. The seminal cases on the desegregation of schools gave rise to injunctions enforced with great fortitude by the judges. Class actions against public services (such as the Police and Fire Brigades) led not only to huge awards of damages (running into millions of dollars) for loss of back pay but also to controversial mandatory orders laying down quotas for the future employment of blacks in the organisation at all levels. Similar relief in the United States has been granted in class actions against industrial and commercial employers. Such class actions provide to the claimants some security against victimisation, since all employees are acting in concert. The scale of damages awarded acts as an incentive not only to complainants to bring the proceedings but to employers to dismantle discriminatory systems before being taken to court.

The very low success rate in complaints brought in this country is a further discouragement to the bringing of claims. The low success rate is partly due to the inherent difficulties of proof which I have mentioned. Another factor is that, with so few cases spread over the whole of the United Kingdom, few tribunals have any real experience of dealing with this type of case. When, as I did for a while, one has seen the same explanations given time after time for the failure to promote a black with superior qualifications one develops a certain healthy scepticism. I recall a case of sex discrimination in which the chairman of the employers' selection panel which had appointed a man in preference to a woman with higher qualifications gave as the reason that the woman was "just not the sort of chap who would fit in"—a Freudian slip which one would have thought would have given some clue to his attitude towards women in his organisation. To my mind surprisingly the Industrial Tribunal held that the decision was not made on the grounds of sex. This type of explanation is given (normally with rather more careful use of words) time and time again. I suspect that an experienced Tribunal which had seen a number of these cases might press for a rather fuller explanation before accepting it at face value.

But the chief reason for the statistically low success rate is the number of applications under the Act which are hopeless from the start. If one has been rejected (for example sacked from one's job), it is only human nature to look for some explanation other than one's own inadequacies: ethnic minorities are not free from this human characteristic. Of the few applications that are brought, far too many are brought by people attributing their misfortunes to racial discrimination on the flimsiest of grounds. Such cases should, and do, fail. But the result is to portray a falsely depressing picture of the chances of success of a genuine complaint.

In addition to the factors I have already mentioned, the higher courts (with the honourable exception of the House of Lords) have tended to construe the Act in a technical and non-purposive way. Although many examples could be given I will refer to only one. In indirect discrimination cases the imposition of a discriminatory requirement or condition is not unlawful if the discriminator can prove that such requirement or condition is "justifiable" on non-racial grounds. The whole concept of indirect discrimination was derived from American case law which had established that practices having a disparate impact on ethnic minorities (even though there was no intention to discriminate) were unlawful unless it could be shown that such practices were *necessary* (and I stress the word necessary) for other reasons. In the debates in Parliament preceding the passing of the 1976 Act, the test of necessity was expressly rejected and the word "justifiable" adopted instead. It is obviously of cardinal importance to the law of indirect discrimination to know by what yardstick one is to judge whether, for example, a requirement that an applicant should have an educational qualification is "justifiable."

In the early cases it was held that such a requirement was only justifiable if it was necessary for some non-racial purpose, *i.e.* the American test of necessity was adopted. If some legitimate objective of the discriminator could be achieved in some way other than the imposition of the discriminatory requirement then he could not justify that discriminatory requirement. Later cases watered down the test of absolute necessity to reasonable necessity. But in *Ojituku* v. *Manpower Services Commission*

(1982) I.R.L.R. 418 the Court of Appeal disapproved of any test of justification related to necessity. In that case, two West African immigrants with sufficient educational qualifications but no previous managerial experience applied to the Commission under the TOPS Scheme for assistance in a course on management studies. The terms on which the scheme had been set up required that applicants for such studies should have previous managerial experience. It was common ground that such a requirement did indirectly discriminate against the applicants since their ethnic group would be much less likely to have had such experience than the indigenous white population. The question was whether the Commission had proved that the requirement of previous experience was "justifiable."

The Court of Appeal upheld the decision of the Industrial Tribunal that such requirement was justifiable because the Commissioners had proved that the scheme would only be effective to obtain employment for those who had previous experience.

I do not in any way disagree with the actual decision. But the reasons given by the majority of the court, if they represent the law, are worrying. The majority said that the word "justifiable" should not be glossed: each Industrial Tribunal should reach its own conclusion as a finding of fact whether they thought the reason advanced justified the discriminatory effect. It was said that if any explanation of the word "justifiable" were permissible it would be that "if a person produces reasons for doing something which would be acceptable to right-thinking people as sound and tolerable reasons for so doing, then he has justified his conduct."

That is one perfectly legitimate possible construction of the Act, if a literal approach is adopted. But I suggest that if a more purposive approach is adopted that could not be the right answer. In the field of racial discrimination, who are "right-thinking people?" One feature we all share is that we think ourselves to be right-thinking people. Without some further guidance as to the yardstick by which one decides what is justifiable, the finding of justification is entirely at large in each case, depending upon the attitudes to racial discrimination of each tribunal. If I were to ask a random sample of people if they thought that the desire of the Manpower Services Commission to limit the scheme to those with previous managerial experience justified the discriminatory effect of excluding West African immigrants from such schemes, I would certainly get a number of different answers. Each person's answer would depend upon the relative importance which he attached to eliminating racial discrimination on the one hand as opposed to the objectives of the scheme on the other. Unless one has some guidance as to the importance to be attached to eliminating racial discrimination as opposed to other matters such as the profitability of a business, the decision will depend entirely on the prejudices and attitudes of each tribunal. A "right-thinking" businessman might well consider the profitability of his business a sound and tolerable reason for a business practice. Therefore if the decision of the Court of Appeal represents the law, widely differing decisions will be given in Industrial Tribunals throughout the land as to whether conduct is or is not permissible. Those decisions, being decisions of fact, are not appealable. Therefore the construction put on the Act by the Court of Appeal in this case has opened the gateway to innumerable claims of justification in cases of indirect discrimination.

Before seeking to draw any conclusions from these matters, there are two other points that I should mention. First, the issue of positive or reverse discrimination.

The justification put forward for quotas and other forms of reverse discrimination is that, unless they are used, there is no adequate way to combat future disadvantage flowing from past racial discrimination. If no blacks have, in the past, been promoted to the first rung on the ladder, they will necessarily not be as well qualified to occupy higher managerial posts as their white counterparts who have had the necessary experience. So, the argument runs, in order to give proper redress and a speedy introduction of ethnic minorities into positions of responsibility, some form of quota or reverse discrimination is necessary.

In this country, there is no doubt that reverse discrimination is as unlawful as any other racial discrimination. The only exception is in the field of education and training. For myself, I would not wish it otherwise. Much as I admire the achievements of the law in the United States, I think reverse discrimination goes too far. For every black who is favoured by reverse discrimination, a white is adversely discriminated against on racial grounds—the very evil which the Act sets out to eliminate. The aim of the 1976 Act is, and should remain, to produce a society in which race or colour is irrelevant for all purposes. To substitute discrimination against white for discrimination against black is no solution. I accept that, without reverse discrimination, it will take longer to produce a balanced society in which ethnic groups are fairly represented at every level on the basis of individual ability. But the back-lash caused by the unfairness to the whites who are discriminated against (now much felt in the United States) would in the long run be far more damaging to the prospects of achieving a society which is genuinely multi-racial.

I have not so far mentioned investigations by the Commission for Racial Equality. The 1976 Act sets up a procedure (of mystifying complexity) under which the C.R.E. was to conduct formal investigations into allegations of racial discrimination and, if found to exist, to seek by way of persuasion or recommendation to resolve the problem. As a last resort, the C.R.E. can issue a non-discrimination notice requiring a person to discontinue unlawful discriminatory practices. Opinions differ as to how effective these investigations have proved to be. It is outside my terms of reference to express any view. But what is clear is that the procedures are quite unduly complicated and decisions of the courts have rendered those procedures even more difficult to operate.

What conclusions can be drawn from all this? The first question is whether the enforcement of civil rights can provide an effective remedy to racial discrimination. I think the answer is affirmatively "yes" as the experience in the United States has demonstrated. In the course of the years, decisions given in class actions under Title 7 have been at the very forefront of the civil rights movement. Only as a result of such civil actions has desegregation occurred, equal educational opportunities been obtained and a substantial shift towards equality of economic opportunity been achieved. This success has been due to vigorous, well-informed and serious black civil rights lawyers working in conjunction with equally vigorous, well-informed serious white lawyers, who have the additional advantage of wealth and status. Generously funded public organisations also aided such litigation. Cases came before Federal Courts presided over by judges of great moral (and sometimes physical) courage who construed the legislation in a purposive manner with a view to achieving the object of the Civil Rights Act. Those courts had the ability to handle the large class actions, giving rise to awards of damages sufficiently large to make even the biggest corporation pause to reflect whether it might not be cheaper, in the long run, to abandon racially discriminatory practices.

To these damages, the American courts could and did add mandatory orders, regulating the future ethnic balance. To the American ethnic minorities the courts have given redress for unlawful discrimination on the same basis as redress for any other legal wrong. The courts are perceived by the ethnic minorities to be their protectors.

Although I have no doubt that the civil law *can* be a major factor in the efforts to achieve racial equality, I fear that in this country the 1976 Act has not come up to expectations. The Act has only been used in comparatively few cases, all of which have been small. The contrast with the United States at almost every point is striking. I cannot think of a single case in this country which achieved a major shift towards equal opportunities for a substantial body of blacks. There has been no organisation of black civil rights lawyers which persistently and with moderation has pursued remedies under the Act. White lawyers (apart from a handful of socially committed barristers and solicitors) have been absent from race cases, except in those few where legal aid or C.R.E. funding is available. The limited funding of the C.R.E. prevents it from supporting many cases which it would like to support. There is no way in which heavy cases, involving elaborate discovery, statistical evidence and difficult points of law, can be brought in the High Court: all cases must be brought in the County Court or Industrial Tribunal which, with the best will in the world, cannot handle such litigation. The damages recoverable are very moderate. The fear of such damages does not provide any spur to large organisations to change their practices. In employment cases no injunctive relief is obtainable. Finally the courts have not been astute to implement the purposes of the Act but have on the whole interpreted it narrowly. The result is that the 1976 Act and the civil rights it confers are perceived as being peripheral to the racial problems of this country, not as the prime defence of the ethnic minorities against discrimination.

I find this conclusion disturbing on both moral and practical grounds. The 1976 Act has purported to give to everyone in the United Kingdom a right not to be subjected to racially discriminatory behaviour. That is as much a legal right as the right to enforce a contract or the right not to be injured by the negligence of another. To revert to my opening, Sammy Davis Junior ought to have the same rights of redress against a person who discriminates against him on the ground that he is a Jewish Negro as against the man who negligently caused the loss of his eye. If there is a right not to be discriminated against, the law ought to provide an effective remedy for its breach. For the various reasons I have considered that is not true of the right not to be discriminated against. Why almost uniquely is the amount of damages limited and injunctive relief unobtainable? To the moral question, "why is the right not to be discriminated against different from any other legal right?" I find it difficult to find a satisfactory moral answer.

The answers normally given are not moral but practical. One does not want the blunt instrument of an injunction loose in the hypersensitive field of race relations: look at the uproar in the United States caused by the high profile intervention of the courts. This country cannot afford the cost of more major legally aided litigation. The financial position of many employers is such that they could not afford the cost of installing and maintaining discrimination-free systems let alone heavy damages. So run the arguments. For myself, I cannot accept them even as practical answers. As arguments against giving any legal rights at all they may have validity. There is a perfectly legitimate case to be made that the law has no place in race relations at all: that race relations are a matter of feelings and attitudes with which the law should not be concerned and cannot effectively deal. But that is not the current position: Parliament has created the legal rights and the law has been introduced into race relations. The question at this stage is not whether there should be legal rights but whether those rights should be second-class rights protected by inadequate machinery. Members of the ethnic minorities know that they have legal rights. Anyone who knows he has a legal right but finds that the law does not protect him will not only feel legitimately aggrieved but will be also more likely to have recourse to other methods to assert his rights. The law exists to enable rights to be enforced peaceably and without civil unrest. Unless the law provides, and is perceived by the ethnic minorities to provide, an adequate means of redressing grievances based on breach of legal rights, society must not be surprised if recourse is had to other means.

The author wishes to draw attention to the unusual period of time that has elapsed between the delivery of this lecture on November 27, 1986, and this publication and to a number of judicial decisions in that period which have a significant bearing on the subject.

INDEX

247